משנה

ArtScroll® Series

Rabbi Nosson Scherman / Rabbi Gedaliah Zlotowitz

General Editors

Rabbi Meir Zlotowitz ז״ל, *Founder and President*

Master Your Words

REAL-LIFE ANSWERS, ADVICE
AND STRATEGIES FOR PROPER SPEECH
Arranged for Daily Study

Published by

ArtScroll®
Mesorah Publications, ltd

A Project of
The Chofetz Chaim Heritage Foundation

Master Your Life

Rabbinical Advisor: Rabbi Moshe Mordechai Lowy

By: Chana Nestlebaum

Editorial Director: Shaindy Appelbaum

FIRST EDITION
First Impressions ... December 2017
Second Impressions ... June 2018
Third Impressions ... December 2019
Fourth Impressions ... February 2020

Published and Distributed by
MESORAH PUBLICATIONS, LTD.
313 Regina Avenue / Rahway, N.J. 07065

Distributed in Europe by
LEHMANNS
Unit E, Viking Business Park
Rolling Mill Road
Jarow, Tyne & Wear, NE32 3DP
England

Distributed in Australia and New Zealand
by **GOLDS WORLDS OF JUDAICA**
3-13 William Street
Balaclava, Melbourne 3183
Victoria, Australia

Distributed in Israel by
SIFRIATI / A. GITLER — BOOKS
POB 2351
Bnei Brak 51122

Distributed in South Africa by
KOLLEL BOOKSHOP
Northfield Centre, 17 Northfield Avenue
Glenhazel 2192, Johannesburg, South Africa

ARTSCROLL® SERIES
MASTER YOUR WORDS, MASTER YOUR LIFE

313 Regina Avenue / Rahway, N.J. 07065 / (718) 921-9000 / www.artscroll.com

---

ISBN 10: 1-4226-1961-3 / ISBN 13: 978-1-4226-1961-2

Typography by CompuScribe at ArtScroll Studios, Ltd.

Printed in the United States of America.
Bound by Sefercraft, Quality Bookbinders, Ltd., Rahway N.J. 07065

In Loving Memory of

לע״נ חיה יפה בת יצחק אליעזר ע״ה

Yaffa Rosenthal, *a"h*

There are few people as worthy of having a *sefer* on Shmiras Haloshon dedicated to their memory as Chaya Yaffa *bas* Yitzchak Eliezer—Yaffa Rosenthal *a"h.*

We could write a book just about the greatness of Yaffa; this is but a tiny glimpse into the life of this beautiful person.

Yaffa loved the Torah and lived by it. Her husband's learning was precious to her, not to be interrupted no matter how challenging the situation. She had great respect for *talmidei chachachim* and would always seek out and follow their guidance. She was close to Hashem; she loved Him and was always thanking Him for the big things and also for little things that usually go unnoticed, and she taught her children and grandchildren to do the same.

Her *ahavas Yisrael* was immeasurable. She often said "I love every Yid," and she meant it. No matter who they were or where they came from, she loved them just because they were Yidden. Her home was filled with people of all types, drawn in by her welcoming smile, comforting warmth, and listening ear. She treated every person with respect and gave them her full attention, joining them in their joy or sadness.

She raised large sums for many causes, the most notable one being her money-lending *gemach,* which she ran with dedication and sensitivity to the borrower's needs. She was involved in *kiruv*, made *shidduchim*, and was always looking for ways to help her fellow Yid. Yet her many accomplishments notwithstanding, she felt that her *raison d'etre* was to be *mechanech* her children. She often told her children, "Even if the only thing you learn from me is '**If you have nothing good to say, say nothing at all,**' then I have accomplished something." Yaffa's life was filled with *tzidkus* in every sense of the word—her *tefillah*, her *emes*, her *tznius*, her *kibbud av v'eim* were all exemplary—but the primary message to her children was *ahavas Yisrael* and *shmiras halashon.* She herself was very careful with *shmiras halashon*, and always had an *ayin tovah* — she saw only good in people.

As one of the first volunteers for the Chofetz Chaim Heritage Foundation, Yaffa was involved in numerous projects, including organizing many Machsom L'Fi schedules. She considered it a *zechus* to be one of the key organizers of the CCHF Tisha B'Av presentation at one of their largest venues, Bais Yaakov of Boro Park. She spent the day overseeing the program and stayed until the end, often driving home some stragglers. She would come home after the fast was long over with a new *chiyus,* and expound on what the speakers had discussed and how it could be implemented.

How appropriate that Yaffa's *yahrtzeit* is Tisha B'Av, a day she devoted for decades to the CCHF Tishah B'Av program. Additionally, it is a day when *Klal Yisrael* strives to perfect their *ahavas Yisrael*, something she truly excelled at. How fitting is this *sefer* on Shmiras Halashon to pass on her message to a wider public: "If you have nothing good to say, say nothing at all!" Through this work, may her legacy continue to inspire *Klal Yisrael* and may her *neshamah* have an *aliyah*.

ח כמת נשים בנתה ביתה בית של תורה וחסד
י ראת ה׳ אהבתו ואמונתו היו אוצרה
ה אמונה שלה בחכמי התורה עברה כל גבוליה

י שרותה בעניני ממון היה לשם דבר לכל מכיריה
פ נים יפות קיבלה כל אדם חסדים גמלה לאחרים בכל מאודה
ה שתתפה עם אחרים בכל לב בעת שמחה ובעת צרה

ב רגש ולב השתפכה לפני קונה בכל איבריה וגידיה
ת פלותיה על חולי ישראל ושאר צרכיהם תפסו כל מעמקיה

י ום יום התפללה עליהם וכתבתם על לוח לבה ועמודי סידורה
צ נועה היתה בכל דרכיה בלבושיה ובהילוכיה
ח ינוך בניה ובנותיה היתה מגמת חייה
ק ירוב רחוקים שעותיה וזמניה לא עלה על חשבון צאצאיה

א ביה ואמה כיבדה בכל כוחה ונשמתה לאות ולמופת כל ימיה
ל שון הרע ואונאת דברים נזהרה והתרחקה מעבור על שפתיה
י ראת שמים הכניסה בילדי ישראל בכתביה
ע שירה היתה כי שמחה בחלקה כאשר יעידו כל רואיה
ז כרה הטוב לא ימוש מכל משפחתה ומעריכיה
ר בים אומרים מי יראנו טוב כי נעדרה ואיננה

ת.נ.צ.ב.ה.

Letter of Approbation from Rabbi Shmuel Kamenetsky שליט״א

בס״ד

שמואל קמנצקי
Rabbi S. Kamenetsky

2018 Upland Way
Philadelphia, Pa 19131

Home: 215-473-2798
Study: 215-473-1212

חודש כסלו תשע״ח

״מי האיש החפץ חיים וכו׳ נצור לשונך מרע״ - דכמו מי שמבקש חיים (כמכריז ר׳ ינאי, מאן בעי חיי), דורש וחוקר תמיד אופנים שונים וחדשים איך להיטיב חייו, לשפר מצבו עלי אדמות כדי שישיג רב תועלת, כן בענין הזה, כסדר צריך לחפש עוד דרכים לשמור פיו מדבר רע.

לכן בואו ונחזיק טובה להמוסד החשוב ע״ש החפץ חיים, שכבר זיכו הרבים בהספרים הקודמים על שמירת הלשון ושאר דברים בענינים שבין אדם לחבירו, וכבר התעוררו הרבה מאחינו בנ״י לשמור פיהם ולשונם מהנגע הגרוע הזה.

ועוד ידם נטויה להוסיף שמירה על שמירה כדרכה של תורה, ולחבר ספר חדש באופן של דוגמאות מצוירות מהניסיון יום יומי, בדרך שאלה ותשובה כדי להשיג רוב תועלת ובירור.

והוא מסודר באופן לימוד יומי שלא יחסר יום אחד מלימוד המוסר ותיקון המידות ושרשיהם כאשר תחזנה עיניכם.

בטוח אני שמי שיקנה וילמוד ספר הזה יבא ברכה לביתו ולכל משפחתו וע״י שמירת הלשון נזכה להגאולה שלימה בקרוב.

שמואל קמנצקי

אליהו ברודנא
1752 E. 18 Street
Brooklyn, NY 11229

נר א׳ דחנוכה תשע״ח

Tonight is a unique night. On one hand, we are all commemorating and celebrating the *teshuah gedolah u'furkan k'hayom hazeh* of the miraculous victory of *m'at min ha'or docheh harbei me'hachoshech*. On the other hand, we are all deeply mourning the passing of the *Oro Shel Olam*, the *Rabban Shel Yisrael*, *HaGaon HaRav* Aharon Yehuda Leib Steinman, *zechuso yagen aleinu, amein*.

This is a uniquely appropriate moment to express feelings of gratitude and admiration to the Chofetz Chaim Heritage Foundation, for continuing to lead the charge to inspire and motivate the *bnei u'bnos Yisrael* to aspire to levels of *segulas Yisrael mi'kal ha'amim*, for which we all exist.

The latest edition of the Chofetz Chaim Yomi, *Master Your Words, Master Your Life*, is part of that holy endeavor. It will *b'ezras Hashem* culminate *b'karov* with the *Geulah Sheleimah* and the day of *hashivah shofteinu k'varishonah v'yo'atzeinu k'vatchilah*.

B'bircas HaTorah,

Eliyahu Brudny

Eliyahu Brudny

לע"נ

הרב הגאון

ר' חיים ישראל בעלסקי

זצוק"ל

ראש ישיבה תורה ודעת ומעמודי הוראה בדורנו

Dedicated in memory of the world-renowned
posek and Rosh HaYeshivah,

HaRav HaGaon R' Yisroel Belsky זצוק"ל

He was distinguished for his incredible intellect and knowledge of *Torah* and related subjects, and renowned for his incredible courage to stand up what he know to be true. HaRav HaGaon R' Yisroel זצוק"ל headed a household that was simply overflowing with *tzedakah* and *chessed*, a *middah* that is abundantly manifest in the home of his daughter Mrs.Tamar Rechnitz, the devoted wife of our dear friend and president, R' Shlomo Yehudah Rechnitz.

ת.נ.צ.ב.ה.

THE CHOFETZ CHAIM HERITAGE FOUNDATION

In memory of my grandparents

Sam & Nina Bellows

Who have instilled in me the values that are in this book.
They literally lived the principles that we all strive for on a daily basis.

Blessed and grateful,

Yoni & Allison Bellows and family

Dedicated

לעילוי נשמת

מורינו הרב שמעון בן הח׳ ר׳ יהודה שוואב ז״ל

רחל (רייכל) ב״ר אברהם שוואב ע״ה

הח׳ מרדכי ב״ר יונה וייסקופף ז״ל

גיטל ב״ר גרשון וייסקופף ע״ה

הרב משה ב״ר אהרן צציק ז״ל

מרים רבקה ב״ר יונה ליפמן צציק ע״ה

ר׳ אברהם ב״ר שלמה זלינגר ז״ל

פעסל רבקה ב״ר דוד זלינגר ע״ה

By their grandchildren

Jeff and Sheva Weiskopf

Monsey, NY

לע״נ

הרב יוסף יעקב לייב בן שלמה ז״ל

Rabbi Yaakov Deitsch *z"l*

נתן בן אריה דב ז״ל ואשתו לאה בת מאיר ע״ה

Mr. & Mrs. Nathan and Lena Seiler *z"l*

שלמה בן משה ז״ל ואשתו פריידל בת פרץ ע״ה

Mr. & Mrs. Samuel and Freida Deitsch *z"l*

רעבעצין הדסה בילא בת אלימלך ע״ה

Rebbitzen Baila Susholtz *a"h*

ת.נ.צ.ב.ה

Dedicated by Zahava Deitsch and family

לע״נ

חי׳ בת דוב בער הכהן ע״ה

לע״נ

ישראל ליב בן מרדכי ז״ל
נלב״ע כ״ד טבת

משה יעקב בן נחום ז״ל
נלב״ע ל׳ תשרי

עטיא פייגא בת ר׳ מרדכי ע״ה
נלב״ע י״ז טבת

בס״ד

לע״נ יוסף חנונו בן שרה ז״ל
נלב״ע י״ט שבט תשל״ג

Yosef Hanono *ben* Sara *z"l*
January 22, 1973

לע״נ ויולט גילסום בת סופי ע״ה
נלב״ע ד׳ אלול תש״ע

Violet Gilsom *bat* Sophi *a"h*
August 14, 2010

May *Hashem* protect and bless our family with ברכה והצלחה,
and the Chofetz Chaim Heritage Foundation
for promoting תורה ומצות.

Dedicated by
David M. Hanono and family
Panama

לע״נ

ר׳ יעקב בן ר׳ יהודה אריה זצ״ל נלב״ע ד׳ אב תשל״ט
ואשתו מרת בריינדל בת ר׳ ברוך ע״ה נלב״ע ו׳ תשרי תשע״ו

ת.נ.צ.ב.ה.

**Dedicated by Avrumi & Elisa Taub
and family**

לע״נ ישראל דוב בן אהרן יעקב ז״ל
נלב״ע ה׳ אדר תשס״ב

Irving Shimoff

Dedicated by Robin & Warren Shimoff

לע״נ

בעלי ישראל בן יצחק דוב ז״ל
יצחק דוב בן אברהם ז״ל ואשתו שרה בת אברהם ע״ה
יהשוע אהרן בן אלעזר יששכר דב ז״ל
ואשתו פייגא בת אשר חיים ע״ה
מלכה בת יהושע אהרון ע״ה
יעקב מנחם בן יחזקאל ישעיה ז״ל
מירל בת אברהם ע״ה

**Dedicated by Mrs. Shoshana Lefkowitz
and family**

בס״ד

With הכרת הטוב to

Michael Rothschild

and the entire staff of the
Chofetz Chaim Heritage Foundation
for your tireless efforts on behalf of כלל ישראל.

Your "Silent Partner"

לע״נ נחמיה אריה ליב פרץ בן אליהו הלוי ז״ל

A true *eved Hashem*
who loved *Hashem's Torah*, and His children

Barak and Erez Baver and families

In loving memory of

Nan Woodrow Mark & Asher Ansel Mark *a"h*

Dedicated by their children, grandchildren and great-grandchildren

THE CHOFETZ CHAIM HERITAGE FOUNDATION

A not-for-profit foundation dedicated to the teaching of Jewish ethics & wisdom

Dear Reader

In the more than two decades since the Chofetz Chaim Heritage Foundation began producing *sefarim* for Shmiras Haloshon Yomi, two major opposing trends have emerged. The first trend is the ever-growing awareness of Shmiras Haloshon that has permeated *Klal Yisrael*. A mitzvah that many thought impossible to keep has become a way of life for some, a goal for many, and at the very least a presence in the awareness of the vast majority of Torah Jews. Our *sefarim* and school programs are helping to propel this change, making information, inspiration and tools for growth available to all.

The other, opposite trend is the great flood of *loshon hora*, a tsunami that has inundated the world, pouring out of the internet and social media. In the guise of news, the media relentlessly push into our view personal attacks and gossip. The boundaries of decency are barely recognizable.

This has affected our world as well. Reputations have been ruined, relationships strained, businesses destroyed and *shidduchim* undone because of the ease and speed with which social media enables people to spread unflattering words and images far and wide.

So, even though we've been promoting Shmiras Haloshon for the past 28 years and *Klal Yisrael's* accomplishments in this area have been magnificent, we are all called upon now to reinforce an entirely new battlefront. It must be strengthened with the best defenses we have, and it is our hope that this new *sefer* will serve that purpose powerfully. As you will see, it is designed to go straight to the heart of the matter in the most practical and motivating way.

As you delve into this *sefer* and let it into your life, you'll be joining the 52,000 students learning our school curriculum, the 25,000 callers a day to our telephone inspiration lines, and the readers around the world of the 450,000 books already in print. *Klal Yisrael* is discovering the beauty of life with Shmiras Haloshon. There's a revolution under way, and we invite you to join it.

The Chofetz Chaim Heritage Foundation

361 Spook Rock Road
Suffern, New York 10901
Tel 845 352-3505
Fax 845 352-3605

Table of Contents

Author's Acknowledgments

In the summer of 1989, a friend asked me to get in touch with a person who was looking for a writer to create some advertising and public relations material for his new organization. That was my first project for the Chofetz Chaim Heritage Foundation and its founder, Mr. Michael Rothschild. I remember driving each day to a copy shop in downtown Concord, NH, to fax my work to the CCHF office, located at the kitchen table of the Rothschilds' home in Flatbush.

From that first ad, I have been blessed with the incredible merit of producing much of the written material this unique organization has created for the benefit of *Klal Yisrael.* I could have been writing stories about small-town politics, as I started out doing, or about the diamond industry, as I did for many years. Instead, I have spent hundreds — perhaps thousands — of days of my life thinking about, synthesizing and communicating thoughts that spring from the Torah and revolve around *ahavas Yisrael.* I don't think there are any words, even in a writer's word-bank, which can adequately say thank you to Hashem for directing my footsteps along this path.

In every major project I have undertaken on behalf of the CCHF, my indispensable partner, **Mrs. Shaindy Appelbaum,** has been the organizer, sounding board, work-flow manager, coordinator, grammar-checker, and most of all, the stickler for perfection that I will never be. She has the unique ability to find every phrase that could be clearer, every inconsistency and every slightly misconstrued idea, all the while making me feel like a genius.

Because one of the cornerstones of this book is its practical approach to *halachos* as they apply to everyday life, a crucial factor is the accuracy of the *halachos* and *hashkafos* we present. I am deeply grateful to **Rabbi Moshe Mordechai Lowy** for his scrupulous review of each example we present. It is only with his expert oversight that I would dare to offer any statement or example of how the *halachah* applies to the various situations we portray.

Tremendous thanks are also due to **Rabbi Avi Neuberger,** who reviewed this book page by page, adding sources for the *halachos* and providing many of the inspiring quotes that are featured in each lesson. His efforts have made this a more accurate and complete resource for our readers.

This book, as all the books I have been privileged to write for the CCHF, is a collaborative effort from beginning to end. The beginning is **Mr. Michael Rothschild,** whose passion for the cause of Shmiras Haloshon and firm belief in *Klal Yisrael's* capacity to reach higher only seems to grow stronger as the years go by. Thank you for entrusting me with the privilege of bringing your vision into reality. Thank you, too, to the **CCHF staff** for your warmth, good humor and support. I believe the Chofetz Chaim would be happy with the spirit of the organization that bears his name.

In this and many other writing projects I have undertaken as an editor or primary writer, I have had the good fortune of working with **ArtScroll Publications,** the premier name in Jewish publishing. I would particularly like to thank **Rabbi Avrohom Biderman** for his generous encouragement and support throughout the years.

Writing about Shmiras Haloshon and the *middos* that nurture it, such as patience, tolerance, compassion and humility, would be impossible for a person whose life did not provide some example of these traits. For this, I offer my heartfelt appreciation to my husband, **Mendel Nestlebaum,** who doesn't need 80,000 words — or even one word — to explain how to "master your words." He simply demonstrates it, every day in every way. May our life's work together be blessed, and may we see only *nachas* from our wonderful children and grandchildren for many years to come.

— *Chana Nestlebaum, December 4, 2017*

Acknowledgments

Our gratitude to Hashem *Yisborach* is beyond words for enabling us to produce this book and continue to spread the concept of *Shmiras Haloshon* in all its facets to communities around the world. With this new volume we have taken the concept of *Shmiras Haloshon* one step further, delving into the personal traits and challenges that color our words and in turn determine the nature of our relationships. All of this we have striven to deliver in brief, clear and memorable segments designed to make an impact.

The Chofetz Chaim Heritage Foundation extends its sincere gratitude to the many people whose talents and devotion made the publication of this book a reality.

Our goal of providing Torah-true inspiration and information necessitates sound guidance, and for that we thank **Rabbi Moshe Mordechai Lowy** *shlita,* Rav of Agudas Israel of Toronto, who meticulously reviewed the manuscript of this book. Rabbi Lowy consistently gives of his precious time to review and answer questions regarding our publishing projects. He also regularly answers questions from educators relating to *Shmiras Haloshon* in **Impressions**, our popular newsletter for teachers, as well as in our popular **Shabbos Menu** newsletter, part of our free **Shabbos Table Machsom** program.

Mrs. Chana Nestlebaum, the writer of this book and so many others of our best-selling titles, has been the voice of our organization since it began 28 years ago. In this new book she has created clear, believable scenarios and insightful postscripts that turn a daily learning text into a readable and engaging daily boost. She is truly a "master of words," who uses her exceptional talents to help us all master our lives.

Mrs. Shaindy Appelbaum, editorial director, is directly responsible for the carefully crafted, progressive flow of this book, designed to elevate the reader step by step. In this and countless other Chofetz Chaim Heritage Foundation projects, she has used her talent, wisdom and perseverance to inspire *Klal Yisrael* and change the world.

Rabbi Avi Neuberger, who has authored several CCHF books including **Positive Vision** published by Artscroll/Mesorah, and the Hebrew *kuntres* ***Ana Yada,*** both on *Shmiras Einayim,* patiently reviewed this book and researched the sources of the *halachos.* We are grateful for his invaluable assistance with finding and crediting the many quotes found in this volume.

Thank you to **Rabbi Zelig Pliskin,** who graciously allowed us to present some material adapted from his book, *Consulting the Wise,* giving our readers access to the wisdom of Torah giants through the ages.

Thank you to **Mrs. Tzippy Lichter** for her diligent, painstaking technical work that was instrumental in guiding the book through the many changes, improvements, reordering and rearrangements that brought it to its final format.

We thank **Mrs. Tova Finkelman** and **Mrs. Miriam Margoshes** for their efficient editing and accurate proof-reading.

The eye-catching cover and engaging layout bear the unique stamp of the incomparable graphic designer **Ben Gasner**.

Chofetz Chaim Heritage Foundation reaches over 100,000 people through its many programs, yet it is only as strong as the people who comprise it. We gratefully acknowledge the staff, volunteers, and leaders who work tirelessly to create a culture of caring and spread the language of *ahavas Yisrael* through the world.

Our success flows from the Torah leaders who map out our path:

The Manchester Rosh Yeshivah, HaGaon HaRav Yehudah Zev Segal, *zt"l,* the founding Rabbinic Adviser of our organization; and **HaGaon HaRav Avraham Pam** *zt"l.* Their wisdom and guidance, as well as their legendary exemplification of *ahavas Yisrael,* will forever influence the path and progress of our organization.

HaGaon HaRav Shmuel Kamenetsky, *shlita,* the Chairman of our Rabbinical Board, is an integral part of the CCHF — the compass that guides us. He invests his heart and soul into the work of our organization, taking time out of his vital work to travel to our dinners, conventions and even accompanies us on fundraising appointments. His clear, Torah-true perspective, provided to us with graciousness and generosity, ensure that our projects uphold the highest standards of *Klal Yisrael.*

Rabbi Yosef Eisen, Rabbi Hillel Litwack, Rabbi Eliyahu Lamm, Rabbi Eliyahu Brog, and Rabbi Mordechai Klein, **Rabbi Dovid Ribiat** who volunteer their time to answer questions on our Sh'ailah Hotline, guiding those who seek to fulfill the mitzvah of *Shmiras Haloshon.*

Much of our impact emanates from our publishing projects that reach schools, *shuls,* and communities around the world. We are grateful to those who give/have given of their precious time and expertise to review all our publications. Thank you to **Rabbi Naftoli Jaeger** for his review of **Chosen Words,** a family bi-weekly newsletter, still being enjoyed after 19 years. Thank you to **Rabbi Avi Shulman,** who has reviewed and improved each issue of our teachers' publication, **Impressions**, for the past 15 years, ensuring that it reflects Torah-true *chinuch* ideals.

We are deeply grateful to the outstanding people of the Chofetz Chaim Heritage Foundation:

To our Chairman of the Board, **Reb Shlomo Yehuda Rechnitz** and his devoted wife **Tamar**, whose vision, enthusiasm, and generosity of spirit have helped us spread the language of *ahavas Yisrael* further than ever before. Reb Shlomo Yehuda's involvement in mapping a strategy to conquer *loshon hora* and *ona'as devarim* is indispensable! The dream of "Every Child, Every Day" truly belongs to them, and we are forever indebted to them for partnering with us to fulfill this dream. May Hashem reward them for their great generosity and grant them much *nachas* from their family and *hatzlachah* in all their endeavors.

To our Board of Directors whose members have been a tremendous help in forging our path: **Rabbi Raymond Beyda, Abraham Biderman, Aba Claman, Nachman Futterman, David Lobel, Yitzchok Mashitz, Ari Parnes, George Rohr, Kurt Rothschild, David Shweky, Gedaliah Weinberger**, and **Moshe Zakheim.**

To the many dynamic speakers who have inspired us over the years, our sincere thanks.

If you have benefited from a *shmiras haloshon* program or publication over the past few years, it is thanks to the selfless dedication of our staff: **Rabbi Yoina Koenig, Mr. Dovid Kogel, Mr. Velvel Kunofsky, Rabbi Avi Neuberger, Rabbi Shlomo Ornstein, Rabbi Yosef Pruzansky, Mr. Boruch Reiss, Rabbi Elchonon Snyder, Rabbi Shea Steinberg, Mrs. Shaindy Appelbaum, Mrs. Chany Bernstein, Hindy Bloch, Mrs. Tehila Danzinger, Mrs. Machla Eichenstein, Mrs. Miriam Eisenberger, Bayla Epstein, Mrs. Tziri Frank, Shevi Greenfeld, Mrs. Miriam Grossman, Mrs. Devorahla Hager, Mrs. Kayla Halpern, Mrs. Michalle Hammer, Mrs. Hindy Housman, Mrs. Chaya Israel, Leahle Kalifon, Mrs. Gitty Kalikstein, Mrs. Breindy Kertzner, Mrs. Tziporah Klitnick, Mrs. Estie Koot, Mrs. Devorah Krawiecz, Mrs. Shira Lazar, Mrs. Esther Leibowitz, Mrs. Blimi Lesser, Rivky Levi, Mrs. Suri Levy, Mrs. Chava Londinski, Mrs. Nechama Lowenthal, Mrs. Sara Gila Margulies, Leahla Mendlowitz, Mrs. Rochel Mendlowitz, Nechama Michael, Mrs. Shoshana Miller, Mrs. Tziporah Esther Mittler, Mrs. Esther Mohr, Mrs. Chana Moskowitz,**

Mrs. Miriam Nieman, Mimi Newman, Mrs. Leah Ozeri, Mrs. Brany Perl, Mrs. Ruchie Perlstein, Mrs. Chayie Schachter, Mrs. Leah Sekula, Mrs. Rivka Sherwinter, Mrs. Frumie Shtierman, Mrs. Chavi Twersky, Mrs. Nechama Weinberg, Baila Weinman, Ruchy Weinstein, Esty Weldler, Mrs. Blimi Wertzberger, Mrs. Sima Zinnes, and Mrs. Esty Zins.

We also thank our staff in Eretz Yisrael: **Rabbi Binyomin** and **Mrs. Shoshana Cohen**, **Sarah Gado, Mrs. Tzippy Gottlieb, Hadar Katan, Mrs. Rochel Orloweck**, and **Mrs. Naomi Rottman.**

The Chofetz Chaim Heritage Foundation is forever grateful to **Rabbi Mendel Kessin**, whose penetrating recorded *shiurim* on *Shmiras Haloshon* inspired us to start our organization.

Our thanks to **Rabbi Heshy Leiner, Rabbi Nochum Stilerman,** and **Rabbi Heshy Augenbraun** for their crucial advice.

To our 700 local coordinators—the *rabbanim,* principals and lay people who have lifted the banner of *Shmiras Haloshon* in their shuls, schools and communities—thank you so much.

We are happy to acknowledge the special partnership we enjoy with ArtScroll/Mesorah Publications that began in 1995 with *The Chofetz Chaim: A Lesson a Day*. Since then this visionary publishing house has been instrumental in our effort to spread the message of *ahavas Yisrael.* **Rabbi Nosson Scherman,** *shlita,* and **Rabbi Meir Zlotowitz**, *zt"l,* general editors of ArtScroll/Mesorah, have taken a strong interest in our projects. Rabbi Zlotowitz approved the format for this book and enthusiastically followed its progress, encouraging us to bring it to life. We will miss his vision, knowledge, and intuitive wisdom. We are, however, fortunate to have the comfort of continuity as we begin with this volume to work with his highly talented son and successor, **Rabbi Gedaliah Zlotowitz**, who continues his father's legacy with professionalism and sensitivity.

Special thanks to **Avrohom Biderman,** who has always been a crucial link in the production of our *sefarim,* and to **Mendy Herzberg** and the entire typesetting/graphics department at ArtScroll, who went far beyond the call of duty to complete this project.

To those who have supported us financially—the major supporters who wish to remain anonymous, the main sponsors of this book, and the families that helped bring this book to publication by sponsoring a day—may the great *zechus* of *Shmiras Haloshon* stand by you and your families, bringing abundant *brachah, shmirah* and *shalom* into your lives.

Above and beyond all else, we humbly acknowledge the clear *siyata d'Shmaya* that has consistently transformed our ideas and visions into momentous forces for positive change in *Klal Yisrael*. This *brachah* is without a doubt the result of the enthusiastic way in which so many individuals from across the country and around the world have embraced our goals. To all of you who have united under the banner of *ahavas Yisrael* and generously given your support to our organization's projects: your idealism and positive vision of *Klal Yisrael's* future is what inspires us to forge on.

May all who work toward the dream of a Jewish nation living together in *achdus*, with compassion and kindness, merit to see the realization of that dream with the coming of the Final Redemption, may it be very soon!

The Chofetz Chaim Heritage Foundation

Who You Are, What You Say, How You Live

Right now, in your hand, you are holding the key to a quality of life that is better, happier and more fulfilling than anything you might think possible. It's a life of loving relationships, secure friendships, strength for meeting challenges, and best of all, peace of mind. You've already grasped this book and begun reading; all you need to do now is to go forward and grasp the clear, down-to-earth information and inspiration that each new page delivers. When you reach the end, you will have taken into your heart the mitzvah of *shmiras haloshon,* the Torah's instructions to all of us — human beings with human foibles — on how to live with, honor, and love one another. You will be on the way to mastering your words, and in doing so, mastering your relationships with the people in your life.

Perhaps you are among the tens of thousands of people who, in the course of the past nearly three decades, have awakened to the power and importance of *shmiras haloshon*. Or, maybe this mitzvah has remained an enigma to you — something good, positive and praiseworthy, but "not for me." Perhaps you've learned the *halachos* of *shmiras haloshon* many times, or perhaps you've never approached this mitzvah in a methodical way.

No matter which of these descriptions fits, this book was written for you. It is a fresh, new, eminently realistic approach. And it is a revolutionary approach — from the inside out.

Shmiras haloshon remains a challenge for many people because achieving it depends as much on our character traits as it does on our knowledge. To shake a *lulav* properly, we need only learn the halachos and have the will to fulfill them. The calculus changes for *shmiras haloshon;* knowing the rules is only the beginning. This is a mitzvah that goes to the heart of how we view others, how we view our relationship with Hashem, and how we view ourselves. Meeting the challenge of negative words and the thoughts that produce them requires us to build our inner world.

This is obvious when we think about people who "never have a bad word to say." They have patience, tolerance and acceptance. *Ahavas Yisrael* fills their hearts. They view the world with an *ayin tovah* — a good eye. They work on themselves consistently, aware that if they don't keep growing, they will begin slipping. The very ones who seem to have perfected their *middos* are the ones who are always seeking further inspiration.

Yet *shmiras haloshon* is not just for elevated souls. It is a vehicle by which every Jew has the opportunity — and the obligation — to *become* a more elevated soul. In this book, you will find a multi-pronged tool for doing just that. First and foremost, we present the rules of the road. How is a Jew to respond, through the prism of *shmiras haloshon*, to the many interpersonal challenges that arise in life? What do you do when your friend needs to "vent"? What do you do when that friend wants to vent every day, in-depth, about the same person? How do you respond when someone asks you, "How did you like that new pizza place?" Who do you tell when you see your friend's daughter's husband-to-be behaving in a way that's not proper? Through real-life situations like these, you'll get a whole new perspective of how *shmiras haloshon* opens the flow of blessing into our everyday life, keeping our interactions productive and sensitive, even when they might sometimes be difficult.

The next prong is the one that can help you dig out the roots of *loshon hora* in your life and replant them with the seeds of *shmiras haloshon*. You will learn from regular people, as well as from the words of Torah giants of the past and present, how to build *shmiras haloshon* from the inside out. You will hear about the practical steps people have taken to cultivate the habits and character traits that give rise to a life of *shmiras haloshon* and all the blessings it brings. A flash of realization, a moment of renewed determination, a commitment to making life better, a book, a five-minute-a-day lecture, a change in schedule or even just one powerful idea taken to heart: all of these have uplifted the lives of people who are just like most of us, sincere but mired in our own personal challenges.

If there is any overall message this book seeks to impart, it is that everyone can grow in *shmiras haloshon*, and that everyone who undertakes the effort will become a better person and live a happier life. This mitzvah has the answer to all our sticky situations, both those that come upon us from outside ourselves and those that are generated by our own sometimes skewed view of the world. This is "Everyman's *shmiras haloshon sefer*."

We invite you to turn the page with an open heart and mind. For those who have learned the halachos before, this book opens up new territory, presenting a wide vista of *middos* development that will instill *shmiras haloshon* firmly into your personality. If you've never embarked on a *shmiras haloshon* learning *sefer* before, this is the one with which to start. It will instantly awaken you to the moment-by-moment relevance this mitzvah has to your life, and introduce you to people who have succeeded in it through small, simple, doable steps.

Everyone likes to be on the winning side, and today, *shmiras haloshon* is winning new victories. There are many new challenges, to be sure, especially in the world of electronic communication, which give every individual the capacity to broadcast his or her words to thousands of people in an instant. However, Hashem has given us the arsenal we need to prevent this potentially devastating trend from overrunning us; He has given us decades to build a new awareness of *shmiras haloshon* throughout the Jewish world. He has helped us imbue new generations with knowledge, tools and sensitivity to the power of words.

Mastery, however, comes only with practice. Every new learning project we embark upon, every right decision we make when we speak, helps us become people who are in charge of our words and therefore, in charge of the impact we make on others in our lives.

As the Geulah comes closer, we feel more acutely the tug-of-war between the powers of purity and impurity in our world, and it becomes ever more important for each of us to add our personal effort to the battle. Here in your hand is an accessible, easily understandable and highly applicable way to bring out the best in yourself, your life and your world. May these pages merit to unlock the doors of our hearts and usher in our long-awaited Redemption.

Note to the Reader

Disclaimer:

The *halachos* of *shmiras haloshon* are very complex, and one small detail can completely change whether you may, may not, or must say something. The purpose of the halachic section of this book is to help people recognize *Shmiras haloshon* issues when they arise, so that they will think twice, and if necessary, ask a rav, before saying something potentially harmful.

Therefore, the scenarios should not be used as a basis for determining what to do in any given situation; consult a *rav* or a halachic expert.

What Is Shmiras Haloshon?

Shmiras Haloshon is the subject of the book you are about to read. Perhaps you've heard the phrase many times before but haven't thought much about what it means; or perhaps it's new to you. To start our journey into the world of words, there are three terms to understand:

Shmiras Haloshon. This means guarding one's tongue. There are several *mitzvos* in the Torah along with an entire body of *halachah* that prescribe how we are to do this. Those *mitzvos* and *halachos* are presented here, divided into daily lessons. In addition, many of the Torah's ethical and spiritual precepts teach the deeper impact of the power of speech.

Loshon Hora. This means evil speech. *Loshon hora* is any true statement that is derogatory or damages another person. Potentially damaging statements are allowed to be said only when they are necessary to protect someone from harm — and even then there are specific rules about how to proceed.

Rechilus. This means peddling, as a peddler goes about selling his wares. In terms of the laws of speech, *rechilus* is defined as a statement made by one person to another which arouses animosity against a third person.

What's Inside?

We are pleased to present you with a fresh new approach to learning and putting into practice the Torah's laws of proper speech. Every day's lesson consists of a comprehensive array of offerings, each aimed at imparting information and inspiration in a different way.

Living the Mitzvah describes a real-life dilemma in which a Shmiras Haloshon question is likely to arise. It includes a general concept, a concrete example, and the *halachah* that solves the dilemma.

Remember provides a quick motto or phrase that encapsulates the *halachah* and makes it easy to remember.

Grow Your Middos is a collection of true stories, strategies and advice designed to help you become aware of the personality traits that influence how people relate and speak to one another. Here is where "Master Your Words" comes to life.

Looking Within asks a question that raises self-awareness of the *middah* being highlighted, while **Building Within** offers an idea to strengthen the *middah* in the context of everyday interactions.

The Quote of the Day is a brief shot of inspiration for Shmiras Haloshon, culled from a wide range of sources.

Tishrei

לע״נ

In memory of

ישראל יצחק בן רב אברהם שלמה ז״ל נלב״ע ל׳ תשרי

Sidney Broome

יוכבד בת יוסף אריה הכהן ע״ה נלב״ע כ״ג תשרי

Evelyn Broome

צפורה בת משה דוד ע״ה נלב״ע ט״ו תשרי

Fay Kasmer Broome

Dedicated by Bernard Broome and family

לע״נ אהרן דוד בן שמעון הכהן ז״ל

לע״נ יעקב קאפל בן אשר ז״ל

ואשתו חי׳ בת חיים הכהן ע״ה

לע״נ רבקה בת יהושע ע״ה

Anonymous

Shevat

לע"נ

רפאל בן רחל ע"ה נלב"ע ד' שבט

Dedicated in loving memory of
Raphael S. Gindi
By his wife and children

לע"נ אבי מורי ר' משה בן לוי ז"ל - *Hochhauser*
נלב"ע כ"ח מנחם אב תשס"א

לע"נ ר' לוי בן גרשון ז"ל
ואשתו איידל חי' טשארנע בת עקיבא הי"ד - *Aftergut*

לע"נ ר' דובער בן מנחם מענדל ז"ל
ואשתו פייגיל בת הרב שבתי ע"ה - *Swerdlin*

לע"נ החבר ברוך בן רפאל ז"ל ואשתו חנה בת יצחק ע"ה - *Wertheimer*

לע"נ החבר מנחם בן יעקב ז"ל ואשתו עלא בת נתן ע"ה - *Lommer*

Dedicated in loving memory by
Leivi and Esther Hochhauser

In memory of
Levi ben Dovid Shlomo Yankelevich z"l
Shmuel Zev ben Levi Yankelevich z"l
Michal Yaakov ben Avraham Yitzchok Broitman z"l

Sivan

In honor of our sons,
Seth, Ian and Zalman and their wives,
Our daughter-in-law Julie Kaplan,
wife of Henuch Lazer ben Aaron z"l,
Our grandchildren,
Josephine, Ezra, Sarena, Gabriella, Jonah, Yaakov Yosef,
Menachem, Eta Fayga and Sara Nechama
From Bubby & Zaidy Shifrin

לע"נ אברהם אליעזר בן יעקב צבי ז"ל נלב"ע כ' סיון
Mr. Abraham Himmel

Dedicated by Rivka & Martin Himmel
and family

לע"נ מאיר בן חיים צבי ז"ל נלב"ע כ"ז סיון
In memory of Mayer Neuhoff

CHAPTER 1

Awareness — Know the Power of a Word

Speech is natural. No one has to tell a baby to speak his first word; he's wired for it. The power of speech, however, is far beyond natural. To use our power of speech for its highest, most life-enhancing purposes, we have to tune into it: to hear our own thoughts and the words they produce; to open our eyes to the impact of our words on the people in our lives. Speech is power. Awareness lets us use that power to light up every corner of our lives.

DAY 1

Living the Mitzvah

What If It's True?

What if you know something is 100 percent true? And you feel other people should know it as well, so that they'll know the truth? Maybe it's not even something so bad...you just really feel other people ought to know the reality. Can that be considered loshon hora?

The Dilemma:
You work for a tyrant. He learns at night with your next-door neighbor, who is telling you what a great guy he is. Shouldn't your neighbor know the truth? May you tell it?

The Halachah:
You may not tell. A true derogatory statement is the very definition of *loshon hora*. Telling a lie — slander or libel — is called being *motzi shem ra.*

The true story can be told only when it's necessary to protect others from harm, and even then, there is a very narrow path defining whom to tell and how much to tell. [See Seven Rules of To'eles, p. 328.]

Sefer Chofetz Chaim, Hilchos Loshon Hora 1:1

א תשרי
1 Tishrei
Cycle 1

א שבט
1 Shevat
Cycle 2

א סיון
1 Sivan
Cycle 3

REMEMBER

True + Negative = Loshon Hora

1 Tishrei – כזכות להצלחתם ובריאותם של יהושע משה בן מאירה ומיכל תמר בת יעל אלה
וילדיהם: דוד נפתלי הרץ, חיה אהובה בלה, דבורה אלישבע ומרים ברכה

1 Shevat – לע"נ פייבל יוסף בן חיים ליב ז"ל ואשתו מרים בת פנחס ע"ה
לע"נ יהודה זאב בן פייבל יוסף ז"ל

1 Sivan – Murray Niedober לע"נ מרדכי בן יצחק ז"ל
Dedicated by his wife, children and grandchildren

Grow Your Awareness

Who's In Charge Here?

You can think a million things in your head. Some nice, some not so nice, some forgiving and some perhaps a little irritable or critical. It's the rare person who truly doesn't ever think a negative thing about anyone. There's no question that training ourselves to see the good and think the good will ensure that we speak the good as well, but until we reach that level, there's one important thing to know.

"Before you speak, you are in charge of the word. Once you speak, it is in charge of you. You are its hostage," says Rabbi Avraham Kohan (Torah Ohr, Great Neck, NY), citing the Chofetz Chaim.

This powerful idea can help us hold our tongues and give us time to process our negative thoughts. Once you've voiced a negative opinion of someone, you've changed reality and you're stuck with that change. Now others will see that person in a different light. If you tell a negative story about someone, others will now know that story; perhaps it will get back to the subject. Perhaps it will cost that person a job, a *shidduch* or a friendship. It may well cost you a friendship, too.

As long as our thoughts are unspoken, we can work on them. "Is it really such a big deal? Am I any better? Can he help being this way? Can I help him change?" The world is a much better place when we are the masters and our words are our servants, accomplishing what we really want to accomplish in life.

Looking Within: Are there times when you wished you could take back what you said? What can you do to contain thoughts that are best left unspoken?

Building Within: When you have a negative assessment or an uncomplimentary story to share, before you say the first word, think to yourself, "I'm about to change reality."

QUOTE OF THE DAY

"The principle way of meriting the World to Come is through guarding one's mouth, which is greater than Torah learning and *mitzvos*, because the mouth is the Holy of Holies..."

(excerpt from a letter [Alim L'Terufah] by the Vilna Gaon)

DAY 2

Living the Mitzvah

When Is a Compliment Not a Compliment?

What could possibly be wrong? You're collecting money for a needy family and you tell someone how much various people gave. You bump into a friend at the store, and you mention to another friend what she bought. Are you speaking loshon hora?

ב תשרי
2 Tishrei
Cycle 1

ב שבט
2 Shevat
Cycle 2

ב סיון
2 Sivan
Cycle 3

The Dilemma:
It's Purim and your yeshivah has sent you and a small group to collect money from alumni. Mr. Asher Kessef — a guy who's said to be worth more than a billion dollars — is on your list! You save him for last, hoping to cap off your day with a huge haul. Finally you arrive at his stately home. A housekeeper leads you into a room filled with people waiting to get Mr. Kessef's ear. When your turn arrives, he asks about his old yeshivah and shares his memories of the Rosh Yeshivah; he then writes you a check for $100. Later, your friends are dying to know: "So? What did you get from Kessef?" What should you say?

REMEMBER
Loshon hora is relative.

The Halachah:
If you state that he gave $100, you would be speaking *loshon hora*, because the amount he gave is stingy relative to his ability to give. Answering "I'd rather not say" implies something negative as well. Therefore, if you have to say something, you should give him the benefit of the doubt: "Mr. Kessef isn't giving a high-school kid his big donation. I'm sure he gives that straight to the yeshivah. But he did give us $100." Make sure that you don't sound sarcastic.

Sefer Chofetz Chaim, Hilchos Loshon Hora 1:1, 5:6

2 Tishrei – לזכות ברכה והצלחה פרנסה, רפואה ושידוכים
for our entire family and all of *Klal Yisrael*

2 Shevat – In memory of Mr. & Mrs. Eli Septon *z"l*
In memory of Mr. & Mrs. Isaac Vaturi *z"l*

2 Sivan – In memory of Isser *ben* Yaakov *z"l*
Dedicated by his daughter Betsy Schrott

Grow Your Awareness

The Flow of Traffic

Chaim was at the wheel and Yisrael was his passenger. They sped along the highway paying no attention to the speed limit. Yisrael peeked over at the speedometer and said, "Chaim, we're hitting 90. Better slow down!" But Chaim wasn't concerned. "I'm going with the flow of traffic," he replied. "As long as everyone else is going 90, I won't get stopped."

Moments later, Chaim noticed a police car closing in on him. He pulled over and waited anxiously as the officer approached. "Do you know you were going 91 miles an hour?" the policeman asked him. "I'm sorry, Officer," Chaim replied. "I wasn't watching the speedometer. I was just going with the flow of traffic." The policeman sympathetically answered, "Yeah, that happens, but you were still speeding." The ticket for going 27 miles an hour over the limit was a whopper. Chaim felt persecuted, but he had no real defense.

This story precisely illustrates what happens when we're in a group of people who are engaged in *loshon hora*. Even if we're aware that we're doing something wrong, we hope that we won't be deemed blameworthy. Why should we be expected to be better than everyone around us? And if all these other nice, well-meaning people don't feel constrained, maybe the conversation isn't *loshon hora* after all! But just as there's no law on the books allowing people to speed even if everyone else is, neither does the Torah make such an allowance for *loshon hora*. Those around us may give us a challenge, but they don't give us justification.

Looking Within: When your friends or family members are speaking *loshon hora,* does that increase your comfort level with speaking or hearing it?

Building Within: When that niggling feeling of wrongdoing rises up in you, think about the futility of the "flow of traffic" excuse and remember that Hashem has each of us on His radar.

QUOTE OF THE DAY

"Hashem said to Israel: 'My beloved children, what do I ask of you? Only that you love one another, respect one another and be in awe of one another.' "

(Tanna D'vei Eliyahu Rabbah 28)

DAY 3

Living the Mitzvah

Are Public Speakers a Matter of Taste?

No one expects everyone to like the same things. People have their individual taste in food and wine. They respond differently to different types of books and music. Most of the time, voicing our preference for biographies over fiction or chicken over beef is nothing more than an expression of our taste. But what about our taste in speakers?

ג תשרי
3 Tishrei
Cycle 1

ג שבט
3 Shevat
Cycle 2

ג סיון
3 Sivan
Cycle 3

The Dilemma:

A well-known speaker is coming to your town and your friend invites you to come along to hear him. You've heard this speaker several times before and, although his material is interesting, you prefer a more dynamic speaking style. *May you tell your friend why you don't want to go to the lecture?*

The Halachah:

Criticizing the speaker is *loshon hora*. Your comments imply that he isn't effective, and may result in people deciding against going to hear him. This is clearly derogatory information that does the subject harm — the definition of *loshon hora*. The case might be different, however, if the inquirer is in charge of hiring a speaker for an event.

Sefer Chofetz Chaim, Hilchos Loshon Hora 5:1, 9:1

REMEMBER
Your critique means empty seats.

3 Tishrei – **Dedicated as a *zechus* for our family**

3 Shevat – לע"נ שיינא ליבא בת יהושע ע"ה
להרבות כבוד שמים בעולם

3 Sivan – **Steven Charles Mendelson *z"l*** לע"נ ברוך יחזקאל בן יעקב הלוי ז"ל
His נשמה **should have** מנוחה ועליה**. Dedicated by the Mendelsons**

Grow Your Awareness

Put Time on Your Side

Are there periods of time in your day that are conducive to *loshon hora*? Lunchtime at work? The school-bus stop, as you stand around with the other mothers? Dinnertime? Shul, during the break between Minchah and Maariv?

If you can pinpoint such times in your day, then you can create a powerful strategy to cut out a great percentage of the *loshon hora* you speak and hear. Even if you usually manage to steer clear of participating in these conversations, you can benefit from a strategy that would save you from having to face that challenge over and over again. So what can you do when "*loshon hora* time" rolls around?

- Identify those times so you can be mentally prepared for what lies ahead.
- Make a plan that minimizes that period of time. For instance, if the school-bus stop is a problem, go out a little closer to the time the bus arrives and leave as soon as the bus departs.
- For set periods like mealtime, think of some interesting topics to introduce so that other people do not become the topic of conversation.

Looking Within: Do you have regular periods of "down-time" that lend themselves to *loshon hora*?

Building Within: Think of one time of day that's a *loshon hora* challenge for you and make a strategy to meet the challenge.

QUOTE OF THE DAY

"Just as people's faces do not resemble one another, so too their thought processes do not resemble one another."
(Bamidbar Rabbah 21:2)

DAY 4

Living the Mitzvah

May I Tell Everyone What We Did?

It wasn't exactly terrible, but it wasn't exactly a shining moment. It definitely was, however, the makings of a great story. If you and some friends engage in a "misadventure," may you tell the story? Because you're including yourself as one of the "guilty parties," you obviously don't feel that the story is really damaging. But what about the others?

ד תשרי
4 Tishrei
Cycle 1

ד שבט
4 Shevat
Cycle 2

ד סיון
4 Sivan
Cycle 3

The Dilemma:

Your newly-licensed son wants to drive a group of friends to an out-of-town wedding. Remembering back to your younger years, you recall a similar situation in which you and two cousins drove through the night at warp speed, got pulled over, didn't have the registration to show the policeman, and ended up spending the day in a small-town police station. *May you tell him the story?*

The Halachah:

Even though you are including yourself among the guilty parties in a story, you are not allowed to tell it if it will cast others in a negative light. The cousins may not want others to know that they behaved irresponsibly. Perhaps the story will get back to their children and reduce the parents' stature in their eyes.

Sefer Chofetz Chaim, Hilchos Loshon Hora 1:9

REMEMBER
Other people's misadventures are not yours to tell.

4 Tishrei – Dedicated as a *zechus* for *Klal Yisrael*

4 Shevat – May today's learning be a *zechus* for our parents and our children.
Dedicated by Meir Yoel & Susan Laub

4 Sivan – לע"נ יוסף בן רחל ז"ל נלב"ע ו' סיון
As a *zechus* for all the grandchildren to follow in his ways

Grow Your Awareness

Turning Down the Flame

Leah Davidson* and her family lived in a Jerusalem apartment. Their upstairs neighbor, Ruth Saperstein, ran a playgroup of 20 children. Every day, Leah had to endure the running, pounding, screaming and crying on top of her head as she tried to go about her day. It was unbearable.

One day, Leah and her husband approached the Sapersteins to see if there was some way to ease the problem. Ruth Saperstein apologized, but staunchly defended her right to earn the money her family needed. They reached a tense impasse, and the two women stopped acknowledging each other's existence.

However, the situation never expanded into a building-wide *machlokes,* as such situations often do. That is because Leah was learning *shmiras haloshon* every day. She states that with that inspiration, she was eventually able to reopen the lines of communication, try to see the situation from Ruth's point of view, and, while continuing to live with the still-touchy situation, refrain from discussing her grievance with other neighbors.

"I learned how to not confuse the issues — disagreement doesn't cancel out *ahavas Yisrael* and the other mitzvos that can make us act with sense, sensitivity and even nobility in the most trying and mundane of situations."

Adapted from *The Quill of the Heart*
(*all names have been changed)

Looking Within: How well-versed are you in the halachos of *shmiras haloshon* and other mitzvos of *ahavas Yisrael*? Are they precise or are they vague in your mind?

Building Within: When you find yourself engaged in a dispute with another person, remind yourself that there are halachos that apply, and find out what your obligations are.

QUOTE OF THE DAY

"Who is mighty? He who makes his enemy a friend."

(Avos D'Rav Nosson Ch. 23).

DAY 5

Living the Mitzvah

If He Doesn't Mind, Why Should I?

Sometimes you know someone who seems to be a real "solid citizen," and yet there are things about his life that might surprise people. When you are privy to such information, are you allowed to disclose it to others if the subject himself is open about it and will even speak about it publicly?

ה תשרי
5 Tishrei
Cycle 1

ה שבט
5 Shevat
Cycle 2

ה סיון
5 Sivan
Cycle 3

The Dilemma:

You attend a wedding with a bunch of old friends. One says something unexpected: "It is so hard to raise kids. I can't tell you how many times I've exploded at them." The friend obviously isn't hiding his flaw, but may you disclose this admission to others?

The Halachah:

The fact that someone discloses negative information about himself publicly and appears unconcerned about doing so does not give us permission to wantonly spread the information any further. Clearly the information stands to reduce the person's reputation in others' eyes, which makes it at the very least *avak loshon hora*.

Sefer Chofetz Chaim, Be'er Mayim Chaim, Hilchos Loshon Hora 2:28

REMEMBER
Don't spread the damaging word.

5 Tishrei – לזכר ולע"נ אחי היקר אליהו בן בנימין זאב יעקב ויהודית גרין ז"ל
Dedicated by the Goodfriend family

5 Shevat – **Dedicated by the Hecht family**

5 Sivan – **Mrs. Chaya Winter** לע"נ חיה בת ר' נפתלי חיים ע"ה נלב"ע ז' סיון
Dedicated by her children the Abish and Winter families

Grow Your Awareness

Make It Short and Sweet

We've already spoken about times of day when *loshon hora* tends to crop up. You might find that there are people, too, who seem to bring out the gossip in you. They might be people you see every day — perhaps members of your own household. Or they might be friends, neighbors, relatives or work associates with whom you speak on occasion.

Just as you can plan ahead for *loshon hora*-prone times, you can plan ways to deal with *loshon hora*-prone people. The simple solution is to keep your communications friendly, direct and as brief as possible. One idea many people find useful is to call people Friday afternoon, shortly before candle-lighting. Then the conversation will be limited naturally. Another method is to direct the topic into neutral territory.

If your "problem person" is a close relative, you can perhaps be direct: "I'm trying very hard to work on *shmiras haloshon,*" you can say. "Help me out and let's change the subject." Without accusing the other person of poor habits of speech, you can still gain control of the situation. In this way, you can neutralize a major prompt for *loshon hora* in your life.

Looking Within: Do you seem to roll seamlessly into a *loshon hora* conversation with certain people?

Building Within: Try to identify where these pitfalls lie and use the strategies above to avoid them.

QUOTE OF THE DAY

"A gentle reply turns away wrath, but a distressing word stirs up anger."
(Mishlei 15:1)

DAY 6

Living the Mitzvah

What If Everyone Already Knows?

Today news travels at the speed of light. If that news includes some derogatory or even scandalous information about a fellow Jew, may we discuss it with others? Is it still loshon hora after thousands of people have already been informed?

ו תשרי
6 Tishrei
Cycle 1

ו שבט
6 Shevat
Cycle 2

ו סיון
6 Sivan
Cycle 3

The Dilemma:

A well-known Jewish businessman is arrested for tax evasion. The story is on the front page of the local daily newspaper and all over the Internet. The cynics have already convicted the man, along with the entire class of people known as "Jewish businessmen." The pundits are already discussing the spiritual failures the crime represents. May you join in these conversations? May you tell others the news?

The Halachah:

Even when information is common knowledge, it is still *loshon hora*. Before the information is verified, it should not even be believed. If it is verified, then it is still proper that it should not be related.

Sefer Chofetz Chaim, Hilchos Loshon Hora 2:2,9,11

REMEMBER

Knowing it and discussing it are two different things.

6 Tishrei – לע"נ אפרים בן ישראל חיים ז"ל ואשתו פיגא בת יעקב ע"ה

6 Shevat – לע"נ יוסף אליעזר בן החבר מרדכי ז"ל
Dedicated by the Pressburger family

6 Sivan – לע"נ איידל חי' בת צבי הירש הכהן ע"ה

Grow Your Awareness

You're On!

Jews are supposed to ask themselves, "When will my deeds reach the level of those of my Forefathers, Avraham, Yitzchak and Yaakov?" This may seem like an unrealistic goal. Are we ever likely to have the opportunity to invite three Arab wayfarers into our homes for a meal in the heat of the day?

We won't. But Rav Elazar Menachem Mann Shach says, in his commentary on the Haggadah, that if that situation somehow happened to unfold in front of our eyes, we would know just what to do. We would recognize that this is our "Avraham moment" and run to lay out the welcome mat. The challenge is to have that realization whenever an opportunity to do a kindness comes our way.

When an unkind or perhaps outright demeaning story comes to mind about someone, it's as if we are there in the desert, facing the three wayfarers who are counting on our kindness. Will we act like Avraham and, out of our kind concern for the subject of our remarks, restrain ourselves?

The temptation to speak *loshon hora* is an "Avraham moment" for every Jew. It's the same test Hashem put before Avraham, only He is customizing it for us in our times and our lives. With that in mind, we can find the strength to grab our moment and run with it.

Looking Within: Do you realize, when *loshon hora* enters the picture, that this is a test Hashem has set out just for you?

Building Within: When you feel somewhere inside that the words you are speaking or hearing are *loshon hora*, focus more sharply so that little blip on the radar screen will become an alarm screaming, "This is a TEST!" Then you will know just what to do.

QUOTE OF THE DAY

With a revealer of secrets, a bearer of tales, or a simpleton of lips, do not mingle.
(Mishlei 20:19)

DAY 7

Living the Mitzvah

Is It My Fault That You Took It Wrong?

When we speak, we never know what might be riding on our words. We might describe someone with an imprecise, ambiguous term that can be interpreted a few different ways. Is it our responsibility if someone interprets such a phrase in a negative way?

ז תשרי
7 Tishrei
Cycle 1

ז שבט
7 Shevat
Cycle 2

ז סיון
7 Sivan
Cycle 3

The Dilemma:

Your neighbor's son is about to enter second grade, where Rabbi Mittelberg will be his rebbi. You son had that rebbi the previous year, and your neighbor calls and asks you, "What's he like?" You answer: "He definitely means well." Your neighbor hangs up dreading the coming year. If you simply meant that the rebbi means well, is it your fault that your neighbor took your words to mean that he's a poor rebbi, albeit with good intentions?

The Halachah:

We are responsible for the impact of our words. Therefore, if we use a term that can be taken several ways, we are obligated to clarify our words.

Sefer Chofetz Chaim, Hilchos Loshon Hora 2:2 with Be'er Mayim Chaim 2; see also Hagahah to 9:3

REMEMBER
Leave no doubt.

7 Tishrei – Meyer Wagh לע"נ מאיר בן יקותיאל יהודה ז"ל
Dedicated by Mr. & Mrs. Yosef & Judy Neiman and family

7 Shevat – Eleanor Krieger לע"נ חנה בת יצחק הכהן ע"ה
Dedicated by her daughter Dorothea Krieger

7 Sivan – לע"נ הרב נתן ומרים בומהאפט ע"ה הי"ד נלב"ע ו' סיון
Dedicated by their grandchildren, Pinchas & Marilyn Newman

Grow Your Awareness

Stay Clear of the Danger Zone

Imagine that you had to walk through a dangerous neighborhood. You'd heighten your awareness of your surroundings, walk quickly and get out as fast as possible. Those same tactics work as well when we are in a spiritually dangerous neighborhood — any place where *loshon hora* is likely to occur.

We've now spoken about navigating around times of day and people in our lives who tend to lead us into *loshon hora*. There are also places we can identify where *loshon hora* is likely to occur. The famous "water cooler" at the office, a table of friends at a wedding, the aforementioned school-bus stop or any place people gather can be a spiritual minefield.

If you can identify those places, you can make a point of avoiding them as much as possible and, with that one step, avoiding a great deal of *loshon hora*. Success depends on taking seriously the need to protect yourself. If you were in a physically dangerous place, you'd be willing to walk a block or two out of your way to avoid trouble. So why not change your seat, change your bus stop, go out for your coffee break? Plan the safest route through your day.

Looking Within: Are there *loshon hora*-prone locations that are part of your routine?

Building Within: Try to motivate yourself to cut one *loshon hora*-prone venue out of your life by making your alternative venue an enjoyable place for you to be.

QUOTE OF THE DAY

"A human is a human and an angel is an angel. But if a human being wishes, he can be greater than an angel."

(Rabbi Leibel Eiger, Otzar Aggados HaChassidim, Vol. 15, p. 68)

DAY 8

Living the Mitzvah

Did I Speak Loshon Hora About My Block?

Loshon hora applies to people and to the Land of Israel. Does it apply to other places, for instance, San Diego, California or Burbank, Alaska? Does it apply to objects, like toaster ovens or car tires or sunglasses? What about animals?

ח תשרי
8 Tishrei
Cycle 1

ח שבט
8 Shevat
Cycle 2

ח סיון
8 Sivan
Cycle 3

The Dilemma:
Your family lives in the heart of a busy Jewish neighborhood. You're in easy walking distance to stores, shuls, yeshivos — everything you need. However, you prefer the grassy suburbs where you grew up. You often complain to your neighbors that you live in a "concrete jungle." Is that *loshon hora*? After all, your neighborhood won't suffer because you spoke about its crowds and noise rather than its great shopping.

The Halachah:
While negative comments about the neighborhood congestion are certainly unrelated to *loshon hora*, it is always better to focus on the positive and minimize the negative. If we do this for the places and things in our lives, we will train ourselves to do it for the people as well.

Shaarei Teshuvah 3:217

REMEMBER
Accentuate the positive.

8 Tishrei – In memory of Falik *ben* Shachna Aryeh *Halevi z"l*
8 Shevat – לע"נ משה בן אליעזר ז"ל
8 Sivan – As a *zechus* for our family for געזונט, פרנסה ונחת
Dedicated by the Rabers

Grow Your Awareness

Shmiras Haloshon at Work

The workplace is often a major challenge in *shmiras haloshon,* as diverse personalities come together under sometimes tense circumstances. Bosses are bound to complain about workers and workers about their bosses. Sometimes the atmosphere can become toxic.

But at sister companies Madison Commercial Real Estate Services in New Jersey and CityBook in Israel, the workplace is the site of tremendous growth in *shmiras haloshon.* Ten years ago, at the behest of some of the employees, the companies started a daily learning program. Today, more than 80 percent of the staff participate in the program, which delivers a lesson a day via email from Rabbi Zelig Pliskin's *Guard Your Tongue.*

After each 24 lessons, the participants take a test on the material. The companies provide a "study break" before the tests, complete with refreshments. After the ninth cycle of learning was completed, the companies sponsored a lavish *siyum* at the Ramada Hotel in Yerushalayim.

The companies' executives value the positive, meaningful bonds that learning together has brought to their employees. The employees value the positive atmosphere their endeavor has brought to the workplace. And, as one manager stated at the *siyum,* "Our employees tell us all the time that it has made a difference in the way they conduct themselves not only at work, but also at home with their families."

Looking Within: Are you immersed in a *loshon hora* environment at work?

Building Within: Rather than accepting that a negative atmosphere is normal in the workplace, think about ways to raise awareness and improve the situation.

QUOTE OF THE DAY

"I would advise those seeking to improve their economic situation to take exceedingly great care in regard *to loshon hora...*" "If one respects another person's feelings and possessions, his own possessions shall certainly be blessed more than if he had performed any *segulah.*"
(Sefer Shmiras HaLoshon, Part 2, Ch. 9)

DAY 9

ט תשרי
9 Tishrei
Cycle 1

ט שבט
9 Shevat
Cycle 2

ט סיון
9 Sivan
Cycle 3

Living the Mitzvah

Isn't Marriage for Sharing?

When someone insults you, to whom do you go for sympathy? When you see or hear something shocking, vexing, disappointing or maybe just very interesting, whom do you want to tell? Married couples who share a close bond in their lives would probably feel the urge to share this type of information as well. Are they allowed to do so?

The Dilemma:

Your store was in chaos today thanks to your incompetent new employee. She managed to get the customers angry, to freeze the cash register and lose several phone orders. When you get home and see the warm, friendly smile of your wife, you just long to unload your woes into her ears and soak up some sympathy. Isn't that what wives are for?

The Halachah:

There is no difference between the rules of *loshon hora* for Jews in general and those that apply to spouses. In fact, sharing negative stories and petty complaints tends to taint a relationship rather than strengthen it.

Sefer Chofetz Chaim, Hilchos Loshon Hora 8:10

REMEMBER

Don't share the poison.

9 Tishrei – לע"נ דוד חי בן שלום הכהן ז"ל
ואשתו חנה בת עזרא ע"ה

9 Shevat – Solomon Spiro לע"נ שלמה בן ר' מנחם צבי ז"ל
Dedicated by the Spiro family, Staten Island, NY

9 Sivan – Leo Krieger לע"נ אליעזר נתן בן משה נחום הכהן ז"ל
Dedicated by his daughter Dorothea Krieger

Grow Your Awareness

Revise Your Second Nature

When you get used to doing something regularly, you might say that the routine has become "second nature." In other words, you barely have to think about it. It's a habit. One person reports how he turned calm interactions into a habit by focusing on the people who got his temper up.

"I thought about people who usually irritate me, and I made a special effort to speak to those people in a soft, gentle way. The more the person irked me, the more I focused on being gentle. It was like a contest with myself. When I felt that little bit of irritation rising up, it was my cue to lower my voice a little, relax my face, maybe even smile.

"Little by little, I couldn't believe it but this kind of reaction started to become natural for me. And you know what? It changed the way I felt about them, too."

In his *Iggeres,* the Ramban tells us to speak gently to *all* people. By dealing softly even with those who annoy us, softness becomes second nature. And first nature, as well.

Looking Within: Can you identify people who you'd like to treat with more patience and friendliness?

Building Within: Set up your new reaction to these individuals as a challenge for yourself. Expect to feel the same irritation, but react to it in a new way, until ultimately, your feelings will also change.

QUOTE OF THE DAY

"Habit and character are closely interwoven. Habit becomes second nature."

(Rambam, cited in Shaarei HaMussar)

DAY 10

Living the Mitzvah

May I Fix the Damage?

Everyone knows the allegory in which a rabbi instructs a man to shake out a feather pillow, and then retrieve the feathers flying through the air. Of course he can't do that, and the rabbi explains that likewise, loshon hora one has sent out into the world cannot be retrieved. But is there anything we can do to make amends?

י תשרי
10 Tishrei
Cycle 1

י שבט
10 Shevat
Cycle 2

י סיון
10 Sivan
Cycle 3

The Dilemma:

Lila's sister-in-law Mindy gets on her nerves. Lila somehow always manages to slip in a negative, critical comment whenever Mindy's name comes up. Her comments are often disguised as jokes or helpful observations, but Lila knows that they're coming from an unwholesome place. Even though Mindy doesn't seem to suspect any animosity, Lila knows she is guilty of *loshon hora*. What should she do?

The Halachah:

Loshon hora is a sin between man and his fellow as well as between man and Hashem. The way to repent is to confess the error out loud, regret it sincerely, and resolve never to repeat it. In the above case, while the speaker must repent before Hashem, she does not have to confess or seek out forgiveness from her victim unless her words caused harm; for instance, the victim was rejected for a job or a *shidduch*, in which case the *loshon hora* is also a sin between man and his fellow, and she would have to ask forgiveness from her sister-in law.

Sefer Chofetz Chaim, Hilchos Loshon Hora 8:4; see Be'er Mayim Chaim 48 there.

REMEMBER
Address your teshuvah to Hashem.

10 Tishrei – לע"נ ברוך יצחק ז"ל בן ישרא-ל מרדכי יבלח"ט נלב"ע כ"ה חשון תשס"ג
Dedicated by his parents Yisroel & Freyda Berger

10 Shevat – לע"נ הרב נתן נטע בן אברהם ז"ל
By his grandchildren and great–grandchildren Tzirel Hecht and family

10 Sivan – לע"נ יצחק יעקב בן ראובן הלוי ז"ל

Grow Your Awareness

Check It Out

A person who owns property has to keep on top of it. A developer wouldn't send his workers off to build a swath of houses and never come by to inspect their progress. He has to make sure he gets the maximum for his investment.

The Talmud (*Chullin* 105a) relates that Rabbi Shmuel compared himself unfavorably to his father, saying that if his father was like wine, then he, Rabbi Shmuel, was "vinegar born of wine." The case in point, he said, was that his father would "examine his holdings" twice a day, while Rabbi Shmuel did so only once a day. The Chofetz Chaim says that the "holdings" that both father and son examined were their spiritual "properties" in *Olam Haba*. While the father scrutinized himself twice a day, the son did so once a day.

We all own some property in *Olam Haba*, but if we speak carelessly or hurtfully, we're not likely to be happy with what is constructed on that property. The solution is to check in regularly; take some time each day to examine our words, habits and interactions. That way, we can continually work to repair the things that inevitably go wrong.

Looking Within: How often do you stop to think about the many interactions you have during the day, and their impact on your "property"?

Building Within: Set aside a few minutes before bed to take stock of your day's interactions. Make tomorrow's goal to repair anything that went wrong and to build upon what went well.

QUOTE OF THE DAY

"One hour of repentance and good deeds in this world is better than the entire life of the World to Come."

(Pirkei Avos 4:22)

DAY 11

Living the Mitzvah

What If It's Indirect?

While talking to a friend, you mention in passing a negative trait of an acquaintance. Word slowly spreads, and two years later the fallout from your offhand remark causes the subject not to be hired for a job he was seeking. Is it loshon hora? After all, you caused him harm, even though in a very indirect way!

י״א תשרי
11 Tishrei
Cycle 1

י״א שבט
11 Shevat
Cycle 2

י״א סיון
11 Sivan
Cycle 3

The Dilemma:

Your sister in Israel told you that she upgraded her kitchen, but was unhappy with the installation and feels she did not get what she paid for. Laughingly, she tells you the name of the contractor, Moshe Bandit. "With a name like that I should have known!" she quips. You share that cute story some time later with your brother and that, you think, is the end of it. Except that several years later Moshe Bandit immigrates to the United States and tries to find work, but somehow your "joke" stuck, and he cannot find employment. Are you at fault?

The Halachah:

Words that cause damage directly or indirectly are *loshon hora.* Since we cannot know how information about another person might impact on his life, the best way to avoid indirect harm is to avoid speaking about others' lives.

Sefer Chofetz Chaim, Be'er Mayim Chaim, Introduction to Hilchos Rechilus 9

REMEMBER
Words that are neutral when said, may be loshon hora when heard.

11 Tishrei – As a *zechus* for *brachah v'hatzlachah* in raising our children *b'derech Hashem*
Dedicated by Mr. & Mrs. Ahron and Yaffa Salamah

11 Shevat – לע״נ חיים יצחק בן אברהם בער ז״ל
Dedicated by Moshe & Shaina Amsel

11 Sivan – As a *zechus* for our grandchildren
Dedicated by Zev & Linnet Jeremias

Grow Your Awareness

Drive-by Conversations

When we're driving down a city street, we might barely notice a new store we are passing. If we're stuck at a red light, however, we pay closer attention. We can see the signs and merchandise in the window and perhaps begin wondering if there's anything in there for us. Once inside the store, our perspective changes completely. We've been lured in, and we'll remain inside until we've gotten everything we want from the store.

This scenario is an analogy for becoming involved in *loshon hora*. It teaches us another strategy we can use to prevent this from happening: step on the gas and drive by the topic. As soon as you notice that people are becoming interested in a negative topic, try to move the conversation quickly past the danger zone. Time is of the essence, because once people have stopped and taken time to ponder, they might see something that attracts them. Then they will walk inside and stay until they're satiated.

The way to "step on the gas" is through the art of distraction. It might seem awkward to introduce a completely new subject, but it can be done easily. "Oh, wait a minute! I just remembered something I wanted to tell you!"

Another distraction method is to take the speaker's topic as a springboard for a tangent. The gossip begins: "Did you see Miriam's new car? I can't believe she bought one that's so…." You jump in: "She's back from vacation? I wonder how she liked it. I'll have to give her a call."

Rarely does the conversation return to its former track.

Looking Within: Have you been involved in *loshon hora* conversations that could easily have been bypassed?

Building Within: Resolve to drive the discussion quickly away from negativity as soon as it gets started.

QUOTE OF THE DAY

"The Satan is powerless to prosecute where there is peace."

(Sefer Chareidim, Mitzvos Asei Hateluyim B'dibbur Ch. 4)

DAY 12

Living the Mitzvah

What's So Embarrassing About That?

You know a lot about a lot of people. Sometimes, a piece of information about someone seems to be just the right thing to add to a discussion. If you relate it, the information may eventually be brought up in front of the subject. Are you sure he won't find the revelation embarrassing?

י"ב תשרי
12 Tishrei
Cycle 1

י"ב שבט
12 Shevat
Cycle 2

י"ב סיון
12 Sivan
Cycle 3

The Dilemma:
You're talking to your teenage son about his difficulties in learning. He says it's too late for him to catch up. You exclaim, "Too late? Are you kidding? Do you know that your rebbi, Rabbi Bornstein, first became religious when he was 20? And look what a *talmid chacham* he is now!" Your son wastes no time telling his friends this fascinating fact, and Rabbi Bornstein now has to deal with a situation he finds uncomfortable. Did you speak *loshon hora*?

The Halachah:
Because the information you related caused embarrassment to the subject, it is *loshon hora*. This is so even if you phrased your words as a compliment.

Sefer Chofetz Chaim, Hilchos Loshon Hora 4:1

REMEMBER
If you talk about someone, make sure he'll be happy to hear what you said.

12 Tishrei – In honor of our dear son Eliyahu Sholom Glenner נ"י
Love, Mommy & Daddy

12 Shevat – In memory of Joseph Naftali Bliksylber לע"נ יוסף נפתלי בן נח ז"ל
By his daughter and son-in-law Rabbi Joel & Chana Hochman

12 Sivan – Avrum Teichman לע"נ אברהם בן שמואל ז"ל נלב"ע ט"ז סיון
Dedicated by Mr. Shmuel & Mrs. Adina Teichman

Grow Your Awareness

Remodeling the Building

This account comes from a Brooklyn high-school girl. See how a group of girls transformed their gossip hour into a time to build positive friendships.

Every Friday night while the men were at shul, a group of girls who lived in the same apartment building would gather together and chat about their week. They entertained each other with tales about school, goings-on in their families, and the low-down on their friends. All of them had the vague feeling that their conversations crossed the line into *loshon hora,* but once they got together, there seemed to be no stopping it.

That is, until one of the girls began learning *Positive Word Power for Teens*. One Friday night, she brought the book along with her and read the first day's lesson to her friends. That launched a discussion that got them thinking more seriously about the way they were talking. They decided to institute a *machsom l'fi* (a designated time for focusing on *shmiras haloshon*) during their Friday-night get-togethers.

Now Friday nights at this apartment building have a whole new upbeat tone. The girls start with a lesson from *Positive Word Power for Teens,* and launch from there into familiar territory of school, friends and family. Except that now, they focus on the good in it all.

Looking Within: Do you have a group with whom you regularly get together (perhaps even your family) that tends to wander into *loshon hora* conversations?

Building Within: When you know you are likely to be sitting and chatting for an extended time, prepare something upbeat, interesting or inspiring to re-direct the conversation in a positive direction.

QUOTE OF THE DAY

"In fact, there is only a single transgression: self-centeredness. Once one frees himself from self-centeredness and loves his fellow man like himself, he can fulfill his [life's] mission and all the mitzvos." *(R' S.R. Hirsch, Bereishis Ch. 5)*

DAY 13

Living the Mitzvah

May I Tell It Like It Is?

Not everyone is fit. You might even consider yourself to be among those who could use a few months with a personal trainer. Is there anything wrong with sharing your honest assessment of someone else's physical weakness?

The Dilemma:
You and your friends went on a hike during your summer vacation. One friend, who rarely exercises, had to rest many times along the way. He was out of breath, his legs were aching, and he seriously considered turning back. If you tell this tale to another friend when he asks about your vacation, have you spoken *loshon hora*? After all, it's not a character flaw to be physically weak.

The Halachah:
Because a person never knows how this information might ultimately be used, it should not be related. In the above example, the "weak" friend might lose out on a *shidduch* opportunity or a job offer because of the impression that he is in poor health.

Sefer Chofetz Chaim, Hilchos Loshon Hora 5:2

י"ג תשרי
13 Tishrei
Cycle 1

י"ג שבט
13 Shevat
Cycle 2

י"ג סיון
13 Sivan
Cycle 3

REMEMBER
A word casually tossed can cause someone a loss.

13 Tishrei – לע"נ משה בן ר' שמואל הלוי ז"ל
לע"נ נחמה בת אברהם ע"ה

13 Shevat – Rabbi Avraham Y. Hirsch *z"l* לע"נ הרב אברהם יצחק בן ר' בנימין ז"ל
By his children, the Hirsch, Chopp, Lapa and Axelrod families

13 Sivan – Mendel Herskovits *z"l* לע"נ חיים עזריאל מענדל בן אברהם ז"ל
In loving memory, by Jeffrey & Dorothy Ackerman and family

Grow Your Awareness

Take a Look Inside

If you approved of everything others did and said, you'd have no basis for speaking *loshon hora*. That means that a feeling of disapproval is often the force that turns the key in the ignition and gets our negative thoughts and words flowing.

Rav Chaim of Volozhin (*Consulting the Wise*, p. 116) suggested that we can use this feeling of disapproval as a cue to look inside ourselves, rather than at the flaws of another person. He pointed out that the Gemara (*Kiddushin* 70b) teaches that we have a strong tendency to be particularly sensitive to our own flaws when we see them in others. This principle can turn disapproval into a helpful exercise in self-assessment rather than a launchpad for *loshon hora*.

Looking Within: What are your pet peeves regarding other people?

Building Within: Use your answer to the above question as a guide to assessing yourself in the same areas.

QUOTE OF THE DAY

"Just as the flaws one sees when looking in the mirror are his own, so the flaws he sees in others are reflections of his own."

(Baal Shem Tov, cited in Pisgamim Nivcharim)

DAY 14

Living the Mitzvah

Do You Really Think the Pizza Took Offense?

You're a connoisseur. Is there any reason you cannot share your negative impressions of a particular product? Aren't you entitled to your opinion?

י"ד תשרי
14 Tishrei
Cycle 1

י"ד שבט
14 Shevat
Cycle 2

י"ד סיון
14 Sivan
Cycle 3

The Dilemma:
Your small town has gotten its first kosher pizza shop. You bring a fresh hot pie home to your family, and everyone eagerly digs in. You, however, who grew up in the big city and know what pizza is supposed to taste like, are profoundly disappointed. When your neighbor sees you in shul that evening, he asks, "Have you tried the pizza yet?" You want to tell him, "Don't bother. It doesn't even taste like pizza." Is that *loshon hora*?

The Halachah:
Your negative assessment would be *loshon hora* because it can dissuade others from patronizing the pizza shop and cause the owner to lose business.

Sefer Chofetz Chaim, Hilchos Loshon Hora 5:7

REMEMBER
Give people the chance to form their own opinion.

14 Tishrei – **Dedicated as a *zechus* by Mr. & Mrs. Yonasan Schwartz**

14 Shevat – לע"נ אלימלך בן חיים משה ז"ל
Dedicated by his family

14 Sivan – **Eve Renee Friedman** לע"נ חיה רחל ע"ה בת נחמן דוד יבלח"ט
Dedicated by the Friedman family

Grow Your Awareness

Living in the Now

Look around you right this second. Unless something unusual is happening, you are probably a) physically comfortable, b) well-nourished, c) adequately clothed, d) thought of fondly by at least a few people in the world, and e) free to grow, think, love, dream and strive according to your abilities.

In other words, you're living the dream of billions of people who came before you, billions of people who have inhabited other times and other places, and even many millions living in the world today.

So why that tightness in your heart? Why the grim expression on your face? Why the tension in your forehead?

Much of our unhappiness in life is the product of our own ruminations. Our critical eye, our inflated expectations, our secret belief that nothing difficult should ever befall us, all conspire to keep us in a state of agitation when in reality, "now" is good.

When our minds wander to the "should haves, could haves and would haves" that tear at our equilibrium, we are wandering into territory that's rife with *loshon hora* and *rechilus*. The cure is to lasso our thoughts and drag them back to the "now," to ferret out the goodness in the moment. Even if it's a tough moment, it's the only moment that counts, because we can't change what was, and we can't know what's coming.

Looking Within: What's your default mode of thought? How often do your thoughts wander to problems, worries and criticism that set you up for *loshon hora*?

Building Within: Defer your worrisome thoughts to the times when the specific issues must actually be addressed, and free yourself to think about the good that is at your fingertips.

QUOTE OF THE DAY

"At the origin of all personal growth lies an awareness of the greatness of man."
(Alei Shur, Vol. 1, p. 168)

DAY 15

ט"ו תשרי
15 Tishrei
Cycle 1

ט"ו שבט
15 Shevat
Cycle 2

ט"ו סיון
15 Sivan
Cycle 3

Living the Mitzvah

What If He Doesn't Care Who Knows?

Your friend has a quirk. It's nothing embarrassing — but it may be monetarily harmful if people find out. Your friend, however, talks about his flaw openly. May you?

The Dilemma:

Your coworker is from the "old days." He is baffled by all kinds of technology. He asks you to show him how to operate his new cell phone, and the "tutorial" takes more than an hour. By lunchtime, he needs you to show him again. You've heard him tell people dozens of times, "When it comes to technology, I'm a dinosaur." Are you allowed to tell your friend about your coworker's tech challenges? Perhaps, down the road, another potential employer may refrain from hiring him due to his "technical deficiencies."

The Halachah:

If the information isn't inherently derogatory and the subject clearly does not care who knows, you are allowed to repeat it, even if in some context it might do harm. If the speaker explicitly gives permission to relate the information, you are certainly allowed to do so.

Sefer Chofetz Chaim, Hilchos Loshon Hora; Be'er Mayim Chaim 2:28

REMEMBER
If it's benign and no secret, it can be shared.

15 Tishrei – לע"נ הרב משה בן יצחק צ'רנר ז"ל
Dedicated by Dr. Mechel & Cheftzi Wiederkehr

15 Shevat – לזכות לראות נחת דקדושה מכל יוצאי חלציו שיהיו כולם זרע קודש ברך ד' הולכים בדרך התורה והיראה תמיד אמן סלה

15 Sivan – לזכות לרפואה שלמה רחל בת אסתר פראדל שתחי'
לע"נ מרדכי בן ר' משה ז"ל ואשתו חי' חנה בת ר' צבי ע"ה

Grow Your Awareness

Win the Debate

Here's a great question: If *loshon hora* is so harmful to us, our families and Klal Yisrael, why do people so often give it a pass? Why aren't we morally offended by it as we are by stealing, or repelled as we are by a pork chop? The reason is that the *yetzer hora,* fully aware of the power of *shmiras haloshon,* makes an especially appealing sales pitch for *loshon hora.*

It feeds us three false claims: (1) *loshon hora* is basically harmless since the subject often doesn't hear it; (2) the subject probably deserves what's being said; and (3) it's an inevitable part of human nature that only a *tzaddik* can conquer. If any or all of those three justifications pop into your head as you're about to speak, you now know where those thoughts are coming from.

Once you know that, you can rally your *yetzer tov* to debunk the claims. Harmless? Think of the subject's reaction if he *does* find out (as often happens), or the stain on his reputation, or the tremendous harm to Klal Yisrael. Deserving derision? Maybe so, but *loshon hora* never was and will never be a way to help someone improve. Human nature? Again, maybe so, but the Torah exhorts us to surmount our nature in many ways, and this is one of them. By definition, that means it can be done by every Jew.

Looking Within: Do you really believe that *shmiras haloshon* is doable?

Building Within: When you are challenged, try to remember that "that's just my *yetzer hora* talking."

QUOTE OF THE DAY

"Man [unlike other creatures] lives to perfect himself… He requires speech for that objective to be realized."

(Beis Elokim [Mabit], Shaar HaYesodos Ch. 46)

DAY 16

Living the Mitzvah

May I Give You a Little Advice About Dovid?

Whether you're a parent, a teacher or a babysitter, you might feel the need to report to someone about a child's less-than-sterling traits. Are you allowed to tell someone negative things about a child?

ט"ז תשרי
16 Tishrei
Cycle 1

ט"ז שבט
16 Shevat
Cycle 2

ט"ז סיון
16 Sivan
Cycle 3

The Dilemma:
You are the math teacher of a seventh-grade class. At the end of the school year, the eighth-grade math teacher wants to review the class roster with you and find out about each student's personality and math ability in order to be prepared for the coming year.

You have several students who are disruptive. On one hand, you want to tell the eighth-grade teacher to beware of those few students — make sure they don't sit together and stop them in their tracks the minute they begin acting up. On the other hand, you wonder if that might be *loshon hora.*

REMEMBER
Loshon hora is dangerous to children.

The Halachah:
Even though most people would not judge a child harshly because of his immaturity, one is still prohibited from speaking *loshon hora* about him or her. Therefore, caution must be taken in the above scenario to assure that what is being said is in fact beneficial for the child and not detrimental. After all, we can still damage a child's prospects by speaking negatively about him. Furthermore, children mature and change. In a new school year, he should have a new chance to prove himself.

Sefer Chofetz Chaim, Hilchos Loshon Hora 8:3

16 Tishrei – As a *zechus* for a *refuah shleimah* for the *cholim* in *Am Yisrael*
16 Shevat – לזכות שרה חי' בת מירל רבקה אביטן שתחי'
In honor of our granddaughter, by Debra & Meyer Abittan
16 Sivan – Dedicated anonymously as a *zechus*

Grow Your Awareness

Is That Me?

Can you hold your tongue when you're with someone you want to impress? Most people can. Yet sometimes, we tell ourselves that we "can't" keep our cool. We're tired, irritated, ill, under a lot of pressure, or in a rush, and whatever is in our mind pops out of our mouths.

Nevertheless, the *Iggeres HaRamban* instructs us to speak gently to all people, at *all* times. The realization that we actually can control ourselves when we must — when we're at work, dealing with a customer, speaking to a parent or an in-law, or a rebbi or *rav* — proves that self-control is possible with the right motivation.

One woman offers this idea for rallying the necessary motivation. "When we're in our homes, we imagine that no one hears us besides our family. We know of course that Hashem hears us, but that's a difficult concept to keep in mind all the time. At one point, I realized that the tone of speech in my house was not something I was proud of. So I turned on a recorder and left it in the kitchen, where most of the family action was. Knowing that what I was saying was being recorded right here in this world did the trick. I didn't want to be horrified by what I would hear when I listened to it."

Looking Within: Would you be embarrassed if someone you respected happened to be at the front door, able to hear you dealing with a tense moment in your home?

Building Within: Use a recorder just one time, and see how it affects your interactions. Then listen to the recording to get an objective sense of how you speak within your own four walls.

QUOTE OF THE DAY

"R' Shimon bar Yochai said: Had I been at Mount Sinai I would have requested two mouths, one for Torah and the other for everything else. But I reconsidered. If we cannot stop speaking *loshon hora* with only one mouth, certainly not with two!"
(Yerushalmi Berachos 1:2).

DAY 17

Living the Mitzvah

Is It Possible to Eat My Words?

What happens if you say something you shouldn't have said, and now you regret it? Is there any way to undo the damage?

י"ז תשרי
17 Tishrei
Cycle 1

י"ז שבט
17 Shevat
Cycle 2

י"ז סיון
17 Sivan
Cycle 3

The Dilemma:

You have a friend who has moved away from the neighborhood. You are one of the few people with whom she has stayed in touch. She calls and asks, "What happened with the Steinbergs? I heard there's trouble there!" You tell her everything you know, including rumors about Mrs. Steinberg's mental health. When you hang up the phone, you feel uneasy. Your words could come back to haunt Mrs. Steinberg, *but what can you do about it now*?

The Halachah:

To do *teshuvah* for hurting someone, the person must ask forgiveness from the one he has hurt. However, in a case like the one above, where the information has not yet done harm, we do not approach the victim. Instead, we do our best to stop the information in its tracks, perhaps by telling the listener that it was not accurate.

Sefer Chofetz Chaim, Hilchos Loshon Hora 4:12 with Be'er Mayim Chaim 4:48

REMEMBER

Don't just regret; retract!

17 Tishrei – In memory of Samuel Weintraub
Dedicated by Ari & Elissa Ciment and family

17 Shevat – לזכות דבורה פריידא בת שושנה רייזל ובינימן יעקב ישראל ברדמן שיחיו
Dedicated by her great–great aunt Judy Z. Lane, in her honor

17 Sivan – May today's learning be a זכות for רפואות וישועות for our entire משפחה.
Dedicated by Reuven & Erica Weinstein

Grow Your Awareness

The Wrong Time to Decide

Your mother-in-law said something to you that you found very insulting, even though she said it in the sweetest voice possible. Now your friend is speaking to you about a recent conflict she had with *her* mother-in-law, and naturally your own wound is beginning to sting all over again.

"Maybe it's all right to talk about it," you think. "After all, if I need to vent my emotions, that's for *to'eles*."

Another inner voice quietly suggests that the need to vent is not all that great. In fact, you've already discussed the situation with a trusted confidante. Furthermore, had your friend not brought up her own story, you would not even be thinking about yours.

"But she's always hurting me," you say to yourself. "Why should I hold back? A little commiseration might help my friend, anyway."

The Ralbag (Rabbi Levi ben Gershon) offers a quick way to settle this inner debate: "Realize that even the greatest people make errors of judgment when they're angry." Therefore, when we're angry, we are in no position to adjudge our negative words to be for *to'eles*. The fact that we're angry is excellent evidence that they are not.

Looking Within: Do you excuse a desire to speak negatively about someone who has angered you by finding a constructive purpose for speaking?

Building Within: When you have an interpersonal situation that you need to discuss *l'to'eles,* limit yourself to one confidante whom you trust to hear you out and advise you.

QUOTE OF THE DAY

"A person accomplishes much more through patience than with all the anger in the world."
(Rabbi Chaim Volozhiner)

DAY 18

Living the Mitzvah

Is It Best Not to Confess?

People make mistakes, and you've made one. You said something about another person and now you find out that he's been harmed by what you said. You know you need to get his forgiveness, but what if you'll only be hurting him more?

י"ח תשרי
18 Tishrei
Cycle 1

י"ח שבט
18 Shevat
Cycle 2

י"ח סיון
18 Sivan
Cycle 3

The Dilemma:

Your dear friend Danny has had a hard time finding his marriage match. In talking about his situation with Eli, a mutual acquaintance, you mention that Danny seems a little slow. "I think he was a premature baby. Maybe he's got a bit of brain damage." The next day, you hear that Danny's latest *shidduch* has fizzled, "just like that." Worse yet, you discover that the young lady was Eli's cousin. Should you tell Danny what you've done and ask forgiveness?

The Halachah:

If your words cause damage to another person, you are required to seek that person's forgiveness. However, Rabbi Yisrael Salanter is reported to have held that if the victim would suffer more by hearing about your *loshon hora,* you must refrain from informing him and forfeit that part of *teshuvah.* One should ask for a general *mechilah* (forgiveness) at an appropriate time, such as Erev Yom Kippur.

Sefer Chofetz Chaim, Hilchos Loshon Hora, Be'er Mayim Chaim 4:48

REMEMBER

Sometimes repairing damage causes further damage.

18 Tishrei – **In memory of my parents, Harold D. Kane** ***z"l, yahrtzeit*** **12 Adar II and Eleanor R. Kane** ***a"h, yahrtzeit*** **18 Tishrei**

18 Shevat – **Harav Yitzchok** ***ben*** **Peretz Klein** לע"נ הרב יצחק בן פרץ ז"ל
Dedicated by Eli & Sandy Klein and family

18 Sivan – ***L'ilui nishmas*** **all the** ***kedoshim*** **of the Fleishman / Sklorovits families**

Grow Your Awareness

Think About the Weather

Pessie R. grew up in a house in which negativity reigned supreme. Both her parents frequently found fault with her, her siblings, each other, the rabbi, some of the neighbors, the schools and so forth.

"I didn't realize until I went away to Eretz Yisrael for seminary that this was not the way all families were," she said. "While I was there, I helped a few American kollel families on Fridays. I was right there in the middle of Shabbos preparations with the whole family home. I knew no one was putting on an act for my benefit. I was seeing real life for these families, and it was nothing like life in my family's house.

"It struck me that when I walked into these apartments it was like walking into a sunny day. There were smiles. There was music playing. I remembered coming home from school to my parents' house and it was so different; it was like a thundercloud hung over the house. This idea stuck with me, and when I got married and set up my own home, I thought about that thundercloud and how I wanted my family never to feel it. Today this image still helps me put aside negative thoughts and keep things positive."

Looking Within: Are you aware that your mood is contagious, and that you can raise or bring down the mood of everyone in your household?

Building Within: Imagine that you create the weather in your home. When you smile the sun shines, and when you're angry, negative or moody, everyone needs to run for shelter.

QUOTE OF THE DAY

"The tongue is the quill of the heart."
(Rabbeinu Bechaya ibn Pekuda, Chovos HaLevavos, Shaar HaBechinah 5)

DAY 19

Living the Mitzvah

May I Just Kind of...Drop a Hint?

You know better than to say something negative about another person. But sometimes it just seems impossible to keep your real feelings from coming through. An eye-roll, a sarcastic smile, a sigh, a laugh, a shrug of the shoulders…are you responsible for negative conclusions people draw?

י"ט תשרי
19 Tishrei
Cycle 1

י"ט שבט
19 Shevat
Cycle 2

י"ט סיון
19 Sivan
Cycle 3

The Dilemma:

Your next-door neighbor is a hypochondriac who often fails to show up where and when he's expected. You were supposed to go together to a fundraising meeting for your children's school, but he opted out. When you get there, the head of the committee asks you where he is. You shrug and turn your hands up in a gesture that says, "What can you expect?" The committee head says, "Oh, another mystery disease?" Did you speak *loshon hora*?

The Halachah:

Facial expressions, gestures or body language that convey something negative are also considered *loshon hora*.

Sefer Chofetz Chaim, Hilchos Loshon Hora 1:8

REMEMBER
Body language can speak louder than words.

19 Tishrei – לע"נ אהרן נתן בן יהודה אלימלך ז"ל

19 Shevat – *L'zechus* Yanky Mandelbaum
With much appreciation, the Blackman family

19 Sivan – Chani Mermelstein לע"נ חנה מינדל בת חיים צבי ע"ה נלב"ע כ"ג סיון
Dedicated by her children

Grow Your Awareness

Flying Under the Radar

Making a grand proclamation of giving up loshon hora forever seems to invite disappointment. Rav Shlomo Wolbe zt"l offers a better strategy in his sefer Alei Shur (Shaar 2), in which he describes an effective strategy for defeating the yetzer hora.

Rav Wolbe was once on the way to Egypt from Eretz Yisrael when he noticed that the plane was flying very low, mere yards off the ground. Rav Wolbe grew concerned and asked the crew if there was a mechanical problem. Their response: the plane was fine, but they were within the range of the Egyptian radar and wanted to remain undetected. Since the radar system could detect only aircraft flying above its height, they were simply "keeping a low profile."

The *yetzer hora*, like the radar system, immediately picks up the signal when we attempt to soar to great heights, and it stands ready to shoot us down. Therefore, we are wise to implement the strategy of the plane and fly low. In other words, if we choose to work on something small, we won't attract the *yetzer hora's* attention. Flying below the radar, we'll ultimately get where we need to go.

Looking within: Do you have big resolutions that you've made over and over again, but have not yet accomplished?

Building within: Choose one small area of your life in which you could realistically increase your level of *shmiras haloshon.* Note your successes and regroup after any setbacks you might experience.

QUOTE OF THE DAY

"It is impossible to assist another, either emotionally or physically, without possessing a positive perspective of people."

(Shem MiShmuel, Bamidbar, Beha'aloscha, 5677)

DAY 20

Living the Mitzvah

What If I Don't Name Names?

You know a story that would really illustrate the point you're discussing with your friend. It puts someone in a negative light, but you can tell the story without naming the subject. Is that permitted?

כ תשרי
20 Tishrei
Cycle 1

כ שבט
20 Shevat
Cycle 2

כ סיון
20 Sivan
Cycle 3

The Dilemma:

Your husband is having a tough time with a super competitive coworker who is always stealing the credit for your husband's work. You used to work with someone just like him, and you learned how to handle the situation. May you tell your husband the story if you don't mention your former coworker's name?

The Halachah:

Even if you don't mention a name, it's *loshon hora* if the listener would be able to identify the subject anyway. Also, if you deride a nameless member of a certain group as a way of ridiculing the whole group, it is *loshon hora*.

Sefer Chofetz Chaim, Hilchos Loshon Hora 3:4

REMEMBER
No name does not necessarily mean no blame.

20 Tishrei – לע"נ מאיר וואלף בן דוב ז"ל
Dedicated by the Leitner family

20 Shevat – **Joseph Dweck** לע"נ יוסף בן סבות ז"ל
Dedicated by Rabbi & Mrs. Eli J. Monsour

20 Sivan – לזכות לבריאות, להצלחה, פרנסה, נחת והרחות הדעת וכל טוב סלה
ללאה יהודית בת שיינדל שתחי' ויצחק מרדכי בן רבקה פיגא נ"י ומשפחתם

Grow Your Awareness

Life Skills

Every skill requires training. The skill of being a successful human being, however, is often left to chance. Because of that, many people adhere to false ideas of what is required to be a success in life. They might equate success with acquiring stuff, being the smartest student, having the most children or the best children, having the best job or the biggest bank account… However, there is one training manual that spells out everything we need to know if we truly want to be successful human beings. That is *Sefer Chofetz Chaim,* or any of its many derivatives that teach the laws of *shmiras haloshon.*

Someone who learns *shmiras haloshon* succeeds. He is beloved; he brings Hashem's blessings into his life; he avoids hurting people; he forges positive relationships with friends and coworkers; he brings positive energy and love into his family life.

The thousands of people who learn Shmiras Haloshon Yomi are testimony to its power. As the Manchester Rosh Yeshivah, Rav Yehudah Zev Segal *zt"l*, said, "I don't know of any family that learns two halachos [of *shmiras haloshon*] a day that hasn't seen a *yeshuah."* For anyone who wants the ultimate formula for finding favor with Hashem and his fellow man, this is it.

Looking Within: Do you see the Torah's laws on human interaction as an area to learn, practice and master like other life skills?

Building Within: Find a way to make learning *shmiras haloshon* a regular part of your life.

QUOTE OF THE DAY

"I don't know of any family that learns two *halachos* [of *shmiras haloshon*] a day that hasn't seen a *yeshuah."*

(Rabbi Yehuda Zev Segal, Manchester Rosh Yeshivah, Founder of Shmiras Haloshon Yomi)

DAY 21

Living the Mitzvah

"He's Come a Long Way": Compliment or Insult?

When people make a turnaround in their lives, we're often awed and surprised by their achievement. If their name comes up in conversation, those who remember them from "back in the day" naturally want to let people know what a high hill they have climbed. Is that a positive statement, or a negative one?

כ"א תשרי
21 Tishrei
Cycle 1

כ"א שבט
21 Shevat
Cycle 2

כ"א סיון
21 Sivan
Cycle 3

The Dilemma:

You know a girl who, in high school, was kicked out of class at least once a week for her outrageous behavior. Now, 15 years later, she's a powerhouse. She runs a large family and a successful business creating custom wedding gowns. Your neighbor recently made her acquaintance and mentions how impressed she was with her. You want to add to her glory by saying, "She's come such a long way since high school. She's amazing!"

May you?

The Halachah:

Implying something negative while sincerely saying something positive is *avak loshon hora,* literally, the "dust" of *loshon hora,* which is a Rabbinic prohibition.

Sefer Chofetz Chaim, Hilchos Loshon Hora 9:1

REMEMBER

Keep the dust from spreading.

21 Tishrei – **In loving memory of Chana Laub** לע"נ חנה שיינדל בת ישראל יהודה ע"ה
Dedicated by Sary & Shlomo Levine, Yudi, Aroni and Yoni

21 Shevat – **Louise Joy Schiff** לע"נ ליבא בת אברהם ע"ה
Dedicated by Zina Schiff

21 Sivan – **In honor of our children Rachel, David, and Yosef Goldstein**
Dedicated by Ben & Magda Goldstein

Grow Your Awareness

A Topic in Your Pocket

An important factor in making progress against *loshon hora* and *rechilus* is to have strategies at the ready. This is especially so because by its very nature, anything to do with speech must include other people. Controlling ourselves is difficult enough, but influencing others is nearly impossible without some forethought.

If you know that someone has a sore subject that always comes up, a sound strategy is to prepare another topic that you can introduce to take the conversation in a different direction. Think of something that is of interest to the person, so that he or she will be truly engaged in the topic rather than waiting for the moment to resume his complaints.

The key is to introduce your topic before the other person gets started. For instance, a person has an intrusive neighbor. Whenever you speak to him, he wants to discuss his neighbor's latest affronts. He goes far beyond the constructive purpose of sharing his burden with a friend, over the borderline into plain *loshon hora*. Therefore, before he gets started, push off strongly in a different direction: "You gotta hear this!"

Once you've accomplished your goal, don't talk too long. Otherwise, your friend is liable to return like a homing pigeon back to his pet topic. Be prepared, be brief and you'll be successful at closing off an avenue of *loshon hora* in your life.

Looking Within: Is there someone with whom my conversations often veer into *loshon hora*? What is the topic that elicits the negativity?

Building Within: When speaking with that person, be alert to his opening up his sore topic, and keep in mind "kosher" subjects he is likely to find interesting.

QUOTE OF THE DAY

"If someone sinned by speaking *loshon hora* or *rechilus*, the antidote is for him to consistently speak words of Torah."
(Vilna Gaon)

DAY 22

Living the Mitzvah

Can "What a Great Guy" Be Harmful Speech?

When you want to mention a good deed someone has done, you are not likely to run those words through your loshon-hora filter. After all, what harm could they do? Nevertheless, when you give some thought to the possible consequences of such a statement, you might realize that it's necessary to squelch your accolades.

כ״ב תשרי
22 Tishrei
Cycle 1

כ״ב שבט
22 Shevat
Cycle 2

כ״ב סיון
22 Sivan
Cycle 3

The Dilemma:

Your children's struggling yeshivah rarely gives tuition breaks. On the other hand, many parents, though affluent, regularly apply for scholarships on the theory that they should not have to pay "full price." This year, you applied for a scholarship and received a generous one because of unusual expenses you're facing. The head of the tuition committee was very generous and sympathetic. May you praise him to your neighbor, who also has children in that school?

The Halachah:

If your praise might encourage others to take advantage of someone's kindness, generosity or hospitality, it could cause financial or emotional hardship to the subject of your praise. Because the words can cause harm, they are not permitted.

Sefer Chofetz Chaim, Hilchos Loshon Hora 9:3

REMEMBER
Appreciate a kindness, but don't advertise it.

22 Tishrei – לע״נ אבינו מורינו דניאל בן יונה ז״ל
למשפחת דן

22 Shevat – לע״נ יוסף דוד בן הרב יצחק אייזק ז״ל נלב״ע כ״ד שבט
לזכות משה דוד בן לאה גיטל נ״י בתורה ובמעשים טובים

22 Sivan – **As a *zechus* for** הצלחה **for our** משפחה **and** כלל ישראל
Dedicated by Rabbi & Mrs. Yehuda Rupp

Grow Your Awareness

See the Satellite View

If we were to see at a glance everything going on in Heaven and on earth the minute we speak a word of *loshon hora*, we would be no more likely to say it than we would be to set our house on fire. On the other hand, if we could see that same view of what happens when we restrain ourselves, we'd run after every opportunity. The problem is to keep these powerful images in mind on a moment-by-moment basis.

One family in Lakewood, N.J. made this a family project. Based on a brochure distributed by the Chofetz Chaim Heritage Foundation, they created a poster with a "satellite view" of the blessings *shmiras haloshon* brings and the troubles brought on by *loshon hora*. One artistic family member designed the poster so that the whole picture was laid out before the viewer's eyes at a glance, neatly contrasting life in this world and in the World to Come for people who guard their tongues and those who do not.

"We framed the poster and hung it in the dining room. We also posted a copy on the refrigerator. My husband and I each brought copies to work, and each of the children made it the first page in their loose-leaf binders," says Miriam B. "It isn't an instant cure, but with those messages all around us wherever we are, it certainly sinks in and makes a huge difference. It helps us see what's going on when we speak, so we don't forget."

Looking Within: How clear a presence is *shmiras haloshon* on your radar as you go through your day?

Building Within: Involve your family in coming up with a strategy that will keep your *shmiras haloshon* awareness at a higher level, such as obtaining a reminder table-card (available free from Chofetz Chaim Heritage Foundation).

QUOTE OF THE DAY

"It never ceases to amaze how people seek *segulos*... I would advise to guard against this sin [*loshon hora*]. Certainly their possessions will be blessed more than if they had performed any *segulah*."

(Sefer Shmiras HaLoshon 2:9)

CHAPTER 2

Ahavas Yisrael — Unite as Hashem's Children

Those who feel a loving bond with their fellow Jews have a hard time hearing or saying anything negative about them. That's why building our sense of *ahavas Yisrael* is one of the fundamental ways to drive *loshon hora* out of our lives. No matter what divides us, we can stand together with compassion and care for each other, giving our Father the ultimate *nachus*.

DAY 23

Living the Mitzvah

Should I Just "Plead the Fifth"?

The Fifth Amendment of the Constitution gives witnesses the right to remain silent rather than say something that would incriminate them. What if we want to remain silent rather than say something that would make us guilty of loshon hora? Are we allowed to "plead the Fifth" rather than give negative information?

כ"ג תשרי
23 Tishrei
Cycle 1

כ"ג שבט
23 Shevat
Cycle 2

כ"ג סיון
23 Sivan
Cycle 3

The Dilemma:

You move into a new neighborhood, next door to your friend's grumpy old widowed uncle. He's already asked you to keep your children off his driveway, to mow your lawn only after 11 a.m., and to cut down a tree that blocks his sunlight. Your friend asks, "So, what do you think of my Uncle Mel? Isn't he a riot?" May you say, "I'd rather not answer that one"?

The Halachah:

Saying you don't want to answer implies that what you have to say is negative. Therefore, that answer is in itself *avak loshon hora*. In this situation the correct response would be, "He seems like a nice man." And leave it at that.

Sefer Chofetz Chaim, Hilchos Loshon Hora 9:1 with Be'er Mayim Chaim 2

REMEMBER

Saying you can't say something is saying something.

23 Tishrei – לזכות למשפחת ווייסמאן

23 Shevat – לזכות ישראל מאיר בן רבקה נ"י

23 Sivan – לע"נ אברהם יוסף בן פנחס ז"ל

Grow Your Ahavas Yisrael

Believe You Can

To many people, the idea of living without envy and animosity toward at least some people in their lives seems foreign. Who doesn't dislike someone? Who doesn't have people in their lives that get under their skin or make them miserable? A boss, an in-law, a neighbor, a teacher — isn't it inevitable?

When we tell ourselves that negative feelings toward other people are an inescapable part of human nature, we actually exempt ourselves from the Torah's injunction, "Do not hate your brother in your heart" (*Vayikra* 19:17). It's as if we're saying to Hashem, "Well, the other 612 I think I can handle, but this one…sorry. It's just not possible."

Yet there is no mitzvah in the Torah that is aimed at *tzaddikim* only. Rabbi Yeruchem Levovitz says that this mitzvah is aimed at everyone, even "the simplest Jew" (*Consulting the Wise,* p. 132). He calls it an "important and basic obligation." So indeed, envy, grudges and animosity might be human nature. But the Torah tells us through this mitzvah that our natures do not have to rule us.

Looking Within: What's holding you back from fully committing yourself to this mitzvah?

Building Within: When you are around a person who annoys you, imagine he or she can read your mind.

QUOTE OF THE DAY

"'Do not cast the sin on [your fellow]' (*Vayikra* 19:17) — i.e., do not cast the entire sin on the sinner. Instead, feel with him and repent yourself for this sin, and your friend will be moved to follow suit."
(Sfas Emes, Kedoshim 5643)

DAY 24

Living the Mitzvah

What If I'm Forced to Speak Loshon Hora?

What if someone in a position of authority — a boss, a teacher, or even your parents — demands information from you that would hurt another person. What should you do?

כ"ד תשרי
24 Tishrei
Cycle 1

כ"ד שבט
24 Shevat
Cycle 2

כ"ד סיון
24 Sivan
Cycle 3

The Dilemma:

Your boss doesn't trust anyone in the office but you. When you meet with him, he often fishes around for negative information about your coworkers [not *l'to'eles*]. One day, he demands information that would certainly be *loshon hora*. Must you risk being fired to avoid speaking *loshon hora*?

The Halachah:

Shmiras haloshon is no different from *kashrus* or Shabbos observance. Just as you would accept inconvenience, financial loss and social derision to keep those mitzvos, you are required to do the same for *shmiras haloshon*.

Sefer Chofetz Chaim, Hilchos Loshon Hora 1:6

REMEMBER
Shmiras haloshon is non-negotiable.

24 Tishrei – *L'zechus* Naomi Malka *bas* Hochana Leah

24 Shevat – As a *zechus* for our family
Dedicated by Mr. & Mrs. Ephraim Bassen

24 Sivan – Rabbi Dr. Samuel Stollman לע"נ הרב שלמה בן הרב יצחק ז"ל
Dedicated by the Stollman family

Grow Your Ahavas Yisrael

The Ties That Bind

- You're away on business in a city you've never visited before. You feel like a total stranger until you walk into the one *minyan* in town for Minchah. All of a sudden, you're at home. When *davening* is finished, you meet a few of the *minyan* members and within two minutes, discover friends in common.
- You're driving down the highway and see a car pulled over to the side of the road. A man in a black hat is standing outside, staring under the hood, while a flock of children stand nearby, clinging to their mother. You pull over and stop to help.
- You live in America, but when Jews in France are being persecuted you speak of them as "us."

These are moments when the ties that bind us hug us tight. We all have such instances, and one woman notes that when she reviews these scenes in her mind, she finds the acceptance she needs to reject preconceptions and *loshon hora* about fellow Jews.

Looking Within: Have you had moments or experiences like the ones described above, in which you feel especially strongly your connection with your fellow Jews?

Building Within: Try to take notice of times when you feel this connection and in doing so, build a greater love and acceptance of all types of Jews.

QUOTE OF THE DAY

"Unity among a people is the gold or silver strand upon which many precious gems are strung."

(Akeidas Yitzchak, Bamidbar, Shaar 74 [Parashas Nasso])

DAY 25

Living the Mitzvah

May I Respond to My Competitor's Lies?

You run a business. One of your competitors seems to be spreading false rumors about your services or merchandise. Can you hit back with some rumors about his business?

כ"ה תשרי
25 Tishrei
Cycle 1

כ"ה שבט
25 Shevat
Cycle 2

כ"ה סיון
25 Sivan
Cycle 3

The Dilemma:
Your auto service-station has been in business for many years and has many loyal customers. A new station opens up in town and some of your customers give it a try. Eventually, a few come back to you and you find out that your competitor has been badmouthing your skill as a mechanic. Can you fight fire with fire and disparage his skills in return?

The Halachah:
There is no basis in Torah for responding to *loshon hora* against you with a return volley of *loshon hora*. Note: You should consult a *rav* for what steps you may take to protect yourself and your business in your particular situation.

Be'er Mayim Chaim, Pesichah Lavin 8,9 ד"ה ומה שציירתי

REMEMBER

Loshon hora isn't self-defense.

25 Tishrei – **In honor of the birth of Aharon Tzvi Berger**

25 Shevat – לע"נ שלום בן ציונה ז"ל
Dedicated by Orna Ben-Samuel and family

25 Sivan – **Aviva Ghatan** לע"נ אביבה יוכבד בת מנחם מנדל ע"ה
Dedicated by her family

Grow Your Ahavas Yisrael

Digging Up the Root

You know it's not right, but some people just drive you crazy. They do something that is in the slightest way insulting or annoying, and it eats at you until you inevitably spit out some *loshon hora* about it. But of course you can't complain to someone else about something so minor, so you build it up into true malfeasance: "He was *davening* so loud that I couldn't hear myself. I mean, great, he has a lot of *kavanah,* but does he have to share it with the entire shul? Does he have to show everyone what a *tzaddik* he is at everyone else's expense?"

On the other hand, there are people who can do no wrong in your eyes. Their sins of omission are written off to forgetfulness. When they do wrong, it's because they're "works in progress." You don't mention their flaws and mistakes to anyone, because you feel protective of their reputation.

Why are we so critical of some people and so tolerant of others? Moreover: Since our critical eye ends up expressing itself through a critical tongue, how can we find a way to build our tolerance for those we find irritating? The Vilna Gaon explains (*Consulting the Wise,* p. 32) that "inner hatred" for another person makes us intolerant, while love for the other person makes us tolerant of their flaws. Getting to the root of our negative feelings and making an effort to change them is a powerful way to nip *loshon hora* in the bud.

Looking Within: Is there someone who gets under your skin to whom you just cannot give a break?

Building Within: Seek out ways to build a more positive feeling about that person, perhaps by doing favors for him, which our *gedolim* say is a way to build love.

QUOTE OF THE DAY

"[*Klal*] *Yisrael* will not be redeemed until they become a unified entity."

(Tanchuma, Nitzavim 1)

DAY 26

Living the Mitzvah

What If Someone Really Needs to Know What I Know?

On one hand, we now know that we are not allowed to say negative things or even make a neutral comment that can hurt another person's standing. But what if withholding the information about one person causes harm to another?

כ"ו תשרי
26 Tishrei
Cycle 1

כ"ו שבט
26 Shevat
Cycle 2

כ"ו סיון
26 Sivan
Cycle 3

The Dilemma:

Your good-natured friend wants to hire a troubled teen to help him in his bagel shop. You know that the boy has a drug problem and has been caught stealing. Should you warn your friend?

The Halachah:

This question falls under the category of *to'eles* — a constructive purpose for which, under certain circumstances, *loshon hora* may be told. While we are not allowed to denigrate others, we are also not allowed to stand by and watch them be harmed, according to the mitzvah of *"Lo sa'amod al dam rei'acha"* (literally translated: "Do not stand by [the shedding] of your fellow's blood," *Vayikra* 19:16).

Sefer Chofetz Chaim, Hilchos Loshon Hora 10:6

REMEMBER
There are times to be quiet and times to speak.

26 Tishrei – Dedicated as a *zechus* for the Sonbolian family

26 Shevat – לע"נ טובא בת צבי ע"ה
Dedicated by Michael & Erica Sommer and family

26 Sivan – Sabina Yochevette Friedman לע"נ שיינדל יוכבד בת יעקב הלוי ז"ל
Dedicated by the Friedman family

Grow Your Ahavas Yisrael

He's Right Here!

One of the hallmarks of speaking *loshon hora* is that the speaker usually takes a quick glance around the room to make sure there's no one there who might take offense at what he's about to say. That should tell us something.

It tells us that no matter how we justify *loshon hora* to ourselves, we know it would offend the person about whom we are speaking, and anyone who really cares about that person as well. That's why we look around us. We don't want to be caught in an embarrassing situation in which we have to explain ourselves.

Therefore, a good way to curtail *loshon hora* is to picture the person about whom you are about to speak. Imagine he or she is standing right there listening to you. Imagine how embarrassed he will be when you put his unflattering moment or personality flaw on display for others to see, mull over and talk about. Imagine the person shaking his head, silently pleading with you to stop.

You don't need to look around before you speak. Just look inside.

Looking Within: Do you have a small part of your consciousness that excuses *loshon hora* with the thought that the subject will never find out, and therefore, it does no harm?

Building Within: Use the strategy offered above — imagining that the person you're discussing is right there — to build your compassion for others, which will in turn motivate you to use this strategy.

QUOTE OF THE DAY

"If people would take just a moment to think about others, they would hear [the subject of their *loshon hora*] begging, 'Please! Don't embarrass me!' — and no one would speak negatively about another person."
(Daas Chochmah U'Mussar, Vol. 1, p. 10)

DAY
27

Living the Mitzvah

May I Try to Get Someone to Help?

You see trouble brewing in someone's life and you want to bring in a person who might be able to help — a teacher, rav, parent, counselor or friend. But obviously that will entail telling someone about the negative situation.

כ"ז תשרי
27 Tishrei
Cycle 1

כ"ז שבט
27 Shevat
Cycle 2

כ"ז סיון
27 Sivan
Cycle 3

The Dilemma:

You have a friend who is the life of the party at every *simchah*. You know he has a drinking problem. Most of his friends laugh it off, but you see that it is beginning to damage his health and his family. Your friend is close to a particular rebbi. May you tell the rebbi about your friend's problem and ask him to intercede?

The Halachah:

While there are still many conditions that must be met before seeking help in this way, this example does illustrate one of the constructive purposes for which *loshon hora* may be told. That is: helping the person about whom we are speaking.

Sefer Chofetz Chaim, Hilchos Loshon Hora 4:5; Hilchos Rechilus 9:1

REMEMBER
Is it really for his own good?

27 Tishrei – לע"נ אליהו יוחנן בן אהרן יוסף ז"ל נלב"ע כ"ח תשרי
27 Shevat – לזכות דוד בן מרגלית נ"י
27 Sivan – הצלחה לברכה בת רודיא צירל תחי' ומשפחתה
לע"נ מנחם מענדל בן ר' יהודה לייב הלוי ז"ל

Grow Your Ahavas Yisrael

How Could You?

A key factor in *shmiras haloshon* is respect for other people. The more we respect someone, the less likely we are to think or say anything negative about him. In addition, if others start saying something negative about that person we will argue, defend him or, if necessary, leave the conversation. No one would stand idly by, for instance, and hear his mother or father insulted.

Rabbi Yeruchem Levovitz (*Consulting the Wise*, p. 137) says that if our goal is to treat others with respect, our best strategy is to ingrain in ourselves the recognition that each person is created in Hashem's image. Each is Hashem's creation, to be treated with care.

Looking Within: Are there any people in your life who you feel are "fair game" for negative comments? If so, why do you see them in that way?

Building Within: Change your negative outlook by purposefully acting respectfully toward someone whom you have trouble respecting. Your "acting" will eventually end up as a new perception of the person.

QUOTE OF THE DAY

"The only way to properly fulfill the *mitzvah* to love our fellow man is by internalizing the awareness that he is created in Hashem's image."
(Rabbi Chaim Mordechai Katz, Be'er Mechokeik)

DAY 28

Living the Mitzvah

May I Help the Victim and Warn Others?

What if you know someone who is being victimized by another person? May you help him/her if it entails hearing or speaking loshon hora? May you get help for the victim from others? May you warn people who might fall victim to that person in the future?

כ"ח תשרי
28 Tishrei
Cycle 1

כ"ח שבט
28 Shevat
Cycle 2

כ"ח סיון
28 Sivan
Cycle 3

The Dilemma:

Your neighbor is married to a woman who is moody and depressive. She puts on a good act in public, but you know the truth because you've seen her in action. Sometimes your neighbor even tells you his problems. Are you allowed to hear his complaints? Subsequently, the couple get a divorce and someone you know begins to date the ex-wife. May you tell him about this woman's emotional issues?

The Halachah:

With the understanding that, first and foremost, there are many parameters and conditions to be met, the simple answer is that helping your neighbor deal with his wife and warning others who might become involved with her are legitimate constructive purposes if you meet the other conditions of *to'eles*. However, a *rav* must be asked what can be said, how much and to whom.

Sefer Chofetz Chaim, Hilchos Loshon Hora 10:1; Hilchos Rechilus 9:3

REMEMBER
Help whenever help is allowed.

28 Tishrei – לע"נ שמעון צבי הירש בן ר' יוסף נחמי' ז"ל
Dedicated by his loving mother

28 Shevat – לע"נ ברכה אסתר ע"ה בת בנימן ז"ל
Dedicated by the Bublick family of Passaic

28 Sivan – Marion Cooper לע"נ מרים בת אלכסנדר ע"ה
Dedicated by Lisa & Ronnie Pachino

Grow Your Ahavas Yisrael

It's Not YOURS!

Every Jewish child learns in school that if you find someone's lost item, you must return it to him. If you hold it for safekeeping, you are not allowed to use it, lend it to anyone else, or exercise any kind of ownership over it at all. It's not yours.

If we extend this well-accepted idea into the realm of other people's names, activities or personalities, we have a strong counterforce to the urge to tell *loshon hora*. This idea comes into play especially when we are talking about our personal lives. Because our loved ones are a big part of our lives and our happiness, we may find it difficult to answer "What's new?" without disclosing other family members' personal information. For parents, "How are you?" is often answered with a report on the children.

Nevertheless, our children's personal difficulties are not our property to share. They, like all the other members of Klal Yisrael, are protected by the rules of *shmiras haloshon*. We can keep our conversations free of *loshon hora* simply by keeping in mind that just as people's possessions belong to them alone, so do their lives.

Looking Within: Have you appropriated your family members' and friends' lives as part of your own daily news feed?

Building Within: Imagine that your near and dear ones have a trademark on their names. Picture the little trademark symbol next to their names, and the next time you want to speak about them, ask yourself, "Do I have permission to use this?"

QUOTE OF THE DAY

"Respect for human dignity is exceedingly precious; there is no *middah* that is more precious."

(R' Menachem HaMe'iri, Beis HaBechirah, Berachos 19b)

DAY 29

Living the Mitzvah

What If I Want to Be the Peacemaker?

Disputes that divide a community are fueled by loshon hora. Anyone who gets involved in any way will hear all the accusations being hurled by both sides. But what if you want to get involved not as a disputant, but as a peacemaker?

כ"ט תשרי
29 Tishrei
Cycle 1

כ"ט שבט
29 Shevat
Cycle 2

כ"ט סיון
29 Sivan
Cycle 3

The Dilemma:
One Shabbos morning, an out-of-town speaker is invited to speak in your shul. His message is a bit controversial, and some people are outraged. The situation turns into a firestorm that causes one group to plan a breakaway *minyan* "where *apikorsus* (heresy) won't be allowed." You are on good terms with the leaders of both camps. May you try to quell the rebellion, even though you will surely hear an earful of abuse about the disputants?

The Halachah:
Machlokes (dispute), especially that which divides a community, is such a corrosive force that anyone who could possibly make peace should try to do so. As in the previous instances of constructive purpose, the parameters of this effort must be defined by a *rav* to ensure that fuel isn't added to the fire.

Sefer Chofetz Chaim, Hilchos Loshon Hora 8:8

REMEMBER
Make peace and pursue it!

29 Tishrei – לע"נ עדינה בת גבריאל אפרים ע"ה
In memory of Adina *bas* Gavriel Efraim *a"h*

29 Shevat – לע"נ אליהו שמואל בן יעקב שלום ואשתו שרה בת ריזא ע"ה
Dedicated by their Son David Jacob

29 Sivan – Dedicated in honor of our family and *Klal Yisrael* on our anniversary
By Dr. & Mrs. Sam Friedlander

Grow Your Ahavas Yisrael

Good for You!

We don't need psychologists to tell us that people try to prop up their self-esteem by putting others down. We can see this phenomenon in action readily in our daily lives. There's something inside the human heart that insists on measuring self-worth by comparison to others. This is the mechanism behind envy, which is the mechanism behind much *loshon hora*.

For instance, a sibling becomes very successful. Other siblings might now feel that their status has gone down in comparison. How do they compensate for the loss of altitude? They do so by finding aspects of their successful sibling's life that they see as inferior to their own, and deeming those areas more important than making a lot of money. "Sure, he's got two houses and an apartment in Yerushalayim. But look how his kids are turning out. He's too busy for them. He should wake up before it's too late."

When envy is the engine, *loshon hora* is inevitably the route our criticism takes. While their analysis may be true, if the siblings were sincerely worried about their brother's family they would approach him directly, with love and concern.

The Vilna Gaon (*Consulting the Wise,* p. 33) teaches that our ability to be sincerely happy for others is directly linked to our ability to be happy in our own lives. Envy destroys our happiness and sense of well-being. On the other hand, the more others' good fortune lights up our hearts, the lighter and brighter our hearts — and our words — will be.

Looking Within: Do you greet others' achievements and good news with a tinge of envy?

Building Within: Try to be aware of your envious thoughts and feelings and tell yourself that another person's good fortune is a good thing for Klal Yisrael, and therefore for you.

QUOTE OF THE DAY

"When one restrains himself, sealing his lips from speaking negatively about his fellow... in Heaven too, the prosecutor cannot open his mouth to speak negatively about him."
(Sefer Shmiras HaLoshon, Shaar HaZechirah Ch. 2)

DAY 30

Living the Mitzvah

Can I Use His Mistake as a Lesson?

If you want to instruct someone on the likely outcome of a poor choice, nothing speaks louder than reality. May you point out someone who is suffering from a mistake he made as a lesson for someone else?

ל תשרי
30 Tishrei
Cycle 1

ל שבט
30 Shevat
Cycle 2

ל סיון
30 Sivan
Cycle 3

The Dilemma:
Your friend is thinking of buying a bigger house — one he cannot really afford. You have a relative who did exactly that, and the result was financial stress which turned into marital stress and ultimately into a heart attack at an early age. May you tell your friend this story so that he may learn from your relative's mistake?

The Halachah:
You may use other people's mistakes as an example to help someone else learn a valuable lesson, provided that the story is well known in any case. However, as in all the previous instances of speaking for a constructive purpose, you must ascertain how much may be said and under what circumstances.

Sefer Chofetz Chaim, Hilchos Loshon Hora 10:4

REMEMBER
A bad choice can be a good lesson.

30 Tishrei – לע"נ מינדל בת פעשע ע"ה

30 Shevat – לע"נ חנה הינדא ע"ה בת ברוך חיים ועדינה כהן יבלח"ט נלב"ע א' אדר תשס"ד
Dedicated by her grandparents Uri & Bracha Mandelbaum

30 Sivan – Rabbi Dr. Leon Green לע"נ אריה לייב בן אהרן יוסף ז"ל
Dedicated by the Green, Slansky, Glass and Newmark families

Grow Your Ahavas Yisrael

Recognizing Your Long-Lost Brother

A Baltimore mother tells this story:

One year, when my children were young, we took the family to Newport, Rhode Island for a summer vacation. We decided to take the kids on a boat tour of the harbor. Naturally, since it was vacation season, the line was long and we were waiting around in the sun. We just stood and watched the people while the kids wandered around. All of a sudden, this little boy came scooting by us, running up to the front of the line. We were surprised to see that he was wearing a yarmulka. My 10-year-old son got all excited — it was another Jew! He started running along behind him.

We followed the boys with our eyes until we saw where they stopped, near the front of the line, where the boy's family was standing. I made my way up there to get my son, but of course, as soon as I met the mother, we started talking. "Where are you staying?" "What are you doing for kosher food?" "Where are you from?"

Eventually, I went back to where my husband was standing and told him all about my new friend. Once we got on board, the two families found each other again.

I always remember that episode because it taught me something. What made them matter to us, out of the 200 or so people standing on line to get on that boat, was that they were Jews — from a different city, from a different background, in a different style of clothes than ours, but we were just so happy to find each other. If we could always feel that way, there'd be no *sinas chinam* and Mashiach would be here!

Looking Within: Can you think of some times when you were delighted to see another Jew even though you didn't know each other?

Building Within: Think about some of your stereotypes about other groups of Jews and work on dispelling them. For example, think about people you admire from that group, or people who disprove a negative stereotype.

QUOTE OF THE DAY

"For a man who follows the Torah, his sense of 'self' incorporates all of Israel, for in truth each member of Israel is a mere limb of a single national body."

(Shaarei Yosher, Introduction)

Cheshvan

*In honor of **Dr. Schick** and the wonderful principals, rebbeim and teachers of RJJ, Staten Island.*

Dedicated by Dr. Louis and Stacey Emmer

*Dedicated as a zechus for the **Farkas** and **Rybstein** families*

Dedicated as a zechus for everyone to find their zivug
By Rena & Marc Kwestel and family

Adar

לע"נ יששכר דוב בן יעקב ז"ל נלב"ע א' אדר

לע"נ מנשה בן דוד ז"ל נלב"ע ג' אדר

לע"נ ישראל בן יצחק דוב ז"ל נלב"ע ט"ו אדר

לע"נ יעקב מנחם ז"ל בן יחזקאל ישעיה יבלח"ט
נלב"ע י"ז תשרי

לע"נ מלכה בת יהושע אהרן ע"ה נלב"ע י"ז תשרי

Dedicated by the Lefkowitz family

לע"נ מאטיל בת ר' מאיר צבי ע"ה

Dedicated by the Kleinberg family

Tammuz

In honor of my dear friends
Rabbi Jack Manne & Mr. Sam Zaks
Dedicated by Mr. Mitchell Feldman

לעילוי נשמות
מורינו ורבינו הרב עמרם בן הרב שמואל דוד זצוק"ל
ואשתו הרבנית יוטא פייגע בת הרב יחיאל אלתר זצוק"ל
הורינו ומורינו:
ר' יחזקאל בן רב יצחק אהרן, ר' חנניה בן ר' דוד,
ר' יונה בן ר' יעקב ואשתו מרת חיה שרה בת ר' יוסף יעקב,
ר' דניאל בן ר' יונה ואשתו מרת איטה מרים בת ר' דוד הכהן,
מרת אלטא חוה הענטשא בת ר' יעקב צבי
אחינו:
רחמים יעקב שמעון בן ר' חנניה,
דבורה דינה בת ר' דניאל, מרת שרה גיטל בת ר' צבי
ונכדנו אלישע ברוך טוביה ז"ל בן רב אורי מנחם יבלחט"א

❖❖❖

וגם לזכות לתורה לחופה ולמעשים טובים לאמונה שלימה לתשובה שלימה ולרפואה שלימה בתוך שאר חולי ישראל לפרנסה ברווח בעושר ובאושר לכל צאצאיהם ולכל משפחותיהם ובמיוחד ליחזקאל בן רב גרשון לוי נ"י, וגם לכל כלל ישראל

DAY 31

Living the Mitzvah

May I Pass Along Information I Heard?

How sure do you have to be about your facts before you offer negative information for a constructive purpose?

א חשון
1 Cheshvan
Cycle 1

א אדר*
**1 Adar*
Cycle 2

א תמוז
1 Tammuz
Cycle 3

The Dilemma:

A woman calls you for information about a young man who has been suggested as a potential *shidduch* for her daughter. Your son knows the boy from yeshivah, and has described him several times as "inconsiderate." May you mention this information?

The Halachah:

Hearsay, which is negative information that you've heard from someone else, may not be repeated. You may only report what you've witnessed yourself [*l'to'eles*]. Even then you must be absolutely sure that you understand the context of what you've seen.

Sefer Chofetz Chaim, Hilchos Rechilus 9:2-4

REMEMBER
If you don't see something, don't say something.

* *During Hebrew leap years, a thirteenth month called Adar Sheni is added to the calendar. During those years, the lessons for the days of Adar should be studied during each of the Adars.*

1 Cheshvan – **In loving memory of my father, Harry Schachner** לע"נ צבי אברהם בן קלמן יצחק ז"ל
Dedicacted by his daughter Susan Tauber

1 Adar – **Shaye Reinharz** לזכות ישעי' בנימין בן רחל הינדה נ"י
Dedicated by his parents, Yitzhak & Renee Reinharz

1 Tammuz – לע"נ רחל בת חיים ארי'ה ע"ה
Dedicated by Chaim & Laya Leshkowitz

Grow Your Ahavas Yisrael

Alternative Reality

What causes people to give themselves permission to speak *loshon hora* even when they know it's wrong? If we can answer that question, then we have a powerful strategy for stopping ourselves.

Rabbi Yeruchem Levovitz, *zt"l*, the Mirrer Mashgiach, attributed the willingness to speak *loshon hora* about another person to a lack of connection with that person. When we don't relate to their pain, we don't consider how they would feel if they knew what we were saying.

The solution, says the Mashgiach, is to get to know the other person. "Think about another person and enter his reality. Then you will have greater rapport with him and become close to him. This leads to a sense of identification and oneness." Putting ourselves in another's shoes is an expression of the mitzvah, *"v'ahavta l'rei'acha k'mocha,"* loving others as we love ourselves.

By learning to care and think about other people's perspectives, we will be far less likely to give ourselves permission to debase them to others. When we feel someone else's pain, we surely don't want to add to it.

Looking Within: Think of someone of whom you tend to be critical. Do you think about his reality and how you would feel if you were in his place?

Building Within: Rabbi Zelig Pliskin (*Consulting the Wise*, p. 131) suggests building *ahavas Yisrael* by asking yourself about others, "What is he probably thinking?" When appropriate, you can even ask that question directly.

QUOTE OF THE DAY

"One who understands words of wisdom will understand that *loshon hora* is the power of lowliness and debasement."

(Maharal, Nesivos Olam, Nesiv HaLoshon)

CHAPTER 3

Assertiveness — Find Your Voice

The gap between knowing what's right and doing it can sometimes seem to be an impossible leap. What will people think? Who am I to speak up? The big surprise is that often we discover that when conversations veer into dangerous territory, people are grateful to be prodded onto a higher road. A little courage can go a very long way, saving someone's reputation and saving ourselves and others from damaging a fellow Jew.

DAY 32

Living the Mitzvah

Is There Any Use in Speaking?

To say that loshon hora is l'to'eles means that it serves a constructive purpose. What happens when your words are aimed at a legitimate purpose, but probably won't do any good?

ב חשון
2 Cheshvan
Cycle 1

ב אדר*
**2 Adar*
Cycle 2

ב תמוז
2 Tammuz
Cycle 3

The Dilemma:
Your good friend has finally found an apartment for her family, right in the location she wants, at just the right price for her shoestring budget. You know that the landlady, a former workmate of yours, is a difficult, argumentative and emotionally unhealthy woman. You're also quite certain that you're ever-optimistic friend will brush off the information if you share it. May you warn her?

The Halachah:
We are only allowed to speak *l'to'eles* if there is a reasonable chance that we will achieve our goal. If a decision has already been made, and/or your words can't or will not likely change it, then the words no longer have a constructive purpose.

Sefer Chofetz Chaim, Hilchos Rechilus 9:3 [in the parentheses]

REMEMBER
If it won't help, it's not l'to'eles.

** During Hebrew leap years, a thirteenth month called Adar Sheni is added to the calendar. During those years, the lessons for the days of Adar should be studied during each of the Adars.*

2 Cheshvan – לע"נ שלמה בן ר' יצחק ז"ל ואשתו שרה בת ר' משה יעקב ע"ה
לזכות אלטר בן חנה נ"י ולע"נ אשתו יוטא בת חיים אלעזר וחנה ע"ה

2 Adar – לע"נ משה בן פריידא ז"ל

2 Tammuz – Shaindel Freier לע"נ שיינדל בת ר' משה הלוי ע"ה

Grow Your Assertiveness

Climate Change

Shlomo HaMelech teaches that when we face a grave challenge, "...you shall wage war for yourself with strategies" (*Mishlei* 24:6). Someone who finds himself locked into a situation where *loshon hora* is the norm has been drafted; he has no choice but to fight or to suffer the negative spiritual and this-world damage that *loshon hora* does. But to win the war, he needs a plan.

For instance, if his workplace is a *loshon hora* zone, he either has to quit his job or do something proactive to make things different. Once he's motivated, he's willing to risk a little social disfavor to save himself and everyone else involved.

The first step when dealing with a group of people is to talk to them one at a time. "Doesn't it seem like we do a lot of talking about other people here? I'd love to change that." They are likely to agree with you. At worst, they might assert that people need to vent their frustrations.

Once you've spoken to each individual, ask everyone to get together and create a group effort to change the climate. With everyone on the same page, *loshon hora* will immediately take on the taint of unacceptable conversation. Little by little, as the new normal sets in, the war will be won.

If you think this is impossible, look back at the era of cigarette smoking. Only a few decades ago, trains and planes had smoking sections. But nowadays, whoever smokes must do it on the sidewalk, away from people. In the same way, you can clear the air of *loshon hora*. It only takes persistence and a small dose of courage.

Looking Within: Do you sometimes feel that the conversation around you is inappropriate, but don't know what to do about it?

Building Within: Think of some possible ways to handle this situation and be alert to an opportunity to take Step One.

QUOTE OF THE DAY

"Love of people is in itself becoming close to Hashem, because you are following in His ways."

(the Alter of Kelm, Rabbi Simcha Zissel Ziv, Chochmah U'Mussar)

DAY 33

Living the Mitzvah

Do I Have to Talk to Him Before Talking About Him?

If you're considering talking to Mr. A about Mr. B's wrongdoing, are you obligated to first try speaking directly to Mr. B?

The Dilemma:
Your neighbor is very harsh to his children. You often witness him shouting at them and hitting them, and you're worried about the children's mental and physical well-being. Should you speak to his *rav* about the situation, or first address the issue directly with the neighbor?

The Halachah:
Generally, we are required to speak directly to the person first. We should reprove him in a manner that is most likely to be accepted and try to awaken him to his mistake. However, in some cases we will only harden his position or put him on the defensive so that he'll be less likely to change his ways. In that situation, we should not speak to him directly, but rather go to a third party who can help.

Sefer Chofetz Chaim, Hilchos Loshon Hora 10:2

ג חשון
3 Cheshvan
Cycle 1

ג אדר*
**3 Adar*
Cycle 2

ג תמוז
3 Tammuz
Cycle 3

REMEMBER
Talk to me, not about me.

* *During Hebrew leap years, a thirteenth month called Adar Sheni is added to the calendar. During those years, the lessons for the days of Adar should be studied during each of the Adars.*

3 Cheshvan – לע"נ משה הכהן בן שמואל הכהן ז"ל
With love from the Atkins family, Marilyn, Marc, Kayla and Judith

3 Adar – Dedicated as a *zechus* for our family
Jay & Michele Levine

3 Tammuz – לע"נ דינה רבקה חי' בת שושנה ע"ה
Dedicated by Homa Lovi and family

Grow Your Assertiveness

Be a Part of the "Stiff-necked People"

In our own holy Torah, the Jewish nation is called "a stiff-necked people" (*Shemos* 32:9). It's the trait that has allowed us to carry on Hashem's mission through the millennia with a loyalty that defies human nature.

To Gershon M. from Brooklyn, the remembrance of the Jewish people's stiff-necked nature acted as an awakening when *loshon hora* was flowing around him:

Waiting for Maariv to begin, Gershon sat between two friends who were talking over him, complaining about the men in charge of the shul's dinner journal.

"I knew I should stop them," Gershon reports. He and his family had recently begun learning *shmiras haloshon* together, and the conversation he was hearing suddenly seemed out of place.

"On the other hand, I thought these guys would think I was nuts if I said something. But then I thought, so what? A Jew has to be ready to defend a mitzvah. Back in Russia my grandparents gave my father a secret *bris* and risked being sent off to Siberia. My wife's grandfather risked putting on *tefillin* in Auschwitz. And I'm afraid of two guys giving me a funny look? I said to them, 'Can we leave off the *loshon hora*?' And they shrugged and said, 'Yeah, sure.'"

When we commit ourselves to following our ancestors' "stiff-necked" ways, keeping *shmiras haloshon* doesn't seem so daunting.

Looking Within: Is standing up against *loshon hora* a bigger problem in your mind than it is in reality?

Building Within: Try to think in terms of defending a mitzvah when you hear *loshon hora* being spoken.

QUOTE OF THE DAY

"It is most surprising that by nature, man is embarrassed before other people but not before his Creator, though the latter observes him at all times."

(Chovos HaLevavos, Shaar HaBechinah Ch. 5)

DAY 34

Living the Mitzvah

Once I'm Talking, May I Tell All?

You have a positive purpose for speaking negatively about someone. You've tried talking to him to no avail and now you're seeking help from a third party. May you lay out all the details of what you know?

ד חשון
4 Cheshvan
Cycle 1

ד אדר*
**4 Adar*
Cycle 2

ד תמוז
4 Tammuz
Cycle 3

The Dilemma:

Your tenant has not paid rent for the past three months. You know that in that time he has taken his family to Florida on vacation and purchased a new dishwasher. You've also heard that he was asked to leave his last apartment for some unknown reason. You want to ask your *rav*, who is also your tenant's *rav*, to intervene and get him to pay the rent. How much information should you impart to him?

The Halachah:

We are permitted to relate only the minimum amount of information necessary to achieve our goal. The best situation is when we can just direct someone to a place where he will see the problem for himself. If that's not possible, we should state our case in the least negative way that will still be effective.

Sefer Chofetz Chaim, Hilchos Loshon Hora 10:2, 14

REMEMBER

The less said, the better.

** During Hebrew leap years, a thirteenth month called Adar Sheni is added to the calendar. During those years, the lessons for the days of Adar should be studied during each of the Adars.*

4 Cheshvan – לע"נ ר' יונה בן שלמה יוסף ז"ל
ואשתו רבקה בת מנחם ע"ה נלב"ע ר' ניסן

4 Adar – In loving memory of my mother Edith Schachner לע"נ נסי בת ר' יוסף ע"ה
Dedicated by her daughter Susan Tauber

4 Tammuz – לע"נ ישראל מאיר בן שלום ז"ל
לע"נ פריידא רחל בת יהודה לייב ע"ה נלב"ע ט"ז תמוז

Grow Your Assertiveness

It Isn't What You Think!

What happens when you unintentionally hear *loshon hora*? For instance, you're at your relative's house for Yom Tov and someone at the table starts talking about a person you know. The Chofetz Chaim says that at times, you can actually do some good by being there.

For instance, you might be able to counterbalance the negative story with positive information about the same person. Chana G. from Monsey tried this and reported her experience.

"We were at my in-laws' home for Pesach. One afternoon I was sitting with my sisters-in-law outside, watching our kids play, when one sister-in-law started talking about a girl I graduated with. This girl had taken quite a long time to get married and then was divorced within the first three months. My sister-in-law said, "Obviously, there's something wrong there."

I was able to state that I knew the girl and that she was very sweet and very smart. I know I did some good because my other sister-in-law said, "You really can't judge like that. Sometimes perfectly nice, normal people have these challenges and you don't know why."

Looking Within: Do you ever let *loshon hora* flow around you because you are embarrassed to stop it or feel your effort won't accomplish anything?

Building Within: Think of a stock answer you can use to naturally and comfortably stand up against *loshon hora* conversations that crop up in your life.

QUOTE OF THE DAY

"The honor of your fellow should be as precious to you as your own."
(Pirkei Avos 2:15)

DAY 35

Living the Mitzvah

May I Add a Little Drama to Make the Point?

You have something important to tell someone — something that could really save him trouble. You want to make sure that he takes your warning seriously. May you exaggerate or dramatize a little to make sure your point gets across?

ה חשון
5 Cheshvan
Cycle 1

ה אדר*
**5 Adar*
Cycle 2

ה תמוז
5 Tammuz
Cycle 3

The Dilemma:

You own a successful business. Another business owner in your community is seeking a new accountant and asks you about someone you used to use. The accountant's rates were very reasonable, but you felt that he missed many deductions that could have saved you tax money. You want to make sure the other business owner isn't tempted by the low accountant fees. May you tell him, "That guy cost me a fortune! Don't go near him. He made a total mess of my taxes"?

The Halachah:

We have no right to exaggerate negative information or omit or alter the facts even if we feel that doing so will serve a constructive purpose.

Sefer Chofetz Chaim 10:2, Be'er Mayim Chaim ad loc. [end]; Hilchos Rechilus 9:2

REMEMBER
Just the facts, please.

** During Hebrew leap years, a thirteenth month called Adar Sheni is added to the calendar. During those years, the lessons for the days of Adar should be studied during each of the Adars.*

5 Cheshvan – **Mr. Sam Mermelstein** לע"נ שלום בן אלכסנדר הלוי ז"ל
Dedicated by the Rich and Isenberg families

5 Adar – **In memory of Trudi & Irwin Kabak**

5 Tammuz – לע"נ חיים מאיר בן ר' מנחם מנדל ז"ל
לע"נ חי' זיסל בת ר' שמואל יעקב ע"ה נלב"ע ה' ניסן

Grow Your Assertiveness

When All Else Fails

Sometimes people are clueless. They start a conversation that is veering toward *loshon hora* and you, in your subtle way, try to change the subject. But they don't want to change the subject. They want to talk about this person whom they find worthy of criticism.

As uncomfortable as you might feel, the only remaining strategy is to ask them to stop. The option of sitting there listening to *loshon hora,* and watching other people all around you fall into its trap, is really no option at all.

So how does a person stop the runaway train? If there's no break in the conversation where you could voice your objection, interrupt. When you do so, keep in mind that what you're saying represents the right path — the path everyone around you would want to take if they were thinking straight at that moment.

Then say what you have to say in a non-accusatory way. Use an "I" message that puts the focus on your needs rather than their misdeeds. "Wait a minute. Before you go on, can I ask you a favor? I'm trying really hard to stay away from *loshon hora* right now. Could we change the subject?"

At worst, people will think there's some deep dark reason that you need this merit. At best, they'll appreciate your wake-up call. But even if they go right on with their *loshon hora,* you will have at least done your best to avoid hearing it and to prevent them from speaking it.

Looking Within: Do you believe that people will look askance at you if you try to interrupt a *loshon hora* conversation? Does that sometimes stop you from trying?

Building Within: Think of some direct but non-accusatory ways of stopping *loshon hora* when hints and other strategies don't work.

QUOTE OF THE DAY

"Receive every man with a pleasant countenance."

(Pirkei Avos 1:15)

DAY 36

Living the Mitzvah

Am I the Right Person for the Job?

Even if you've determined that your negative information is accurate and you've tried to discuss it directly with the subject, you still might not be the right person to handle the situation. That may be the case if the subject is someone you dislike.

ו חשון
6 Cheshvan
Cycle 1

ו אדר*
**6 Adar*
Cycle 2

ו תמוז
6 Tammuz
Cycle 3

The Dilemma:

You worked for a woman who you considered to be a tyrant. She was critical and condescending, and never uttered a word of praise. You disliked her intensely and ended up getting fired. Someone you know is considering allowing her son to go out with your former boss's daughter. Should you tell her what kind of mother-in-law he might end up acquiring?

The Halachah:

If you would enjoy describing her many flaws, you can't be certain that your only purpose is a constructive one. A person has to rid himself of negative feelings before speaking. If he cannot do that, and the information can be obtained from someone else, it's better to refer the questioner to the neutral source.

Sefer Chofetz Chaim, Hilchos Loshon Hora 10:2; Hilchos Rechilus 9:2, Be'er Mayim Chaim ad loc. 3

REMEMBER

To'eles isn't a weapon.

** During Hebrew leap years, a thirteenth month called Adar Sheni is added to the calendar. During those years, the lessons for the days of Adar should be studied during each of the Adars.*

6 Cheshvan – לזכות זיווג הגון בקרוב לאריאלה לאה בת שרה תחי'

6 Adar – As a *zechus* for our family
Dedicated by the Levine family

6 Tammuz – In honor of our children Yosaif and Leah Rodbell
Dedicated by Bubbe & Papa Vogel

Grow Your Assertiveness

Right Goal, Wrong Strategy

You're sitting with a group of people who begin talking about someone's flaws. They're taking one side in a heated dispute, and you know that if you try to stop their *loshon hora,* they will cling to their righteous indignation even harder.

The Ralbag offers this advice: "Utilize your ingenuity. Your approach should be to show them that you are basically in agreement with the outcome they desire. But you think it would be preferable for them to take a different course of action in order to achieve that outcome" (*Consulting the Wise*, p. 57).

For instance, your friend Michael has split with his business partner, Aryeh, and everyone feels that Aryeh is trying to walk away with an unfair percentage of the business. Your friends are discussing Aryeh's greediness, lack of character, poor business sense and demanding wife.

You could say, "Well, I think we all agree that we want to see Michael get his fair share out of the business. But you know we're really not accomplishing anything by talking about it. How about we call Rabbi Klein right now and ask him to offer to mediate? Maybe it'll work or maybe not, but it's better than just sitting here and talking about it." By starting off on common ground, your ability to influence people is much greater.

Looking Within: When *loshon hora* is going on around you, do you feel helpless to stop it?

Building Within: When *loshon hora* revolves around some problem or issue, get the participants in the conversation to focus on the goal of resolving the issue.

QUOTE OF THE DAY

"If a person keeps to himself, he is not pursuing peace. Rather, he should go out and actively look for ways to make peace wherever he can."

(Avos D'Rav Nosson 12:6)

DAY 37

Living the Mitzvah

What If I'm Starting Really Big Trouble?

You might want to prevent harm by speaking negatively about someone, and you might meet all the conditions for doing so. But what if the fallout from your words spells disaster for the subject?

ז חשון
7 Cheshvan
Cycle 1

ז אדר*
**7 Adar*
Cycle 2

ז תמוז
7 Tammuz
Cycle 3

The Dilemma:

You see your neighbor's 15-year-old son standing with a group of friends outside a local pizza shop smoking a cigarette. On one hand, you want his parents to know about it so that they can perhaps curtail this harmful habit. However, if you know that his parents are likely to react extremely harshly to the news, should you still speak?

The Halachah:

If the consequence of your speaking will cause undue harm, then the constructive aspect of your words is nullified. Certainly we are not allowed to cause more harm to a person than the halachah would allow for that specific misdeed.

Sefer Chofetz Chaim, Hilchos Loshon Hora 10:2; Hilchos Rechilus 9:2

REMEMBER
Consider the fallout.

** During Hebrew leap years, a thirteenth month called Adar Sheni is added to the calendar. During those years, the lessons for the days of Adar should be studied during each of the Adars.*

7 Cheshvan – Sophia Ashkenazi לע"נ צופה חי' בת פרידה ע"ה
Dedicated by Rabbi & Mrs Eli J. Mansour

7 Adar – לזכות משפחת סולומון,
להצלחתם בכל הענינים בס"ד לעבודת ה' יתברך.

7 Tammuz – לזכות עטרה רחל בת שרה מרים תחי'

Grow Your Assertiveness

Stop the Stewing

A large percentage of *loshon hora* comes from the distaste most of us have for confrontation. It doesn't take much courage to swallow an insult and then tell everyone else about how hurt we are and how unfairly we've been treated. If we would instead approach the person who insulted us and let him or her know we feel hurt, we might find that they are sorry, or that we've misinterpreted something. We would be left with no anger to spew, and the urge to vent our feelings would disappear.

Constructive criticism, constructive argument and calm assertiveness are all ways to settle an issue before it has time to fester and spur us on to *loshon hora*. Often we hold back our feelings because they seem petty. We think we should be "bigger than that." So instead of clearing the air, we violate the mitzvah forbidding us to "hate another Jew in your heart." We act like a friend but speak about the person as an enemy.

The solution is simple: Calmly, honestly, tell the person how his or her words or actions made you feel. Tell why you had this reaction. Give a chance to explain. Even if he or she does not succeed in soothing your hurt completely, you might find that there's nothing left to say to anyone else about the matter.

Looking Within: When you swallow an insult or disappointment, are you really letting it go or simply stashing it away?

Building Within: Practice ways of addressing slights and insults that certain people in your life may insensitively send your way. Try to be direct, firm and calm in your response so that you won't appear overemotional or angry.

QUOTE OF THE DAY

"Do not withhold good from the one who needs it when you have power in your hand to do it." *(Mishlei 3:27)*

DAY 38

Living the Mitzvah

Isn't It Better to "Live and Let Live"?

Someone you care about keeps repeating the same behavior that causes him grief. Is it better to solicit a wise person's help in getting your friend out of his rut, or to give him the benefit of the doubt and leave him be?

ח חשון
8 Cheshvan
Cycle 1

ח אדר*
**8 Adar*
Cycle 2

ח תמוז
8 Tammuz
Cycle 3

The Dilemma:

Your brother is a hothead. He is highly intelligent and a hard worker, but he can't hold a job. You've tried to help him see how his behavior antagonizes people, but he's not listening. Do you say, "This is who he is. I'll just focus on his many good points," or do you ask his *chavrusa*, whom he respects, to speak to him?

The Halachah:

The companions and relatives Hashem put into our lives are there to help us refine our natures, pointing out flaws that we cannot see in ourselves. It's not only permitted, but it's important to offer constructive criticism or have others offer it.

Sefer Chofetz Chaim, Hilchos Loshon Hora 10:3, Be'er Mayim Chaim ad loc. #23

REMEMBER
Your real friends will tell you the truth.

* *During Hebrew leap years, a thirteenth month called Adar Sheni is added to the calendar. During those years, the lessons for the days of Adar should be studied during each of the Adars.*

8 Cheshvan – **Susie Elbaum** לע"נ שרה בת משה ע"ה
Dedicated by her sister Hilde Klugmann

8 Adar – **In memory of Masha Chaya *bas* Dan *a"h***
Dedicated by Nosson Shine and Pinchas & Yona Shine & family

8 Tammuz – **In honor of our children**
Dedicated by Lani & Dovid Harrison

Grow Your Assertiveness

Speak to Me, Not About Me

One of the best ways to conquer *loshon hora* is to learn the art of assertiveness. Saying what needs to be said in a way that's empathetic and yet direct can settle an issue with the party involved, leaving nothing to say to third parties.

This was the experience of Meir N., a father and grandfather of a large family:

My newly married son was constantly asking for money. It seemed to me that he wanted a lot of things that we didn't have until I had been working for quite a few years. For instance, we used to drive a 12-year-old beat-up station wagon that lasted us at least five years. But when my son needed a second car, it had to be a late-model lease.

I didn't feel like I could say anything to him. I didn't want him to feel inferior to his friends, who had all these things. I didn't want to cause friction in his marriage, either, because maybe it was his wife who had the expensive ideas. So what I did instead was complain about him nonstop to my wife. Finally, one day, she said, "Why don't you tell *him* these things instead of me?"

I gave a lot of thought to how I'd say what was on my mind without creating hard feelings. Finally, one day when he called for more money, I said, "We need to talk about this." The conversation was difficult for me, but in the end, he completely understood. Not only did I lose my need to vent my frustration with him, but I ended up realizing what a sincere, good boy he really is.

Looking Within: Do you tend to harbor resentment rather than addressing the problem directly?

Building Within: Learn about effective communication and begin using it to tackle difficult situations head-on.

QUOTE OF THE DAY

"The tongue of the righteous is choice silver." *(Mishlei 10:20)*

DAY 39

Living the Mitzvah

Someone Who's Usually Reasonable Has Hurt Me. May I Ask a Third Person to Intervene?

You thought you knew this person, when all of a sudden, he did something completely out of character. You want to publicize his actions so that someone will talk to him about it, but is it loshon hora to report what happened?

ט חשון
9 Cheshvan
Cycle 1

ט אדר*
**9 Adar*
Cycle 2

ט תמוז
9 Tammuz
Cycle 3

The Dilemma:
Your father-in-law, a man with a refined nature and positive attitude, was walking with you to shul on Shabbos when he began lambasting you about the way you're raising your children. He seemed agitated and even called your parenting methods "lazy." You want to tell your wife about the conversation and get her to intervene with her father. Is this considered a constructive purpose, which would allow you to tell your wife a negative story about her father?

The Halachah:
When someone acts out of character, we must try to understand what happened and see it in a positive light. If it's clear that the person really did speak or act incorrectly, we have to assume that he realized it and immediately regretted it. Speaking to someone else about the incident is not considered *to'eles*; it is simple *loshon hora*.

Sefer Chofetz Chaim, Hilchos Loshon Hora 4:4

REMEMBER
When reasonable people act unreasonably, there's probably a reason.

** During Hebrew leap years, a thirteenth month called Adar Sheni is added to the calendar. During those years, the lessons for the days of Adar should be studied during each of the Adars.*

9 Cheshvan – לע"נ עטיל בת משה ע"ה
Dedicated by Chaim & Chaya Goldberg
9 Adar – לע"נ ר' דוד יהודה ז"ל בן יקותיאל פנחס הכהן יבלח"ט נלב"ע ח' אדר
Dedicated by the Fulop, Wolf and Reichman families
9 Tammuz – לע"נ מרים בת נתן ע"ה

Grow Your Assertiveness

Polish Your Marketing Skills

When a business tries to sell its product, it advertises the benefits the consumers will enjoy if they make the purchase. It omits or underplays the expense and difficulty that might be involved in arriving at those benefits. We see an ad of a happy couple zooming along the highway in their new Acura. We don't see them scraping together the monthly payments for the car.

That same marketing strategy works for selling people on positive changes in their lives. The Ralbag states that the first step is to tout the benefits. Once a person begins to envision what life will be like after the change, he's more willing to undertake the difficulties involved in making the change. "His desire to attain those benefits will decrease the pain involved," the Ralbag explains (*Consulting the Wise*, p. 56).

The "product" of *shmiras haloshon* may seem overwhelmingly difficult to many people, but we can market its benefits by both modeling and telling about the peace and happiness it brings to life. Then the difficulties involved in developing this quality will pale against the benefits it bestows.

Looking Within: When you think about *shmiras haloshon,* is your initial impression one of constant self-restraint and struggle, or of a positive outlook on people and life?

Building Within: Think of someone in your life whom you consider lovable, positive and good to be around. "Channel" that person's manner of speech when you feel yourself becoming irritated.

QUOTE OF THE DAY

"We are required to appoint individuals to promote peace between spouses and between fellow men... The [appointees] should be happy individuals who know how to placate and appease people and to bring peace among men."
(Iggeres HaTeshuvah, Rabbeinu Yonah 41)

DAY 40

Living the Mitzvah

May I Get a Third Party to Reprove Someone Whom I've Seen Doing Something Wrong?

You're certain that you've seen someone do something really wrong, but you're not the one to stop him. May you get someone else involved?

י חשון
10 Cheshvan
Cycle 1

י אדר*
**10 Adar*
Cycle 2

י תמוז
10 Tammuz
Cycle 3

The Dilemma:

You work at the desk next to the company's top salesman. You've heard him making travel arrangements that he passes off as business trips but are really personal getaways for himself and his wife. He's stealing money from the company, but given his egotistical personality, you know that he will never accept reproof from you. However, you *daven* at the same shul as he does. May you ask your *rav* to speak to this individual, even though the *rav* has no firsthand knowledge of his shady practices?

The Halachah:

Even the *rav* may not act on hearsay, which means that theoretically he should not intervene in any situation that he doesn't see for himself. For that reason, the better alternative is for you to try to address the person directly. If that's not possible, you should describe the situation to the *rav* and ask him to look into it. Even if he doesn't come to a point where he has firsthand information, he could tactfully discuss the situation with the errant salesman without making accusations.

Sefer Chofetz Chaim, Hilchos Loshon Hora 4:5

REMEMBER

Firsthand is the first choice.

** During Hebrew leap years, a thirteenth month called Adar Sheni is added to the calendar. During those years, the lessons for the days of Adar should be studied during each of the Adars.*

10 Cheshvan – As a *zechus* for our family
Dedicated by Arthur & Tziviah Toran

10 Adar – לזכות דבורה בת רינה שתחי'

10 Tammuz – לע"נ הורינו ז"ל
מאת ישראל ופריידא ברגר

Grow Your Assertiveness

Grab the Steering Wheel

As we've discussed on previous days, we can mitigate a lot of damage by keeping ourselves away from places and people that tend to lead us into *loshon hora,* and spending as little time as possible in problematic situations. But in most of these cases, we will find it impossible to eliminate these situations altogether.

That's when the fallback strategy of grabbing the conversational steering wheel comes to the rescue. You would be surprised to learn how very little most people really care about the topics they discuss. Of course, there are instances in which someone is hurt or upset and driven to talk about it. Often, however, *loshon hora* is truly idle time-filler conversation.

When that is the case, you can easily steer the conversation onto a different topic. The most effective idea is to take some time to write down topics or questions that you can interject. You can even interrupt with, "Before I forget...," or "Do you mind if I change the subject?" It's much easier to do than you might think. And it works.

Looking Within: Do you ever find yourself trying to change the subject when it begins to hit too close to home?

Building Within: Nothing builds confidence like success. Practice rerouting casual conversations once in a while and see for yourself how easy it is to do. Then you'll be ready to steer away from *loshon hora.*

QUOTE OF THE DAY

"He who guards his mouth and tongue, guards himself from trouble."
(Mishlei 21:23)

DAY 41

Living the Mitzvah

Do I Have to Judge People Favorably When They're Making the Same Mistake Again?

You've seen this person do the same thing wrong many times, and now you're seeing him do it again. Do you have to assume he's innocent until proven guilty, or can you believe your eyes?

The Dilemma:

Your wife loses her temper and gives your 5-year-old a hard smack. She's generally calm and gentle with the children, but you've seen her lose her cool before. Is it now your obligation to judge her favorably and assume there were extenuating circumstances, and that she regrets her act and will try not to repeat it? Or is it your obligation to find a way to offer some reproof?

The Halachah:

If you've seen someone do the wrong thing and there's no other possible explanation, you have a mitzvah to try to set the person straight. That is the case here. The husband has to address what he's seen but tread cautiously, using a respectful, sincere approach that will encourage his wife, not insult her.

Sefer Chofetz Chaim, Hilchos Loshon Hora 4:4

י"א חשון
11 Cheshvan
Cycle 1

*י"א אדר
**11 Adar*
Cycle 2

י"א תמוז
11 Tammuz
Cycle 3

REMEMBER

Even a favorable judge relies on the evidence.

** During Hebrew leap years, a thirteenth month called Adar Sheni is added to the calendar. During those years, the lessons for the days of Adar should be studied during each of the Adars.*

11 Cheshvan – Annette Rose Stein לע"נ נעכה רייזה בת ר' אברהם הכהן ע"ה
Dedicated by her grandchildren and great–grandchildren

11 Adar – לע"נ אברהם יעקב בן שלמה יהודה ז"ל
Dedicated by his children

11 Tammuz – לע"נ הרבנית צפורה פיגא פרידמאן מסדיגורה בת הרב יוסף אריה פעלדמאן ע"ה
By her children and *einikelech* Rabbi & Rebbetzin S.Z. Scharf and family

Grow Your Assertiveness

Don't Just Sit There

Most people occasionally find themselves surrounded by people who don't share their sensitivity to *loshon hora*. It could be at a wedding, at the office, standing at a bus stop, or sitting at someone's Shabbos table. The conversation takes a bad turn and there seems to be no way to reroute it to a kosher topic.

In that case, the Chofetz Chaim urges us to leave the scene or clamp our hands over our ears. However, he acknowledges that such dramatic moves might make matters worse.

A man once consulted Rav Avraham Pam *zt"l* about a situation that often ended in his hearing *loshon hora*. The man waited each day for a bus home from work, and a neighbor sometimes passed by in his car and offered the man a ride. However, the driver always launched into *loshon hora* as he drove. Rav Pam advised the man to forego the ride rather than subject himself to *loshon hora*.

Looking Within: When you find yourself "stuck" in the midst of *loshon hora*, how do you respond?

Building Within: Summon the courage to change the conversation: Network with others for *shidduchim*, job opportunities or other helpful purposes, so that the conversation stays constructive.

QUOTE OF THE DAY

"One should flee from a group of idle chatterers as from a fire."

(Sefer Shmiras HaLoshon, Shaar HaZechirah Ch. 14)

DAY 42

Living the Mitzvah

When Should I Believe a Negative Public Statement About Someone?

Your local beis din published a negative notice about your neighbor in your local Jewish newspaper. Isn't it loshon hora to besmirch someone publicly?

י"ב חשון
12 Cheshvan
Cycle 1

י"ב אדר*
**12 Adar*
Cycle 2

י"ב תמוז
12 Tammuz
Cycle 3

The Dilemma:

In the midst of a long, angry inheritance fight, the oldest son decides to put the family house up for sale. Since the issues are far from settled and a *beis din* is in the process of mediating the case, the *rabbanim* urge him several times to take the house off the market. When he refuses, they print an announcement naming the son and stating that his attempt to sell the house violates the *beis din's* ruling. Now his neighbors are looking askance at him and his children are being teased in school. Is the announcement *loshon hora*?

REMEMBER

Justice is a just cause.

The Halachah:

Since social pressure is often the only means Rabbinic courts have to enforce their rulings, public announcements have traditionally been used to prod a recalcitrant person into compliance. Such announcements are not considered *loshon hora* and may be believed.

Sefer Chofetz Chaim, Hilchos Loshon Hora 4:7

* *During Hebrew leap years, a thirteenth month called Adar Sheni is added to the calendar. During those years, the lessons for the days of Adar should be studied during each of the Adars.*

12 Cheshvan – לע"נ נחמה בת ברוך אורי ע"ה
Dedicated by the Rogoff, Strauss and Frid families

12 Adar – לע"נ רבקה בת גיטל ע"ה

12 Tammuz – לע"נ יוסף בן רפא–ל הלוי ז"ל ואשתו חי' רעכיל בת משה ע"ה
לע"נ משה שמוא–ל בן אשר אנטשיל ירוחם ז"ל ואשתו פערל בת ישרא–ל ע"ה

Grow Your Assertiveness

What Am I Afraid Of?

Rochel G., a young wife and mother from Lakewood, N.J. began learning Shmiras Haloshon Yomi with a neighbor in the development in which she lived. She tells this story of how she finally managed to put her learning to work:

My friend Shoshana and I were learning on the phone about five minutes a day. We found right away that the learning influenced our own conversations with each other, but that was about it. Whenever we'd sit at the playground with other mothers, we'd end up in the middle of *loshon hora* conversations. We were both too intimidated to say anything, especially since we were younger than most of the other women there.

Then one Shabbos, I was reading a story about a rabbi who was sent to Siberia during the Soviet times. He decided that he would keep Shabbos no matter what, and he went through incredible suffering to do it. Not only that, but he had to keep his purpose a secret or he'd be killed. As I read this, I realized that I was more afraid of a group of religious women not liking me than this man was of Russian guards who could kill him.

When I told this to Shoshana, we decided that the next time the playground conversation got into *loshon hora,* we would say very politely, "Do you think that maybe we shouldn't be talking like this?" We had a chance to use that line the very next day and we were shocked; everyone agreed. Now our conversations are much more positive.

Looking Within: What reaction do you fear from others that keeps you from speaking up when *loshon hora* begins?

Building Within: Role-play with someone, or in your own mind, ways of derailing a *loshon hora* conversation and dealing with any negative reactions you might provoke.

QUOTE OF THE DAY

"Better to experience embarrassment on this world than to be shamed in the World to Come before the entire Heavenly Assembly."
(Sefer Shmiras HaLoshon, Shaar HaZechirah Ch. 16)

DAY 43

Living the Mitzvah

May I Discuss My Non-Religious Neighbor's Transgressions?

When a non-religious Jew behaves in ways that fly in the face of the Torah's requirements, are you allowed to express your disdain?

The Dilemma:

While you're having your Shabbos lunch, your non-religious next-door neighbor is having a pool-side barbecue. May you criticize his actions in your conversation with your Shabbos guests?

The Halachah:

Although we are not prohibited from speaking *loshon hora* about a heretic, today's non-religious Jews are generally not defined as heretics. Rather, they're compared to a *tinok shenishbah* — a Jewish child who was kidnapped and raised without Torah. Therefore, he falls into the category of Jews about whom *loshon hora* is prohibited.

See Beis Yosef, Yoreh Deah 159; Shulchan Arch, Yoreh Deah 159:3; cf. Shach ad loc. #6

י"ג חשון
13 Cheshvan
Cycle 1

י"ג אדר
**13 Adar*
Cycle 2

י"ג תמוז
13 Tammuz
Cycle 3

REMEMBER

Fight ignorance with love, not loshon hora.

** During Hebrew leap years, a thirteenth month called Adar Sheni is added to the calendar. During those years, the lessons for the days of Adar should be studied during each of the Adars.*

13 Cheshvan – **Chaya Zylberberg** לע"נ חיה שפרינצא בת ר' יעקב ע"ה נלב"ע י"ג חשון
Mendel Zylberberg לע"נ מרדכי מנחם מענדל בן ר' יעקב יצחק ז"ל נלב"ע כ"ז חשון

13 Adar – **Leah Simon (Konigsberg)** לע"נ לאה בת ר' שלמה ע"ה נלב"ע י"ג אדר
Dedicated in loving memory by her children

13 Tammuz – לע"נ שמואל דן ז"ל בן יוסף חיים יבלח"ט
Dedicated by his parents

Grow Your Assertiveness

Waiting for Applause

A little boy goes to the playground with his mother. He runs off to the slide and as he sits at the top, preparing for the plunge, he calls out, "Mommy! Watch!"

Children naturally look for their parents' approval. Later, they look for their friends' approval. But the Alter of Novardok states that if they don't shed this need for approval as they reach adulthood, it will turn into a great obstacle to spiritual growth. "A person who seeks honor from others will never be able to keep his positive resolutions if other people disapprove of him because of his ideals. … His behavior will be entirely dependent on the environment in which he finds himself."

The Alter teaches us how to steer clear of *loshon hora* when the people around us are all taking part in it. First, we have to be willing to give up the moment in the spotlight that our bit of gossip affords us. Second, we should be able to withstand a smirk that might greet words such as, "I don't want to hear *loshon hora*." Caring a little less about our social status frees us to care a lot more about what matters.

Looking Within: How much does your happiness and self-esteem rest on other people's approval? Are you able to voice a dissenting opinion, even if it's unpopular?

Building Within: When you stand up for someone whose reputation is being diminished by *loshon hora,* imagine the applause you will surely receive in *Shamayim.*

QUOTE OF THE DAY

"May your fear of G-d be as great as your fear of your fellow man!"

(Rabbi Yochanan ben Zakkai, Berachos 28b)

CHAPTER 4

Compassion — Feel for Others

What does it mean to have compassion? It means to feel for another person, to step into his world and experience life through his eyes. With the simple question, "How would I feel?" we can neutralize anger, soothe irritation, restrain impatience and stop the engine of *loshon hora* in its tracks. In the time it takes to look another person in the eye and see the humanity there, we can shift the entire landscape of our heart.

DAY 44

Living the Mitzvah

Do I Have to Confront Him First?

May you protect others from a harmful individual without confronting that person first?

י"ד חשון
14 Cheshvan
Cycle 1

*י"ד אדר
**14 Adar*
Cycle 2

י"ד תמוז
14 Tammuz
Cycle 3

REMEMBER
Flattery gets you nowhere.

The Dilemma:

You notice your coworker spending a good portion of her working day shopping and schmoozing on the Internet, in effect stealing from your employer. May you behave toward her as if she is your good friend, while reporting her misconduct to upper management?

The Halachah:

One may not speak *loshon hora* about another person even *l'to'eles* (i.e., for the benefit of preventing people from sustaining harm) without trying to reprove that person first. After all, the individual may very well change upon hearing the rebuke. Avoiding confrontation and acting toward that person in a way that hides your disapproval is prohibited also, because it is flattery. While we should always treat others with respect and concern, we should not pretend to approve of their actions when that is not the case. Furthermore, there is a positive command to rebuke one's fellow. [The law is different where the person will certainly not accept the rebuke. See Day 71]

Sefer Chofetz Chaim, Hilchos Loshon Hora 10:2

** During Hebrew leap years, a thirteenth month called Adar Sheni is added to the calendar. During those years, the lessons for the days of Adar should be studied during each of the Adars.*

14 Cheshvan – **Carl Aaron Friedman** לע"נ יחזקאל אהרן בן יוסף יהודה הלוי ז"ל
Dedicated by his children

14 Adar – לע"נ אברהם בן דוד ז"ל

14 Tammuz – ***L'ilui nishmas*** **Yittel bas Yehuda *a"h***

Grow Your Compassion

Refuse to Testify

You might dislike someone quite a bit. However, it's the rare situation in which one Jew wishes actual harm upon another. And certainly, we would be horrified at the idea of being the agent of that harm. Being an informer or an agent of destruction is a terrible identity to bear.

But that is the role we play when we speak *loshon hora*. We know that Hashem is merciful and always seeks ways to give us the benefit of the doubt. The Heavenly Accuser always has a full agenda of cases to prosecute, but he's largely stopped from doing so by one of the key requirements of the *beis din*, both in heaven and on earth. That is the requirement for two witnesses. The Accuser needs corroboration.

Loshon hora provides just what he needs. When we point out someone's sins and flaws, we become the second witness. Our words wipe out the doubt and set prosecution in motion.

This is a powerful image to think of when we're about to say something negative about another person. Do we really want to be the instrument of his suffering? Just for disappointing us in some way or falling short of his spiritual potential? Or do we want for him what we want for ourselves — patience, tolerance and another chance to try?

Looking Within: If you say something negative about someone, and it's unlikely that the story will do the subject any real harm, do you have a sense that you're not hurting anyone with your words?

Building Within: Before you say something negative about someone, imagine that your words are being transmitted to the Heavenly prosecutor's office — because they are.

QUOTE OF THE DAY

"One who speaks *loshon hora* below is the very one who empowers the Satan above."
(Zechor L'Miriam Ch. 3)

DAY 45

Living the Mitzvah

What Do I Do If Someone Comes to Me for Help?

If you're someone people trust to handle difficult situations, you might be the one they turn to for advice on how to steer someone onto the right path. And to do that, they've got to tell you what the person is doing wrong. May you listen to it?

ט"ו חשון
15 Cheshvan
Cycle 1

ט"ו אדר*
**15 Adar*
Cycle 2

ט"ו תמוז
15 Tammuz
Cycle 3

The Dilemma:
Two of your sons are in business together. One believes that the other is being stubborn, refusing to seek advice and making bad decisions. He decides to come to you for advice on how to reprove his brother, or perhaps for you to intercede. He wants to tell you all about the foolish decisions his brother has made. May you listen?

The Halachah:
If you're not personally aware of your stubborn son's doings, you should first check out the facts to make sure you're getting an accurate picture. In any event, you are allowed to listen to the information if it's for the constructive purpose of steering your son in the right direction or settling a dispute between your two sons.

Sefer Chofetz Chaim, Hilchos Loshon Hora 6:10 with Be'er Mayim Chaim 4:29; Be'er Mayim Chaim 9:9 ד"ה והנה אחר

REMEMBER
Hear, validate and help.

** During Hebrew leap years, a thirteenth month called Adar Sheni is added to the calendar. During those years, the lessons for the days of Adar should be studied during each of the Adars.*

15 Cheshvan – **Boruch Dov Wydra** לע"נ ברוך דוב ז"ל בן משה חיים יבלח"ט

15 Adar – **Dedicated as a *zechus* for *brachah* and *hatzlachah* for my family**
Rabbi Yekusiel & Mrs. Mindy Janklowicz

15 Tammuz – **In memory of Reb Tuvia *ben* R' Binyomin Brodie *z"l***

Grow Your Compassion

He's His Own Biggest Challenge

In life, there are people who seem to energize us and others who seem to drain a little life out of us. People who are needy, who have a lot of troubles, whose thought patterns don't seem to make sense to us, who have irksome habits — all challenge our ability to think, speak and act in a positive way.

Rabbi Yisroel Reisman offers a strategy to deflate our irritation and allow our better selves to shine through: compassion for people who have an emotional deficiency, just as if they had a physical deficiency.

How does this help? Think, for example, of a person whose in-laws are difficult. That person can look at their demands and think, "They are emotionally needy. If they had a physical handicap, G-d forbid, I'd have to do whatever I could to help them. I'd have to drive them, shop for them — whatever it would be, I'd do it! So, thank G-d, they don't have a physical handicap but sadly, they have an emotional one, and it also requires my attention." By seeing people's demands in that light, with compassion for their cluelessness or neediness, we can deal with them in a way that is caring rather than callous. We see our own actions as compassionate rather than burdensome, and our urge to speak negatively about them falls away.

Looking Within: Everyone has people in their lives who tend to be draining. How do you interact with that person?

Building Within: Think, when dealing with a difficult or needy person, how grateful you are to Hashem that you do not have their challenges.

QUOTE OF THE DAY

"A safety fence for wisdom is silence."
(Pirkei Avos 3:13)

DAY 46

Living the Mitzvah

Is It Loshon Hora to Report My Student's Misbehavior to the Principal?

You're at the end of your rope with a certain disruptive student. Under what circumstances are you allowed to discuss his case with the principal?

ט"ז חשון
16 Cheshvan
Cycle 1

ט"ז אדר*
**16 Adar*
Cycle 2

ט"ז תמוז
16 Tammuz
Cycle 3

The Dilemma:
You have a class of rowdy fifth-grade boys. Most of them respond when you put your foot down and call the class to order. But one child is especially disruptive and impulsive. He talks too loud, interrupts too often, and jumps out of his seat for no discernible reason. You know he's taking medication for ADHD, but you think he just needs someone to put some fear into his heart. Today you were especially tired and he drove you crazy. Is it time to tell the principal about his behavior?

The Halachah:
While there may be many sound reasons for a teacher to discuss a student's behavior with the principal, other teachers or the child's parents, anger and frustration are not among them. To talk about the child's flaws within the limits of *to'eles*, your motivation has to be purely to help the child. If you were able to deal with him when you were in a better mood, then perhaps your motivation in this instance is not what it should be. Before speaking to the principal, make sure you're doing so for the child's benefit.

Sefer Chofetz Chaim, Hilchos Rechilus 9:2

REMEMBER
Frustration is not a constructive purpose.

** During Hebrew leap years, a thirteenth month called Adar Sheni is added to the calendar. During those years, the lessons for the days of Adar should be studied during each of the Adars.*

16 Cheshvan – **Maier Cahan** לע"נ ר' מאיר בן ר' משולם פייביש הכהן כהנא ז"ל
Dedicated by the Cahan family

16 Adar – לע"נ מרדכי בן אברהם מנחם טייטעלבוים ז"ל
Dedicated by Chuny & Lisa Teitelbaum

16 Tammuz – **Miriam Breiner** לע"נ מרים בת דוד הכהן ע"ה
Dedicated by Karen & Marc Silverman and children

Grow Your Compassion

Something That Might Actually Help

Most people know someone they definitely do not admire: someone who treats others poorly or has self-destructive habits or seems detached from spirituality or is in some other way on a fast train to nowhere. When that person's name comes up in conversation, *loshon hora* is all but inevitable. His troubles are all his own doing, and we sometimes cannot help but point that out. However, our "wise" commentary changes nothing.

Rav Eliyahu Dessler *zt"l* suggests that rather than condemning such a person, we should do something that will actually help him: pray to Hashem to inspire him to do *teshuvah*. "Develop compassion for the true situation of people who continuously transgress," he says. "They are the most unfortunate of people." Compassion, not condemnation, is the approach that can make the difference (*Consulting the Wise*, p. 224).

Looking Within: Does it give you any satisfaction to condemn another person or look down on him?

Building Within: If you begin to focus on another person's weaknesses, think about your own weaknesses and why you have not yet been able to conquer them. In this way, you can feel compassion for the difficult task the other person faces.

QUOTE OF THE DAY

"Stars appear as tiny specks in the sky when in reality each is a mighty world. So too a Jew may appear puny and insignificant when in reality he is an immense world."

(Baal Shem Tov al HaTorah, Lech Lecha §27)

DAY 47

Living the Mitzvah

May I Report Misbehavior to a Student's Parents If They Are Likely to Overreact?

You have an aggressive student in your class who's always starting fights. You know his parents could rein him in, but may you tell them the problem?

י"ז חשון
17 Cheshvan
Cycle 1

י"ז אדר*
**17 Adar*
Cycle 2

י"ז תמוז
17 Tammuz
Cycle 3

The Dilemma:
One of your students took another child's catcher's mitt without permission, and then dropped it in a puddle. The mitt's owner jumped on the boy and started punching him, screaming, "My father's gonna *kill* me if I wreck this mitt!" According to the school rules, the child who started the fight should be suspended and his parents called. But you know for a fact that the father does indeed have a bad temper and is quick to hit his children. What should you do?

The Halachah:
One of the conditions of *to'eles* is that there will be a benefit [to the child] in sharing the information. In a situation in which a child might be embarrassed or punished physically because of a teacher's report to the parents, the teacher has to weigh the situation and decide if the consequences are necessary for the child's growth.

Sefer Chofetz Chaim, Hilchos Rechilus 9:2

REMEMBER
Consider the outcome before reporting.

** During Hebrew leap years, a thirteenth month called Adar Sheni is added to the calendar. During those years, the lessons for the days of Adar should be studied during each of the Adars.*

17 Cheshvan – לע"נ יצחק בן אברהם שפרן ז"ל ואשתו בתי' בת מאיר יהודה ע"ה
Dedicated by their children, Safran, Persoff and Fogel families

17 Adar – לזכות בריאות, ברכה, הצלחה, ופרנסה
for the Roberts family

17 Tammuz – לע"נ מינדל בת מרדכי ע"ה
Dedicated by her grandchildren

Grow Your Compassion

Put Your Thumb on the Scale

You know that scale of justice? The one that's often used to represent Heavenly judgment of our deeds? For many of us, that scale seems more like a seesaw that shifts from up and down as the balance shifts between our good deeds and our sins. While most people consider themselves generally good people, worthy of a good life in this world and a nice spot in *Olam Haba,* we never really know where we stand.

But there is one way to ensure that our good deeds will far outweigh the sins. That is to be forgiving of others' mistakes. If we did only one thing right in our life, that would be the thing to do.

That is because the Heavenly court operates on the concept of *middah k'neged middah,* measure for measure. When we're harsh with others, Heaven is harsh with us. When we demand our due and overlook nothing, Heaven overlooks nothing from us.

But a great boon lies on the other end of the spectrum. When we give others the benefit of the doubt, Heaven does the same for us. When we judge others with compassion, realizing, "He did the best he could under the circumstances," then that is how we are judged. So if we can't be perfect, our next-best option is to be forgiving.

Looking Within: Have you said or done things that you would like Hashem to overlook?

Building Within: Before passing judgment on someone, stop yourself by asking, "How would I want to be judged if I were him?"

QUOTE OF THE DAY

"If your words will be negative, then seal the gates made by Hashem — the teeth and lips — and do not breach the fences of the King of All Kings."

(Pele Yoetz 62:95)

DAY 48

Living the Mitzvah

May I Report a Crime?

You're aware that someone has cheated another Jew out of money. What can you do with that information?

The Dilemma:

You are an accountant for a large, Jewish-owned company and you have discovered that the chief financial officer has been siphoning money out of the business's funds. What should you do with this information?

י״ח חשון
18 Cheshvan
Cycle 1

*י״ח אדר
**18 Adar*
Cycle 2

י״ח תמוז
18 Tammuz
Cycle 3

The Halachah:

Helping someone receive restitution for a loss is considered a constructive purpose, and therefore you would be allowed to relate what happened. First, you should verify your suspicions if you're not certain; then you should speak to the perpetrator if possible. However, a problem arises if reporting the incident would cause consequences that are beyond what halachah would allow. Since halachah doesn't allow people to be jailed for monetary offenses, reporting such an incident to the police — or to someone else who would then report it to the police — would be problematic. In cases like this, a competent *rav* must be consulted.

Sefer Chofetz Chaim, Hilchos Loshon Hora 10:1 ff., Rama Choshen Mishpat 388:7 [at the end]

REMEMBER

Righting a wrong is right.

** During Hebrew leap years, a thirteenth month called Adar Sheni is added to the calendar. During those years, the lessons for the days of Adar should be studied during each of the Adars.*

18 Cheshvan – **Dedicated as a *zechus* for** כלל ישראל

18 Adar – לע״נ בילא נעכא בת ר׳ יעקב ע״ה
Dedicated by Nachum & Tzippy Schaum and family

18 Tammuz – **In honor of Faigy, Yocheved, Esty, Avi, Chaya, Shana and Batsheva**
Love, Mommy & Daddy

Grow Your Compassion

Cruel? Who, Me?

What benefit does a person derive from speaking negatively about someone else? Usually, none at all. He doesn't become more important by making someone else sound less important. He doesn't get smarter by pointing out someone else's foolishness. He doesn't gain talent by pointing out someone else's lack of talent. The only upshot of negative words is the cloud it casts over another person's reputation. It's a lose-lose proposition.

For that reason, explains Rav Yechezkel Levenstein *zt"l* (*Consulting the Wise,* p. 249), the Talmud (*Taanis* 8a) designates speaking *loshon hora* as evidence of a cruel person. He explains that many people believe they're far from such a heinous trait as cruelty, and yet they belie that belief if they speak *loshon hora.* It has no purpose other than demeaning another person, which makes it the very definition of cruelty.

Many people think of *loshon hora* as something that's hard to control. However, when we think about it as an act of cruelty we recoil. We have to admit that it's true; *loshon hora* has no purpose but pain and damage. When we see it that way, we can see our way to freeing ourselves from its grip.

Looking Within: Do you think about the destruction of another person's reputation or image when you hear or speak *loshon hora*?

Building Within: Link the idea of *loshon hora* to the words "character assassination," "destruction" and "cruelty" to help you develop a true distaste for it.

QUOTE OF THE DAY

"If you have done your fellow man a slight wrong, let it be a serious thing in your eyes. But if you have done him much good, let it be a small thing in your eyes."
(Avos D'Rav Nosson, Nuschah Alef, #41)

DAY 49

Living the Mitzvah

May I Report Dangerous Behavior to the Police?

You have firsthand knowledge of dangerous behavior committed by a fellow Jew, yet you know that the title "informer" is a title to avoid. Should you report the crime to the police?

י"ט חשון
19 Cheshvan
Cycle 1

*י"ט אדר
**19 Adar*
Cycle 2

י"ט תמוז
19 Tammuz
Cycle 3

The Dilemma:
Your neighbor has a troubled son. Although he is too young for a driver's license, he often takes his father's car out for a joyride. You've seen him careening recklessly around town and you fear that he will cause serious damage or injury. You've spoken to his parents, but they can't seem to get him under control. Right now, he's weaving in and out of traffic on the road you're on. Should you pull over and call the police on him?

The Halachah:
Questions of reporting misconduct to secular authorities are very sensitive and whenever possible, should be decided in consultation with a *rav*. Where there is a clear threat to others, the person may be reported to prevent harm.

See Rama, Choshen Mishpat 388:7

REMEMBER

Ask when possible; report danger when necessary.

** During Hebrew leap years, a thirteenth month called Adar Sheni is added to the calendar. During those years, the lessons for the days of Adar should be studied during each of the Adars.*

19 Cheshvan – לזכות שלמה אריה בן העניא עטיל נ"י

19 Adar – לזכות ס"ד ושדוכים לכל המשפחה

19 Tammuz – Matie Rubinfeld לזכות מאטיל לאה בת מינדל תחי'
Dedicated by R' Yossi Rubinfeld

Grow Your Compassion

The Only Thing to Do

A woman whose husband was fighting a devastating illness sought advice from HaRav Chaim Kanievsky, *shlita*. He told her, "A woman who is going through a difficult time has special power, and in this case the best way to use that power is to get women to work on *shmiras haloshon* together."

Why *shmiras haloshon* above any other mitzvah? The woman didn't know, but her heart was devoted to doing all she could to save her beloved husband. She spoke to her sister, who recommended "Purity of Speech," an English adaptation of *Sefer Chofetz Chaim*, for the group to learn. In the introduction Rebbetzin Kanievsky *a"h* writes: "In recent months we have witnessed numerous tragedies and illnesses. One day a group of people came to my husband, HaRav Chaim Kanievsky *shlita*, to ask him why these tragedies are occurring. The Rav opened a Gemara and pointed to the answer: 'Improper speech is the cause and we can alleviate the situation ONLY by guarding our tongues.' "

With these words as her inspiration, the woman began a network of WhatsApp groups around the world, all learning two halachos a day as a *zechus* for her husband. There were 3,100 members in a host of countries, including the U.S., Canada, Israel, Hong Kong, South Africa, France, Switzerland, England and Brazil. Although her husband did not recover, the learning done in his *zechus* continues to bring healing and blessing into the world.

May it bring an *aliyah* to the *neshamah* of Rafael Daniel Mordechai *ben* Nochum Meir Haleivi *z"l*.

Looking Within: Do you perceive your own way of speaking as something that has an impact on the health and well-being of other Jews?

Building Within: When you're tempted to say something negative, try to remember that by holding back you may be sparing others, or yourself, from tragedy.

QUOTE OF THE DAY

"A person who avoids *loshon hora* and utilizes his power of speech in a positive way is forever enhancing the spiritual power of his words. Thus, the Torah study and prayer that emanate from his lips are endowed with an exalted spiritual light."

(Sefer Shmiras HaLoshon, Shaar HaZechirah Ch. 10)

DAY 50

Living the Mitzvah

May I Tell Others That My Adversary in a Dispute Refuses to Come to a Beis Din?

It takes two to bring a dispute to beis din, and your opponent refuses to participate. May you pressure him by telling others that he won't heed the summons?

כ חשון
20 Cheshvan
Cycle 1

כ אדר*
**20 Adar*
Cycle 2

כ תמוז
20 Tammuz
Cycle 3

The Dilemma:

Your tenant recently moved out owing you one month's rent. He says the money is his because he paid to fix a plumbing problem. You disagree that you are responsible for that expense. You ask him to settle the matter with you before a *beis din,* but in his eyes, there's no issue. "The money is mine fair and square," he says. May you tell people that he refuses to come before a *beis din* as a way of pressuring him to behave in accordance with the Torah's standards for settling disputes?

The Halachah:

Assuming that he is merely mistaken in his belief that he's entitled to the money without any question, he is still considered *amisecha* — a fellow member of the Jewish nation — whom you aren't permitted to embarrass. You could speak to someone who might be able to influence him, but this must be done without causing him shame. Only the *beis din,* if its summons is ignored, can publicize the person's refusal.

Sefer Chofetz Chaim, Hilchos Loshon Hora 4:8

REMEMBER

A misguided Jew is still a Jew.

** During Hebrew leap years, a thirteenth month called Adar Sheni is added to the calendar. During those years, the lessons for the days of Adar should be studied during each of the Adars.*

20 Cheshvan – לע"נ אמי מורתי ינט בת יואל הכהן ע"ה

20 Adar – In memory of Yocheved *bas* Matisyahu *a"h*

20 Tammuz – In memory of our grandfather Sol Ginnis *z"l*
In memeory of our uncle, Steve Fhiston *z"l*

Grow Your Compassion

Be Just a Little Holier

You have certain ideals. You work hard to uphold them, steeling yourself against the temptation of the moment and focusing your strength on doing what you know Hashem wants of you.

But other people? They can be so weak! They can be so blind! You find it so frustrating that you sometimes join with like-minded people to shake your head and wonder about what makes some people tick.

Thus, in your zeal, you end up speaking *loshon hora*. Rav Moshe Feinstein *zt"l* (*Consulting the Wise,* p. 199) says that Avraham Avinu teaches the right attitude toward those who don't live up to our ideals. He prayed for the welfare of the people of Sodom, even though they lived in a way that was complete anathema to Avraham.

The more elevated a person is, the less likely he is to think and speak *loshon hora*. If we find that because of our idealism we think poorly of others, that is a sure sign that we need to become just a bit more idealistic, perhaps by following Avraham's lead. Don't talk about others' shortcomings; pray for their well-being.

Looking Within: What are your inner thoughts about people who appear to be stagnating at a lower spiritual level than your own?

Building Within: Whenever you begin thinking or speaking about another person's spiritual failings, add this phrase: "But *loshon hora* is worse."

QUOTE OF THE DAY

"One must seek far-fetched justifications for his friends' actions just as he would for himself; if he fails to do so, it is because he does not love his fellow as himself."
(Michtav M'Eliyahu, Vol. 5, p. 431)

DAY 51

Living the Mitzvah

May I Criticize a Beis Din Ruling That Seems Clearly Wrong to Me?

You saw the whole thing and you're 100 percent certain that the beis din's decision is 100 percent wrong. May you tell others about this injustice?

כ"א חשון
21 Cheshvan
Cycle 1

כ"א אדר*
**21 Adar*
Cycle 2

כ"א תמוז
21 Tammuz
Cycle 3

The Dilemma:

You were the only one in the parking lot who saw what happened: Mr. Klein backed into Mr. Bloom's car and then pulled away without even leaving a note with contact information. You waited for Mr. Bloom and told him everything he needed to know about the big dent in his fender. When Mr. Bloom contacted Mr. Klein, he denied any wrongdoing. The two men agreed to bring their dispute to a *beis din* and much to your shock, the rabbis decided for Mr. Klein! You're furious over the injustice and want everyone to know that they shouldn't count on this *beis din* for an honest decision.

The Halachah:

If a person witnesses a crime that is brought before a *beis din* and the accused person is acquitted, the witness is not allowed to criticize the *beis din*. That is because we assume that a court of Torah scholars has done its best to ascertain the relevant facts and apply the law properly. Here, for example, since there is only one witness, his testimony is invalid. If a person is one of the litigants, he's even less likely to be able to judge the fairness of the outcome objectively. If someone believes that the judges truly made an error, he should seek the advice of a Rabbinic authority.

Sefer Chofetz Chaim, Hilchos Loshon Hora 6:8 in Hagahah

REMEMBER
Don't judge the judge.

** During Hebrew leap years, a thirteenth month called Adar Sheni is added to the calendar. During those years, the lessons for the days of Adar should be studied during each of the Adars.*

21 Cheshvan – **In memory of my mother Helen Samoukhian** לע"נ חנה רחל בת איוב ע"ה
Dedicated by her daughter Esther

21 Adar – לע"נ רחל בת בנציון ע"ה
Dedicated by Benzion & Masha Wellson

21 Tammuz – לע"נ אברהם ציון בן נאוה ז"ל
Dedicated by Natalie & Max Mizrachi

Grow Your Compassion

"It's My Business to Know"

When someone owns a business, he knows every aspect of it. He remembers sales figures for the past ten years. He has a mental list of all his vendors, shipping rates, currency exchanges and the tax laws of four different countries. The breadth and depth of his knowledge seems astounding to others, and he learns more every day.

"How do you keep so much information in your head?" someone might ask him. No doubt his answer will be, "It's my business to know."

When a person is motivated, his mind can absorb vast amounts of information. Therefore, the only reason someone might be murky on what constitutes *loshon hora* is that he hasn't yet found the motivation to learn. He hasn't yet decided that "it's my business to know."

But if we want success in the 120-year enterprise we call "life," this is information we can't do without. There are many ways to learn, from books, emails and audio, with partners, in shul, on a phone line. None of them take more than 5 minutes a day, and all of them impart the details we need to observe the mitzvah correctly. Then we'll know.

Looking Within: Do you have any consistent plan in place to learn and review the laws of *shmiras haloshon?*

Building Within: Just do something and do it every day. Whether it's learning or using one of the strategies you learn in this book, your small daily effort will transform *shmiras haloshon* into a growing presence in your life.

QUOTE OF THE DAY

"The longer one persists in guarding his tongue, the easier it becomes."
(Sefer Shmiras HaLoshon, Preface)

DAY 52

Living the Mitzvah

May I Tell Someone That He's Been Victimized If He Might Seek Redress That's Harsher Than Halachah Would Allow?

כ"ב חשון
22 Cheshvan
Cycle 1

כ"ב אדר*
**22 Adar*
Cycle 2

כ"ב תמוז
22 Tammuz
Cycle 3

Someone has caused another person harm. The victim doesn't know who did it, but you do. May you tell?

The Dilemma:
You're shopping at a local men's clothing store when a boy comes in, tries on a pair of shoes and runs out the door wearing them. You know who the boy is; he's a troubled kid who seems to have a penchant for nice clothes and shoplifting. The owner notices the boy pass by the cashier and break into a sprint. The owner runs after him out the door, but the boy disappears around the corner. "If I find out who that kid is, I'm going to smack his face and drag him off to the police!" he says angrily. "He can sit in jail!" May you tell him the identity of the boy?

The Halachah:
If the victim can be expected to try to retrieve his possessions or money using methods that are not acceptable by halachah, the witness should not identify the wrongdoer for him.

Sefer Chofetz Chaim, Hilchos Rechilus 9:13 (#37)

REMEMBER
Don't ignite a wildfire.

** During Hebrew leap years, a thirteenth month called Adar Sheni is added to the calendar. During those years, the lessons for the days of Adar should be studied during each of the Adars.*

22 Cheshvan – לע"נ דוד בן יצחק ז"ל נלב"ע כ"ה חשון
Dedicated by his children and grandchildren

22 Adar – לע"נ טילא רייזל בת חנה חיה ע"ה

22 Tammuz – *L'zechus* my wife who personifies the words אשת חיל
Dedicated by BMM

Grow Your Compassion

For the Road

For some people, it's a long ride from home to work. There are many options: music, a *shiur*, the news, or perhaps a hands-free phone conversation. One commuter decided to start every commute with a Shmiras Haloshon Yomi telephone *shiur* by Rabbi Ephraim Eliyahu Shapiro. He set up his car's Bluetooth to call into the Chazak Inspiration Line whenever he started the engine.

That way, he hears a daily three-to-five-minute *shmiras haloshon* lesson as he sets out for his day's activities. "It puts me in the right frame of mind before I begin dealing with everyone at work," says the young man. "Then on the way home, it helps me process the day's events before I begin catching up on phone calls and carrying on conversations that might otherwise turn into complaints about things that happened during the day."

Often he drives during the course of his workday as well, and his automatic setup provides him with that day's lesson once again. "Someone asked me if it's annoying to hear the same thing three or four times a day," he says. "But if you're listening to the radio, the traffic and weather report comes on every five minutes during rush hour. Most people don't consider that annoying. If I really feel like I don't want to hear it again, I just shut it off. But more often than not, it's just what I need to hear."

Looking Within: Have you made *shmiras haloshon* learning a regular part of your day, so that you can stay on track and keep moving forward?

Building Within: Knowing that *middos* change slowly, try to find a way to keep *shmiras haloshon* messages flowing into your life on a regular basis so that the message will seep in.

QUOTE OF THE DAY

"Even someone who has completed the entire *Sefer Chofetz Chaim* will not guard his tongue properly if he fails to study it consistently. The only recourse is a commitment to study this holy *sefer* constantly."
(R' Isser Zalman Meltzer, approbation to Sefer Ikkarei Dinim)

DAY 53

Living the Mitzvah

May I "Vent" to Ease My Emotional Burdens?

When big problems weigh heavily on our minds, we often seek someone with whom to share the burden. Are we allowed to tell our problem to a confidant when the information we would be relating reflects poorly on someone else?

כ״ג חשון
23 Cheshvan
Cycle 1

כ״ג אדר*
**23 Adar*
Cycle 2

כ״ג תמוז
23 Tammuz
Cycle 3

The Dilemma:

You have been married for six months and your wife doesn't appear to be adjusting to married life. Her formerly confident, sunny personality has become morose. She doesn't respond to your efforts to make her happy. You're confused, disappointed and don't know what to do. May you tell your best friend what's going on?

The Halachah:

You would certainly be allowed to discuss the situation with a *rav* or counselor. The Chofetz Chaim says that even outside the context of counseling, a person may be allowed to share such information simply to relieve stress (within the confines of *to'eles*). This would apply only to truly challenging situations, not everyday irritations. In either case, a person should share only as much information as necessary, and be careful that no harm should be caused to anyone by this revelation.

Subnote to Sefer Chofetz Chaim 10:14 and sources cited in Lesson a Day, note 113

REMEMBER
Share only as needed.

** During Hebrew leap years, a thirteenth month called Adar Sheni is added to the calendar. During those years, the lessons for the days of Adar should be studied during each of the Adars.*

23 Cheshvan – לע״נ ר׳ יהושע זעליג בן אברהם שמואל הכהן ז״ל
Dedicated by Reuven & Tzila Miller

23 Adar – לע״נ אהרן דוד חיים בן ישראל איסר ז״ל ואשתו שינדל רחל בת ר׳ עוזר ע״ה
לע״נ יעקב בן דוד צבי ז״ל

23 Tammuz – לזכות דוד בן פשה נ״י

Grow Your Compassion

The THINK Strategy

We often hear that the best way to avoid a mistake is to take a moment to think before we speak or act. But when it comes to our words, what should we be thinking?

Sometimes, the thoughts that flit through our brains are completely unhelpful. "Does she deserve what I'm about to say? Yes!"

"Is what I want to say the truth? Yes!"

"Shouldn't I get this off my chest? Absolutely!"

"Will the person I'm talking about ever find out what I've said? Oh, probably not."

"Are other people saying pretty much the same kind of thing I want to say? Sure, everyone is."

With these types of thoughts, we give ourselves the wrong advice and dive right into *loshon hora* or *rechilus*. Therefore, it's not enough just to think for a few seconds. We have to be prepared with the right thoughts to think. They have to be our "default mode" when we're about to say something that we probably already suspect is not quite right.

One way to put ourselves on track is to remember the **THINK** strategy. Instead of the questions above, ask yourself:

Is what I'm about to say **T**rue? **H**elpful? **I**nspiring? **N**ecessary? **K**ind?

With this strategy we ensure that when we speak, those who hear us will feel better for having been in our presence.

Looking Within: Do you have a reliable way to intercept your own *loshon hora*?

Building Within: Review the THINK strategy and use it as often as you can so that it will become second nature.

QUOTE OF THE DAY

"The mouth of the righteous is a fountain of life."

(Mishlei 10:11)

DAY 54

Living the Mitzvah

May I Debase an Abusive Person to His Victim?

Some people have trouble controlling their temper and end up saying hurtful things to the people in their lives. If a victim comes to you for comfort, are you allowed to say anything negative about the perpetrator?

The Dilemma:

Your husband's office just hired a new manager whose assignment was to "whip the sales force into shape." In the course of his first week on the job, the manager has convinced your husband that he's inept, lazy, and bound for failure. To comfort your husband you say, "Your new manager is obviously on a power trip. You know you're none of those things. He doesn't know what he's talking about." Is this *loshon hora*?

The Halachah:

We're permitted to speak negatively about a verbally abusive person in order to comfort the victim. It's also important to help the victim devise a strategy for dealing with the abuser so that the problem won't be an ongoing one.

Sefer Chofetz Chaim, see subnote to Hilchos Loshon Hora 5:3

כ"ד חשון
24 Cheshvan
Cycle 1

כ"ד אדר*
**24 Adar*
Cycle 2

כ"ד תמוז
24 Tammuz
Cycle 3

REMEMBER

Don't hold back the encouraging word.

** During Hebrew leap years, a thirteenth month called Adar Sheni is added to the calendar. During those years, the lessons for the days of Adar should be studied during each of the Adars.*

24 Cheshvan – לזכות לברכה והצלחה לכל בני משפחתנו

24 Adar – Rochelle Berkowitz לע"נ רחל בת אליהו יצחק ע"ה
Dedicated by Mr. & Mrs. Tuvia Berkowitz

24 Tammuz – לזכות יצחק בנימין מעללער וכל המשפחה

Grow Your Compassion

No Doubt About It; Learning Heals

Suri tells this unusual story of a clear message from Hashem:

As a young girl, pretty, outgoing Suri had one noticeable flaw — her chapped, swollen lips. This initiated a habit of licking them, which caused more chapping. No medication seemed to help.

The problem became a crisis as her oldest brother's bar mitzvah approached. She dreaded the occasion, imagining the shame she would feel as she posed for family pictures and saw the looks on the guests' faces.

One night, Suri's mother asked her to fetch the "Family Lesson a Day" from the shelf so she could learn the daily lesson she had undertaken as a merit for a friend. "Why don't you learn with me?" Suri's mother suggested. "Maybe learning *shmiras haloshon* every day will be a merit to help your lips heal." Suri was happy to try.

Amazingly, the next morning, the chapping had visibly subsided, and before long it was gone. A few weeks later, Suri skipped a night of learning. In the morning, she noticed some redness returning. Quickly she got back on track. She proudly wore a glowing, healthy smile at her family's *simchah* and ever since, Shmiras Haloshon Yomi has been a daily essential.

Looking Within: Do your attempts at improving in *shmiras haloshon* tend to be short-lived? How likely are you to restart an abandoned effort?

Building Within: Think of a difficult situation for which you would like to see a solution and take upon yourself some quick daily learning as a *zechus.* Every time you learn, imagine the solution to your problem inching a bit closer.

QUOTE OF THE DAY

"If a Jew feels his love for his fellow Jew increasing daily, he can rest assured that his love and fear of Hashem is increasing likewise."

(Yid HaKadosh, cited in Tiferes Yehudi 87)

DAY 55

Living the Mitzvah

What If I Know Someone Intends to Harm Another Person?

An occasion may sometimes arise in which you find out that someone plans to do something that would harm an unsuspecting person, either financially, emotionally or physically. What are you supposed to do with that information?

The Dilemma:

Your neighbor on the left has had it with the mess on the lawn of your neighbor on the right. He's certain that you agree with him that something has to be done to restore the environmental quality of the block. He tells you that he intends to report the situation to the town's Public Works Department, which will result in a costly ticket for the messy neighbor. Should you warn him?

The Halachah:

Even though you will no doubt be raising animosity between your two neighbors, the Torah directs us, "Do not stand aside while your fellow's blood is shed" (*Vayikra* 19:16), which is broadly interpreted to cover any kind of harm. We are therefore obligated to speak up, as long as we meet the conditions of *to'eles*. A *rav* should be consulted.

Sefer Chofetz Chaim, Hilchos Loshon Hora 10:6 with Be'er Mayim Chaim 25; Hilchos Rechilus 9:3 with Be'er Mayim Chaim 14

כ"ה חשון
25 Cheshvan
Cycle 1

כ"ה אדר*
**25 Adar*
Cycle 2

כ"ה תמוז
25 Tammuz
Cycle 3

REMEMBER

Don't just stand there! Do something!

** During Hebrew leap years, a thirteenth month called Adar Sheni is added to the calendar. During those years, the lessons for the days of Adar should be studied during each of the Adars.*

25 Cheshvan – לע"נ שמואל אליהו בן נתן ז"ל

25 Adar – **Rabbi Leib Potashnik** לע"נ הרה"ג ר' יהודא ארי' בן ר' משה מנחם זצ"ל
Dedicated in loving memory by Chavie Feuer and Dina Einhorn

25 Tammuz – **As a *zechus* for *gezunt* and *menuchah* for our respective mothers-in-law**
Dedicated by Shoshana & Isaac Jaroslawicz

Grow Your Compassion

You're Going to Love the View

Two steps forward, one step back. That's the pattern most people encounter when they're trying to improve themselves. This gives rise to a sense of futility: "What's the sense of climbing higher when I can't stay at that level? Aren't I just fooling myself into thinking that I'm better than I am?"

Rabbi Levi Yitzchak of Berditchev tells us that our "visit" to the higher plane is never a wasted effort. "When you reach a high level, impressions of that level always remain, and will enable you to more easily rise up out of the lower levels into which you sometimes fall," he says. "Eventually, you will once again return to the higher levels" (*Consulting the Wise*, pp. 232-233).

In *shmiras haloshon,* this pattern is especially important to acknowledge because the situations that give rise to *loshon hora* are so varied and ongoing. It's hard to be prepared for everything that comes our way. However, little by little, we find ourselves responding with more self-control and compassion than we previously had. Progress unfolds over time, and we eventually realize that our setbacks are merely downward blips on an upward graph.

Looking Within: Do you believe that slip-ups in *shmiras haloshon* negate any progress you've made? Does that thought keep you from resuming your effort?

Building Within: When you feel as if your *shmiras haloshon* effort is futile, look back over a period of time and ask yourself if your responses to *loshon hora* challenges are different than they used to be.

QUOTE OF THE DAY

"One who habitually refrains from *loshon hora* will eventually be free of all transgressions between man and his fellow."

(Sefer Shmiras HaLoshon, Shaar HaZechirah Ch. 1)

CHAPTER 5

Consistency — Habits of Greatness

No one succeeds at life without mastering his power of speech, and no one succeeds at mastery without practice. There are dozens of tools we can use and habits that we can adopt to instill in ourselves a keen awareness of our words and a solid understanding of what the Torah requires of us in our interactions with others. Big changes come from small acts done every day.

DAY 56

Living the Mitzvah

May I Warn Customers About a Merchant?

When a merchant keeps mischarging you or selling you defective merchandise, are you allowed to warn other customers to beware?

כ"ו חשון
26 Cheshvan
Cycle 1

*כ"ו אדר
**26 Adar*
Cycle 2

כ"ו תמוז
26 Tammuz
Cycle 3

The Dilemma:

The owner of your local grocery store gives fast, friendly service. However, several times upon examining your receipt, you notice that some items are being rung up twice. The owner always provides a refund when you point it out, but it happens fairly regularly. Do the other customers know? How many of them actually look at their receipts? Should you warn them?

The Halachah:

Your first stop should be the owner. However, if the situation doesn't change, you are obligated to warn the other customers to check their receipts carefully. You should not imply that the owner is dishonest; he may be careless or have trouble scanning the items. However, the other customers should be warned in order to prevent a loss.

Sefer Chofetz Chaim, Hilchos Rechilus 9:10, 11

REMEMBER

Buyer be warned.

* *During Hebrew leap years, a thirteenth month called Adar Sheni is added to the calendar. During those years, the lessons for the days of Adar should be studied during each of the Adars.*

26 Cheshvan – לע"נ יוסף בן משה חיים ז"ל
Deidcated by the Ranbod family

26 Adar – **As a *zechus* for *shidduchim* for our family**
Dedicated by R.S.M.

26 Tammuz – לע"נ ר' אברהם בן ר' שמואל בנימין זאב ז"ל
ואשתו שיינא פייגא בת ר' משה הכהן ע"ה

Grow Your Consistency

Glad I Called!

Sometimes schoolchildren play pranks on each other, thinking more about the laugh they'll get than the hurt they might cause. The girl in this story credits the Chofetz Chaim's TicTalk hotline with preventing her from compounding the damage of a prank and for opening the way for reconciliation.

My friend and I played a practical joke on a girl in our class. We wrote a letter, pretending it was from someone else, and left it on her desk to see how she would react. A few weeks later, we asked her if she got that letter. She said she did, and she was upset about it. We realized we shouldn't have done it, but still, I was bursting to tell someone about the story.

When I got home, I was all set to call someone and share the joke, but I realized that I hadn't called TicTalk yet that night. Our school really encourages us to call every night, so I decided to call TicTalk before I called my friend. By the time I finished with TicTalk, I realized that there was no reason to tell anyone else about our joke. The story didn't go any further, and I'm very happy that I decided this, because it was the kind of story that would have gone viral. If I would have repeated it to one girl, she would have passed it along and everyone would have known.

My friend and I apologized to the girl we played the trick on, and we're very good friends now. I'm happy that I didn't repeat the story and grateful to TicTalk for giving me the inspiration.

A small, well-timed awakening was all it took to prevent an innocent girl from becoming the brunt of embarrassing gossip.

Looking within: Do you have any instant reminders that will stop you in your tracks when *loshon hora* creeps into your life?

Building within: Find one small thing that you can incorporate into your daily routine that will help you strengthen your *shmiras haloshon.*

QUOTE OF THE DAY

"That which you give another does not deplete your own; it is an expansion of yourself. For through [giving] you sense yourself within the other. That connection is called love." *(Michtav M'Eliyahu 1:36)*

DAY 57

Living the Mitzvah

May I Steer Someone to a Store That Offers a Better Deal?

Your friend is heading to a store to make a major purchase. You think he'll get better value for his money at a different store. Is your advice loshon hora?

כ"ז חשון
27 Cheshvan
Cycle 1

כ"ז אדר*
**27 Adar*
Cycle 2

כ"ז תמוז
27 Tammuz
Cycle 3

The Dilemma:

Your sister bought a house and wants to replace the carpeting before she moves in. She doesn't shop around; she heads straight to Carpet Castle, where her friend works as an interior designer. You know that the same brands are selling for a much lower price at Floors nMore. May you share this information with her without speaking *loshon hora* about Carpet Castle and harming its proprietor?

The Halachah:

You're allowed to advise friends of a store where they can get better quality or better prices, but that allowance comes with several conditions: (1) You have to know that this is the case firsthand. If not, specify that "I don't know for sure but I've heard..." (2) You must be sure that the lower-priced merchandise is of comparable quality to that of the higher-priced store. (3) You must be certain that it's not stolen merchandise or an illegal knock-off. (4) Finally, you have to relate the information without implying anything negative about the higher-priced merchant. (5) Above all, this kind of conversation is allowed only if someone is actually considering a purchase. Otherwise, it's *loshon hora.*

Sefer Zera Chaim, Hilchos Rechilus 9:10

REMEMBER

Don't pay a price for your free advice.

** During Hebrew leap years, a thirteenth month called Adar Sheni is added to the calendar. During those years, the lessons for the days of Adar should be studied during each of the Adars.*

27 Cheshvan – **Dedicated as a *zechus* for the Paneth and Werner families**

27 Adar – לע"נ מרים בת דוד פנחס הכהן ע"ה
Dedicated by her grandchildren Wendy & Alan Gerson

27 Tammuz – **In memory of Harav Simcha Bunim *ben* Harav Chaim Benzion Finkelman *z"l***
In memory of Perel Basia *bas* Tzvi *a"h*

Grow Your Consistency

Repairing Wear and Tear

When you grow up in a home that encourages *shmiras haloshon,* your language is controlled and refined. You just don't spout negative stories, criticize others, or laugh at people's flaws and foibles. It feels wrong.

But what happens when you enter a different environment? What happens if your workplace, school, shul or community has low standards for acceptable speech? Little by little, your sensitivity goes away. Things that sounded harsh in your ears begin to sound normal. And you carry this new, desensitized way of speaking into the rest of your life.

That's why thousands of adults, whether they spend their days in offices or in classrooms or at home with their children, make the learning of *shmiras haloshon* a part of their day. By learning for just a few minutes, they scrape off the corrosion that may have accumulated in their speech. It's a daily bit of maintenance that restores the luster to their words and their relationships.

Looking Within: Are you on the way up or on the way down in your attention to *shmiras haloshon?*

Building Within: Use one of the many available learning formats to create a consistent strategy for yourself to ensure that your sensitivity to speech stays strong and grows.

QUOTE OF THE DAY

"Happy is one who avoids this sin [*loshon hora*], for he is blessed by all of Israel together."
(Sefer Shmiras HaLoshon 2:23)

DAY 58

Living the Mitzvah

May I Tell Others That a Product Is Unsafe?

כ"ח חשון
28 Cheshvan
Cycle 1

כ"ח אדר*
**28 Adar*
Cycle 2

כ"ח תמוז
28 Tammuz
Cycle 3

If a Jewish manufacturer puts something on the market that you believe is unsafe, are you allowed to warn people about it?

The Dilemma:
You purchased a skin cream made by your local holistic, organic, vegan, no-animal-testing health product store. The proprietor makes the cream herself, using her own secret recipe. You try it and instead of smoothing your skin, it gives you a rash. May you tell your neighbor, who is thinking of purchasing the same cream?

The Halachah:
First of all, you must bring the problem to the manufacturer's attention and try to resolve it directly. Second, you may not call something "dangerous" unless it really is. If you had an allergic reaction to something or over-indulged in or misused a product, that doesn't qualify it as "dangerous."

Sefer Chofetz Chaim, Hilchos Loshon Hora 10:2

REMEMBER

Caution with caution.

* *During Hebrew leap years, a thirteenth month called Adar Sheni is added to the calendar. During those years, the lessons for the days of Adar should be studied during each of the Adars.*

28 Cheshvan – As a *zechus* for our children to be *matzliach* in *limud haTorah*, to find their *shidduchim*, good health and wealth until 120.

28 Adar – לע"נ ברוך שרגא בן שלמה יהודה ז"ל

28 Tammuz – As a *zechus* for the Kahn and Schon families
Dedicated by Shloimie & Malkie Kahn

Grow Your Consistency

The Shmiras Haloshon Diet

Someone who has to cut back on salt for health reasons might find that at first everything tastes like cardboard. If, however, he cuts back little by little, his taste buds will adjust. Eventually, he'll be wondering why others dump so much salt on their food.

Cutting out *loshon hora* operates on a similar principle. Gedalia B. describes his experience of "losing his taste" for *loshon hora*:

Rosh Hashanah was coming and I was having some big personal problems. I decided that being careful with *loshon hora* might be just the *zechus* I needed. My first big test came at PTA at my son's yeshivah. I was waiting with two friends for a turn to see the math teacher and they started complaining about him. I sidled over to a couple of other friends nearby, but I was still straining to hear the other conversation.

Two nights later at a wedding, a big *loshon hora* conversation got started. I said, "Hey, there's my old yeshivah friend. I'm going to go sit with him for a while," and I moved on. But I couldn't help looking over every so often to the other table, wondering what they were saying.

Then on Shabbos, I was walking home from a *kiddush* and two friends were walking ahead of me. Their heads were together in deep conversation. For a second I thought I'd speed up and join them, but I said to myself "What for?" I realized that I didn't have the feeling that I was missing out. I know there are plenty of challenges ahead, but I was encouraged to see that change was really happening.

Looking Within: Do you stick with your *shmiras haloshon* resolutions long enough to build new habits and see a difference?

Building Within: Keep up your efforts, even after you backslide, so that *shmiras haloshon* can have a chance to become ingrained in you.

QUOTE OF THE DAY

"Speech is the most sublime of Man's powers. It is that which distinguishes Man from all other creatures."

(Derashos al HaTorah, R' Yehoshua Ibn Shu'aib, Parashas Shelach)

DAY 59

Living the Mitzvah

May I Share My Doubts About a Product's Kashrus?

Most observant Jews take kashrus very seriously. If we come to doubt the kashrus of a product, we steer clear of it. May we discuss our suspicions with others, who would also want to be protected from violating this prohibition?

כ"ט חשון◆
29 Cheshvan
Cycle 1

כ"ט אדר◆*
**29 Adar*
Cycle 2

כ"ט תמוז
29 Tammuz
Cycle 3

The Dilemma:
The local pizza shop has been under your community's kosher supervision since it opened five years ago. It has recently switched to another organization's *hechsher,* and you've heard from a friend in the know that the reason for the switch was the owner's unwillingness to abide by some of the community supervisor's standards. Should you tell others about this?

The Halachah:
Casting doubts on the *kashrus* of a product is bound to put the proprietor out of business. Therefore, it is *loshon hora.* If there are doubts, a competent *rav* should be consulted. Generally, the *rav* of a community decides *kashrus* issues for his congregation.

Sefer Chofetz Chaim, Hilchos Loshon Hora 10:2; see Mesillas Yesharim Ch. 20

REMEMBER
Keep it all kosher.

◆ *When the month has only 29 days the lesson for the 30th day should be studied today.*

* *During Hebrew leap years, a thirteenth month called Adar Sheni is added to the calendar. During those years, the lessons for the days of Adar should be studied during each of the Adars.*

29 Cheshvan – In memory of my parents Shmuel & Leah *a"h*
Dedicated by Golda Rivka

29 Adar – In memory of BatTova *bas* Michel Chuna *a"h, Yahrtzeit* 28 Adar
Dedicated by R' Chaim & Leah Tatel

29 Tammuz – לע"נ מנחם מענדל בן ר' יוסף ז"ל
Dedicated by Rabbi Chaim & Mrs. Gittel Bausk

Grow Your Consistency

Keep Flapping Those Wings

Improving in *shmiras haloshon,* like all self-improvement, is often a "two steps forward, one step back" gradual process. When that is the case, the most important tool is persistence. To keep going when setbacks keep coming takes dedication, persistence and a strong belief that the effort is worthwhile.

Sometimes it's easier to say, "This is as good as it's going to get. I can't be perfect, so why keep trying?"

Rav Yisrael Salanter (*Consulting the Wise*, p. 26) offers a visual image that helps answer that question and provide fuel for the continued effort. He says to look at a bird in flight. It must flap its wings to maintain its altitude and rise higher. If it stops flapping, it begins descending. There's no doubt that as long as it wishes to remain airborne, it needs to keep flapping. There will never be that one, great flap that keeps it afloat for the rest of its journey, enabling it to coast the rest of the way.

Similarly, on our spiritual journey through life we're either ascending or descending. The only thing that keeps us from going down is our continuing efforts to stay aloft. That's why we keep trying.

Looking Within: Do you really believe that *shmiras haloshon* demands constant effort, or do you believe that it comes naturally if you just have the right intention?

Building Within: Build some kind of reminder into your day to keep you focused on *shmiras haloshon.*

QUOTE OF THE DAY

"If you see your service of Hashem today as the same as yesterday, know that you have in fact fallen, because a person is always moving and never stationary."
(Yid HaKadosh, Niflaas HaYehudi)

CHAPTER 6

Discernment — Wisdom and Understanding

Since very few people set out to do damage to themselves or to anyone else, we can be sure that most of the words people speak are not meant to harm. We have dozens if not hundreds of ways to justify our criticisms, insults and jokes. We have loads of rationalizations for the fights we fight. It takes wisdom to know when we're fooling ourselves, to see the truth through the fog of pride and emotion. The more we recognize the truth, the less we fall into traps of our own making.

DAY 60

Living the Mitzvah

May I Speak Against Someone in Order to Vindicate Myself?

What if you are unjustly blamed for something that another person did or said? Are you allowed to name the perpetrator in order to clear your own name?

ל חשון*
30 Cheshvan
Cycle 1

ל אדר*
**30 Adar*
Cycle 2

א אב
1 Av
Cycle 3

The Dilemma:

You are one of two salespeople in a store. Both you and your coworker use the cash register to ring up sales. After a customer leaves, you hear the other salesperson tell a stock-boy, "Uh-oh. I thought those shirts were on sale." At the end of the day, your boss finds a shortage and blames you for it. May you tell him that it was your coworker who made the mistake?

The Halachah:

The answer is complicated. If a person makes an innocent mistake (and you are therefore not obligated to inform the storekeeper) you are not allowed to name the person just to clear your name. You are, however, allowed to say that you did not do it. If there are only two possible culprits, as in this case, you can make that denial if the other person's actions were, in fact, improper; for instance if the sales person had been negligent. In general, accepting the blame is considered meritorious, unless you will be unjustly penalized. You are not obligated to suffer any financial loss or compromise your current or future job prospects, and are even allowed to name the culprit to prevent any loss on your part.

Sefer Chofetz Chaim, Hilchos Loshon Hora 10:17 with Be'er Mayim Chaim 43; Hilchos Rechilus 9:14

REMEMBER

Don't throw mud to clean your name.

** When this month has only 29 days the lessons for the 30th day should be learned together with that of the 29th.*
** During Hebrew leap years, a thirteenth month called Adar Sheni is added to the calendar. During those years, the lessons for the days of Adar should be studied during each of the Adars.*

30 Cheshvan – **Dedicated by Young Israel of Great Neck**
30 Adar – **With profound appreciation for our *maggidei shiur* R' Berish Goldenberg and R' Chaim Trainer (S.M., L.A.)**
1 Av – **Dedicated as a *zechus* for my family**

Grow Your Discernment

A Minute in His Shoes

We often hear the aphorism that you can't judge another person until you've "walked a mile in his shoes." In truth, however, we could curtail a lot of *loshon hora* by spending even one quick minute in the other person's shoes, because that's how long it takes for us to take offense or feel disapproval for someone else.

A brusque answer when we're asking for help, a bland expression when we're seeking a smile, a "no" to a simple request — any of these can be affronts, even when coming from someone we normally consider a friend or ally.

What we can't know in the moment of our reaction is what that person is thinking, feeling or experiencing at that time. The bland expression says to us, "He isn't happy to see me," when in fact it means "I'm operating on two hours' sleep." The "no" to our request tells us, "He's so selfish. I would certainly do this for him," when in reality it means, "My time (or money or resources) is already taken."

The practice of assuming the best of others, especially those who have proven their friendship and loyalty over time, prevents misjudgments from spilling over into hurt, resentment and *loshon hora*.

Looking Within: Are you easily hurt or insulted?

Building Within: When someone seems uncharacteristically unfriendly toward you, try giving him a second chance at a later time or date.

QUOTE OF THE DAY

"Do not judge another until you've stood in his place."
(Pirkei Avos 2:4)

Kislev

לע"נ
ר' אפרים צבי בן ר' שלמה הלוי ז"ל נלב"ע ט' כסלו תשס"ד
מרת בלומא בת ר' אליהו צבי חיימאוויטש ע"ה
נלב"ע כ' ניסן תשס"ד
ר' חיים מאיר בן ר' נפתלי פרידמאן ז"ל
נלב"ע ג' תמוז תשס"ו

Dedicated by Mr. & Mrs. Naftuli Friedman

לע"נ
דבורה בת נחום ע"ה
ר' יצחק הכהן בן ר' שלמה דב הכהן ז"ל
סימא בת יצחק אהרן ע"ה
ריזל בת ר' יצחק הכהן ע"ה

Dedicated by their children, grandchildren and great-grandchildren
Adena, Dov, Shmuel Yaniv, Shayna, Leora and Atara Goldman

לע"נ מיידא הודיא בת משה ע"ה נלב"ע כ"ב כסלו

Helen Polonsky

Dedicated by Alex & Amy Polonsky

Nissan

Horace A. Bier z"l - לע"נ אברהם צבי בן ברוך ז"ל נלב"ע כ"ז ניסן
Pauline Bier a"h - לע"נ פעשא לאה בת יהודה ע"ה נלב"ע כ"ג חשון
Dr. Leon Hirschfus z"l - לע"נ יהודה צבי בן אלחנן יצחק ז"ל נלב"ע א' כסלו
Reyetta Hirschfus a"h - לע"נ רחל אסתר בת משה ע"ה נלב"ע ו' ניסן

Dedicated by Bryan and Andrea Bier

לע"נ הרב הגאון יעקב יוסף מרדכי בן הרב הגאון יהושע ליב ז"ל
נלב"ע ז' חשון

ואשתו הרבנית פערל פנינה פרומט בת משה דוד גודלבסקי ע"ה
נלב"ע י"ב ניסן

In honor of the Chofetz Chaim Heritage Foundation for all they do for Klal Yisrael.

Dedicated by Paul & Lisa Glaser and family

Av

In memory of Yosef Faham - ל"נ יוסף בן רחל ז"ל
In memory of Yosef Mizrahi - לע"נ יוסף בן מרים ז"ל

Dedicated by the Mizrahi family

Dedicated in the memory of our beloved and dear mother and grandmother
לע"נ אמי מורתי האשה החשובה והצנועה המפורסמת במידותיה
מרת חיה גיטל וואלצער בת הרה"ח ר' צבי שלום מיללער ע"ה
נפטרה ט"ו מנחם אב תשע"א לפ"ק
ולע"נ אמה זקנתי מרת רבקה מיללער ע"ה
בת ר' אברהם אבא בערגער ע"ה הי"ד
נפטרה שב"ק ה' סיון תשע"ו לפ"ק
נודב ע"י בנה ר' יעקב שלמה וואלצער נ"י ומשפחתו שיחי'

May all the learning in the month of Av
be a zechus for a speedy and complete recovery for
Aliza bat Sarvar, Lielle Devorah bat Golda, Sarvar bat Miriam
Netanel ben Aliza, Ariela bat Aliza, Esther bat Sarvar
Golda bat Esther, Esther bat Tooba, Eliyahoo ben Saltanat
Dedicated by Gavriel ben Sarvar and Golda bat Esther

DAY 61

Living the Mitzvah

May I Name the Guilty Party If I'm Wrongly Accused?

Somehow you've gotten blamed for something you didn't do, and you know who did it. May you deflect the blame?

א כסלו
1 Kislev
Cycle 1

א ניסן
1 Nissan
Cycle 2

ב אב
2 Av
Cycle 3

The Dilemma:
You're having Shabbos lunch with your family at your fancy Tante Eva's house. While she's in the kitchen your cousin, who's sitting next to you, carelessly knocks over a wine glass and leaves a big red puddle on the white linen tablecloth. Tante Eva returns and says sharply to you, "You need to be more careful around nice things." You don't want to embarrass your cousin, so you keep quiet. But later, when you're alone in the kitchen with Tante Eva, she mentions it again. May you set the record straight?

The Halachah:
In this situation, where there's no other purpose than to vindicate yourself, you are not allowed to shift the blame to the guilty party. You could, however, say, "I wasn't the one who spilled the wine." However, if doing so leaves your cousin as the only other option, you should not even say those words. The rule is different if you are being accused of something that is immoral or improper or would be a *chillul Hashem*; then you can deny your involvement, even if doing so automatically implicates someone else.

Sefer Chofetz Chaim, Hilchos Loshon Hora, Be'er Mayim Chaim 10:43

REMEMBER

One person's denial can be another's indictment.

1 Kislev – לע"נ שפרה בת ר' יעקב צבי ע"ה
Dedicated by Yocheved Kail

1 Nissan – לע"נ מיכלא בת מרדכי ע"ה
Dedicated by Yitzchok & Livia Cohen

2 Av – לע"נ יוסף יהודה בן ר' משולם שרגא פיוויש ז"ל נלב"ע כ"א תמוז
ואשתו גרנע בת אליעזר ע"ה נלב"ע ב' אב

Grow Your Discernment

How "Outside the Camp" Turned Into "Under the Chuppah"

A woman relates this story:

One *Chol HaMoed* when I was busy hosting my married children and grandchildren, I took a night off. My friend took me out to view "Outside the Camp," a film produced by the Chofetz Chaim Heritage Foundation.

At the time, my son Meir was in *shidduchim.* We had gotten a suggestion for a seemingly wonderful girl named Esti. Everyone gave glowing reports of her personality, but one person hinted that she had experienced some setbacks in seminary.

With a list of girls to consider, I put Esti's name aside. My husband, however, wasn't comfortable with this summary dismissal.

"Outside the Camp" changed everything. The film told the story of a wonderful girl whose reputation was besmirched subtly by another girl in her high school class. This rumor resurfaced years later to destroy this girl's *shidduch* possibilities. At the end of the film, the friend who had started the rumor realized the damage she had caused and tried to repair it.

When I told my husband about the plot, he immediately connected it to Esti. I agreed to make a few more phone calls to verify the information we had heard, and I found out that there was nothing to it. Meir and Esti were engaged three weeks later. I shudder to think of what would have happened, and not happened, if I had accepted the rumor and passed over the extraordinary girl who married my son!

Looking Within: Do I jump on any negative *shidduch* information I may get, feeling that I finally got the truth?

Building Within: When someone gives you negative *shidduch* information, listen with the same wise discernment you would want from others, should they hear negative information about you.

QUOTE OF THE DAY

"If people are so careful not to swallow a live ant, why are they not afraid to swallow a live person?"

(the Rebbe Reb Boruch MiMezhibozh [cited in Pisgamim Nivcharim])

DAY 62

Living the Mitzvah

May I Take a Stand Against My Rebbi's Opponent?

Your rabbi or rebbi decides a matter one way, and another rabbi decides it the other way. May you, out of dedication to your rabbi and his authority, speak up against the opposing rabbi?

ב כסלו
2 Kislev
Cycle 1

ב ניסן
2 Nissan
Cycle 2

ג אב
3 Av
Cycle 3

The Dilemma:

Rabbi A., head of your son's yeshivah, believes the boys should learn to translate the Chumash into Yiddish as well as English. A new yeshivah opens up headed by Rabbi B. who believes in bypassing Yiddish, going straight into English. Parents in your school begin clamoring for Rabbi A. to follow suit. You are furious at their audacity in challenging the principal, who is highly respected and experienced. Rabbi B., on the other hand, already has one failed school on his record. May you discredit him in your effort to support your principal?

The Halachah:

You may not do so. Getting involved in the disputes that arise between Torah scholars leads only to *loshon hora* and *machlokes*. *Machlokes* often results from the dangerous delusion that one is fighting for a Torah ideal, when in fact he is motivated by ego and pride. Scholars can differ without personal animosity, yet those who carry their banners often turn constructive differences into destructive battles.

Sefer Chofetz Chaim, Pesichah, Lavin 12

REMEMBER

If the feelings are personal, the fight isn't about principles.

2 Kislev – **In memory of Rabbi Benjamin Sincoff** ***z"l*** לע"נ ר' בן ציון בן שאול ז"ל
By his children and grandchildren Joey & Atara (Shira) Zolty

2 Nissan – **Dedicated as a** ***zechus*** **for the Rosenwald** ***mishpachah***

3 Av – לזכות לבלומא בת רחל מרים שתחי'

Grow Your Discernment

Really Honor Your Parents

Family loyalty is one of the strongest of all bonds. Therefore, if someone wrongs our parents we are very likely to jump into the fray.

However, the Chofetz Chaim warns that this is almost always a mistake. We know the saying that "love is blind," which means that out of love and honor for our parents, we will almost surely be blinded to the truth of the situation. They may very well be right, but they may bear some fault as well, as is almost always the case in a *machlokes*.

If a child gets involved on his parents' behalf, he will merely add more fuel to the fire. By bolstering his parents' arguments, he will cause them to fight harder and resist compromise.

If he talks to others about the situation, he is likely to add *loshon hora* to the mix. In addition, he will no doubt look for validation of his family's side of the argument, and may in the process expand the *machlokes* to include new participants, who will take sides in a feud that doesn't even pertain to them.

Therefore, the Chofetz Chaim advises children to take a supportive role, rather than becoming active combatants. Help your parents process the situation and move toward a resolution. The best way to honor them is to guide them away from the terrible destruction of *machlokes* and toward the blessings of *shalom*.

Looking Within: Do you automatically feel enmity toward people against whom your parents have a grievance?

Building Within: Work on discerning the fine line between supporting your parents and fanning the flames, and if possible, try to lower the flames instead.

QUOTE OF THE DAY

"Guard your tongue from evil, and your lips from speaking deceit. Turn from evil and do good, seek peace and pursue it."
(Tehillim 34:14)

DAY 63

Living the Mitzvah

Is It Loshon Hora to Tell the Truth About a Potential Shidduch?

Sometimes a friend is looking for a shidduch, business partner or an employee and you think you've got just the right person. The only thing is, the person you have in mind doesn't have the traits your friend says he requires. Should you mention that when suggesting the connection?

ג כסלו
3 Kislev
Cycle 1

ג ניסן
3 Nissan
Cycle 2

ד אב
4 Av
Cycle 3

The Dilemma:

Your brother has been dating for several years and hasn't yet found his *bashert*. He has clearly stated that he wants a very intellectual and well-read girl with a Master's degree and a well-paying profession. You know a wonderful young woman with sterling *middos* but who is not particularly brilliant; in your opinion, she is really what your brother needs. May you push the match despite her non-intellectual nature if you think it might work?

The Halachah:

When suggesting a relationship, a person has to avoid transgressing the prohibition against "putting a stumbling block before the blind," which Chazal interpret as offering unsound advice. If someone has clearly stated a preference, you are in fact required to tell him that the relationship you are suggesting varies from that preference.

See Sefer Chofetz Chaim, Be'er Mayim Chaim, examples at the end of Hilchos Rechilus

REMEMBER
No tricks.

3 Kislev – לע"נ חי' בת ר' מנחם מענדל ע"ה
Dedicated by the Safrin and Kantor families

3 Nissan – **May we have *nachas* from our children, grandchildren and great-grandchildren.**
Dedicated by Berel & Esther Kriger

4 Av – **Mr. Selig Wolf** לע"נ אבינו מורינו ר' אשר זעליג בן ר' אביגדור ז"ל
Dedicated by his children

Grow Your Discernment

"Righteous Anger"

Something's got to be done! But ask yourself: are you the right one to do it? For example, your company has a new employee. He is your son's former rebbi, a person who you blame for ruining your son's eighth-grade year and causing your son difficulty in getting into a good high school. Wisely, in your opinion, he's left the classroom. But now he has joined your company as a manager. His take-charge personality comes through once again in the office, where his workers chafe at his new rules.

"It's ridiculous that someone who can't get along with people has been given such a position!" you think. You're not going to sit by and watch the company fall apart because of this arrogant man who thinks he knows everything. Arrogance is a terrible trait that can only damage the company and the people who work there. You absolutely must tell the boss that he's hired a monster who is driving everyone away.

But wait, says Rav Shmuel of Ahalinov, a disciple of Rav Chaim of Volozhin (*Love Your Neighbor*, p. 85, citing *Minchas Shmuel*, p. 36). First ask yourself: "Would this behavior bother me if I liked this person? Isn't it possible that he was hired to take charge and get the office running more smoothly? Aren't there other managers in the company who have a similar style? If you find that it's not so much *what* happened but rather, *who* was involved, then your gripe is personal, not principled.

Looking Within: Do you tend to react "on principle" toward people you don't really like, while relaxing those principles for those you do like?

Building Within: When you find yourself thinking, "That's not right!" use this as a cue to assess your personal feelings toward the person who has affronted you.

QUOTE OF THE DAY

"Hatred arouses strife, but love covers all offenses."
(Mishlei 10:12)

DAY 64

Living the Mitzvah

Is It Ever Acceptable to Conceal Negative Shidduch Information?

Although we've learned that we have to respect people's stated preferences when they're in search of a shidduch, there are occasions when we're allowed to temporarily conceal facts that might stop the match before it gets started.

ד כסלו
4 Kislev
Cycle 1

ד ניסן
4 Nissan
Cycle 2

ה אב
5 Av
Cycle 3

The Dilemma:

You know a boy who was on the streets for a few years. After those years of difficulty, he straightened out and his true brilliance and goodness surfaced, and he emerged as a solid *bachur*. He would be perfect for your highly intelligent, idealistic niece, but if she hears up front that this boy had "a bumpy ride" she will reject the *shidduch* out of hand. May you tell her about the boy without mentioning his long-ago difficulties?

The Halachah:

That is a judgment call that should be made by a *rav* and not a *shadchan*, who has an interest in getting the sides together. A *rav* will consider whether the issue at hand is objectively serious enough to block an initial meeting. If not, he may allow the information to be temporarily concealed until something of a relationship exists. However, it would have to be disclosed before the parties have a chance to develop strong positive feelings for each other.

Oral ruling by HaRav Shlomo Zalman Auerbach zt"l

REMEMBER
Sometimes it's not *what* you say, but *when* you say it.

4 Kislev – *L'ilui nishmas* Menachem Mendel Yitzchok *ben* Aharon *z"l, yahrtzeit* 4 Kislev
L'ilui nishmas Yael *bas* Zev *a"h, yahrtzeit* 4 Adar

4 Nissan – In gratitude to the Almighty for all His kindness
Dedicated by Rabbi & Mrs. Yehuda Abrams

5 Av – לע"נ ראובן בן אהרן הכהן ז"ל
לע"נ שמעון בן ראובן הכהן ז"ל

Grow Your Discernment

Don't Be Naïve

Think of all the times you've been misled. You draw a conclusion based on something you see or hear, and the truth turns out to be the 180-degree opposite. How much more, then, can you assume that what you hear from others is incomplete or inaccurate in some way? Even history books can get it wrong.

However, if you happen to stumble into a group of people speaking *loshon hora,* you may find yourself believing every word you hear, especially if it seems in character with the person they're discussing. How can you avoid jumping to that conclusion?

Realize that the report you are hearing is likely to be highly imperfect. Therefore, taking the information as the whole truth is illogical.

Does that mean you must turn a deaf ear to information that could be important for you to know for your own or another Jew's protection? It doesn't, but it does mean that you should never assume you've got the whole picture until you've investigated thoroughly.

Looking Within: Do you use the same discernment regarding another person's reputation as when making a big purchase or an important decision?

Building Within: When you hear a story that reflects badly on someone, think of one possible way the information could be skewed.

QUOTE OF THE DAY

"He who walks in his world without contemplating whether his path is good or not is like a blind man walking along a riverbank..." *(Mesillas Yesharim, Perek 2).*

CHAPTER 7

Forgiveness — Break Free of Grudges

A person who carries around unresolved anger is someone who has chained himself to a very demanding master. He is not allowed to be happy or relaxed. He is not allowed to sleep peacefully or experience closeness to others. Instead, he is bound to his insulted pride, frustration and sense of persecution. He is like a slave who refuses to set himself free. Yet he can. When he forgives his adversary and drops his grudge, he discovers the wide world of freedom, light, friendship and goodness that was there all along.

DAY 65

Living the Mitzvah

How Can I Decide Whether or Not to Suggest a Shidduch?

On one hand, few acts of chessed compare to helping to build a Jewish home. On the other hand, so much can go wrong in transmitting information back and forth. How does a person know whether or not to suggest a match?

ה כסלו
5 Kislev
Cycle 1

ה ניסן
5 Nissan
Cycle 2

ו אב
6 Av
Cycle 3

The Dilemma:

You feel that a young woman you recently met would be perfect for your nephew, although you can't pinpoint exactly why. In fact, she is 5-foot-2 and your tall nephew has said he doesn't want a short girl. She's also from New York and your nephew says he wants an out-of-towner. However, she was at your Shabbos table and seemed very pleasant, mature and kind-hearted. Should you suggest her?

The Halachah:

We may suggest a *shidduch* without doing research; that's the parties' responsibility. However, we should not suggest a match unless: we know of no reason why the relationship would harm either party; we believe that the match has a reasonable chance of resulting in an engagement; we know of no medical, emotional or character flaw that would make either party an unfit spouse; we feel that neither party will have a negative influence on the other; neither party has a strong objection to any trait of the other.

Sefer Chofetz Chaim, see Tziyurim

REMEMBER
Make suggestions that make sense.

5 Kislev – **Avrohom Rumstein** לע"נ אברהם בן משה ז"ל
Dedicated by the Stahl family

5 Nissan – לע"נ אסתר בת מרדכי ז"ל
Dedicated by her children Yanky & Mindy Amsel

6 Av – לע"נ אלטע חי' שרה בת חיים יצחק ע"ה
Dedicated by her children Shloimy & Rochel Gruen

Grow Your Forgiveness

How to Get on Hashem's Good Side

Giving other people the benefit of the doubt is a guaranteed way of steering clear of *loshon hora*. Nevertheless, it's a mindset that most people find difficult to adopt. Why *should* they give the benefit of the doubt when the other person has hurt them?

A kollel student in Lakewood, N.J. explained how he finally grasped this concept. "It was right before Rosh Hashanah at the end of a year that had been very difficult for my family. I thought about the previous Rosh Hashanah, and how in spite of my hopes and my *tefillos,* things had turned out differently from what I would have wanted. I was upset with a lot of people, and I was also worried if this year my *tefillos* would be answered.

"There was still a lot of unfinished business and it wouldn't get straightened out before Rosh Hashanah. I had recently heard someone discuss the concept that if you give others the benefit of the doubt, Hashem does the same for you.

"So I forced myself to think through the various situations that had troubled me during the year and see them from the other person's side. By the time I was done, I really felt at peace. It helped my *davening* tremendously and it seems to have helped my situation as well."

Looking Within: If you are angry at someone, ask yourself what you have to do to be able to let go of the hurt and get rid of the burden of a grievance.

Building Within: Motivate yourself by remembering that by forgiving others, you gain the great benefit of Hashem's forgiveness for your wrongdoings and mistakes.

QUOTE OF THE DAY

"Before praying, one should accept on himself the *mitzvah* of loving each and every Jew like himself, for by doing so his prayers will be included in those of all of *Klal Yisrael*."

(Rabbi Chaim Vital quoting the AriZal, intro. to Shaar HaKavanos)

DAY 66

Living the Mitzvah

May I Give My Opinion When Asked for a Reference?

Someone has given your name as a reference for a shidduch and the caller asks for your opinion about the person in question. May you offer a negative opinion?

ו כסלו
6 Kislev
Cycle 1

ו ניסן
6 Nissan
Cycle 2

ז אב
7 Av
Cycle 3

The Dilemma:

A girl's mother calls a boy's learning partner and asks, "Do you see him as the type of boy who will remain in yeshivah for the long term?" If the partner's opinion is negative, may he answer the question honestly or is that *loshon hora*?

The Halachah:

In factual matters, a reference should be honest about important relevant facts such as a bad temper. In matters that are peripheral, rather than report a negative fact the reference should say "I don't know." But when asked for an opinion, a reference should not venture into territory that is difficult to quantify. Instead, refer the questioner to a rebbi, *rav* or teacher — someone with the wisdom and experience to fairly assess the person's intelligence, seriousness, spiritual striving, and so forth.

Sefer Chofetz Chaim, Hilchos Rechilus 9:13

REMEMBER
Share your facts but save your opinions.

6 Kislev – לע"נ הרה"ג ר' פלטיאל בן ר' דוד ישעי'הו ז"ל נלב"ע ב' תמוז
ואשתו מרת גאלדא חנה בת ר' חיים אלטר ע"ה נלב"ע ו' כסלו

6 Nissan – R' Chaim Friedman *z"l* לע"נ ר' חיים בן ר' שלום ז"ל
Dedicated by the Friedman, Braun and Weissman families

7 Av – Jack Fogel לע"נ ר' יעקב זאב בן ר' יהודה ארי–ה פאגעל ז"ל
Dedicated by Shalom & Ettie Fogel

Grow Your Forgiveness

Breaking Up Without Breaking Down

When two people throw their lot in with each other, whether in business, a *chessed* project, or a marriage, their lives become tied together in many ways. They get to know each other on a deeper level. They share their creativity. They go out of their way for each other because they have common goals. For all these reasons, if the partnership, dissolves people feel betrayed. Pain and resentment rush into the void: "After all I did for you!"

Recognizing this situation as a breeding ground for *loshon hora, rechilus* and *ona'as devarim* and a whole host of vengeful feelings, Rabbi Chaim Zaitchyk *zt"l* (*Consulting the Wise,* p. 266) offers this advice: Shift your focus from the wrongs you feel were done to you in the final, difficult period of the relationship to all that you gained from your partner. Focus on the aspects of the partner that you appreciate: the kindness he did for you, even if it was rare; the goals he helped you achieve; the talents he brought to the table.

By doing this, you crowd out feelings of resentment. Then you may even be ready to take one more giant step: Do what you can to help him, even if he wronged you. You'll be doing yourself the greatest favor of all by pruning away the tangle of negativity in your heart and clearing the path forward.

Looking Within: Have you let difficulties that have arisen in a close relationship crowd out the positive reasons the relationship started or the good that it produced?

Building Within: Try to shed the burden of negative feelings by following Rabbi Zaitchyk's advice and changing your focus.

QUOTE OF THE DAY

"Hashem loves only those who love the Jewish people. And the more one increases his *ahavas Yisrael,* the more [love] Hashem showers upon him."

(Mesillas Yesharim Ch. 19)

DAY 67

ז כסלו
7 Kislev
Cycle 1

ז ניסן
7 Nissan
Cycle 2

ח אב
8 Av
Cycle 3

Living the Mitzvah

May I Volunteer Vital Negative Information?

What if you hear about a shidduch in the making and you know that one of the parties is hiding a major shortcoming? May you offer your information unsolicited?

The Dilemma:

Your friend reveals to you that he is dating a young woman and will probably soon become engaged. When he tells you her name, you recognize it as the name of a girl who was a classmate of your sister. You remember that the girl had to leave school for several months because of a seizure disorder. Does your friend know of this severe health challenge? Should you find a way to make sure he knows?

The Halachah:

Someone who knows important negative information should make sure that it is revealed because of the mitzvah of "Do not stand aside while your fellow's blood is shed" (*Vayikra* 19:16), which refers to any situation in which we are able to prevent someone from being harmed. However, there are many conditions that weigh into whether a person should speak up, how much should be said, and to whom it should be said. A *rav* must be consulted to avoid the many stumbling blocks inherent in this situation.

Sefer Chofetz Chaim, Tziyurim [at the end] #4

REMEMBER
Prevent harm.

7 Kislev – לע"נ הענך בן נתן ז"ל ואשתו שרה בת אהרן ע"ה
לע"נ יוסף בן פישל ישראל ז"ל ואשתו רחל בת לייזר ע"ה

7 Nissan – As a *zechus* for our family
Dedicated by Shlomy & Shelley Berger

8 Av – לע"נ חוה בת מרדכי ע"ה
Dedicated by the Einhorn family

Grow Your Forgiveness

Upholding the Real Principle

Sometimes a person feels that his values are so rock-solid that he cannot forgive someone who wrongs him. "I am not friends with someone who does such things," he maintains. "I have my standards."

The Ralbag (*Consulting the Wise*, p. 61), however, points out that Yosef HaTzaddik also had "his standards," and very high ones. However, when his brothers appeared before him in Egypt and he revealed his identity, he did not maintain that "I don't forgive people who try to kill me." Instead, he saw that Hashem was in control of the situation at all times. "I fear Hashem," he told them as an explanation of why they needn't worry about his revenge.

Someone who refuses to forgive someone who has sincerely asked to be forgiven is considered cruel, not righteous. He may abhor cheating, but when the person who cheated him comes to make amends, the "high road" and righteous act is to forgive.

Once we purge the anger and the grudges from our hearts, the fuel that feeds *loshon hora* is greatly reduced. The power some people feel from their righteous indignation is nothing compared to the dignity and peace of mind they attain by dropping their grudge.

Looking Within: Do you have a list of offenses that you consider unforgivable?

Building Within: When someone asks you for forgiveness, remember that Hashem will be better pleased with you if you forgive than if you maintain your grudge on moral grounds.

QUOTE OF THE DAY

"He who is slow to anger is better than a mighty person, and the ruler of his spirit [is better] than the conqueror of a city."
(Mishlei 16:32)

DAY 68

Living the Mitzvah

Is There Anything Wrong With Listening to Loshon Hora?

When matters are in our control, we can understand being accountable for our words and actions. But when we are "innocent bystanders," do we really bear responsibility for what others say in our presence?

ח כסלו
8 Kislev
Cycle 1

ח ניסן
8 Nissan
Cycle 2

ט אב
9 Av
Cycle 3

The Dilemma:

You call a childhood friend to whom you haven't spoken in months. You're both catching up with the events in each other's lives when your friend mentions that his younger brother was kicked out of yeshivah and has begun dabbling in drugs. Do you bear responsibility for hearing this *loshon hora*?

The Halachah:

Listening to *loshon hora* gives it a certain amount of believability, and therefore, a person who pays attention to such stories transgresses the Torah's commandment, "Do not accept a false report" (*Shemos* 23:1). Listening to and speaking *loshon hora* both harm the subject of the report and are both considered lowly activities, beneath a person created in Hashem's image.

Sefer Chofetz Chaim, Hilchos Loshon Hora 6:2, Be'er Mayim Chaim 2

REMEMBER
It's low to keep listening.

8 Kislev – לע"נ יעקב זאב בן יהושע ז"ל
לע"נ חי' מרים בת יעקב זאב ע"ה נלב"ע ט' כסלו

8 Nissan – לע"נ אברהם מנחם מענדל בן משה יחזקאל ז"ל
Dedicated by his two daughters

9 Av – In loving memory of Yaffa Rosenthal לע"נ חיה יפה בת יצחק אליעזר ע"ה
By her children and grandchildren Chaim & Hadassah Shapiro and family

Grow Your Forgiveness

Keep the Best and Dump the Rest

Imagine you had only enough space in your living room for either a soft, luxurious leather couch or a large pile of decaying, splintery old lumber. Then imagine you chose the lumber. That's what you decided to live with day in and day out, and the couch is what you decided to reject from your home.

This is essentially the choice people make when they choose their grievance against someone in place of their relationship with him. A person who has meant something to us in our lives — a friend, sibling, parent or child — is a precious asset. This is someone with whom we share memories and experiences, someone who knows us well enough to understand us and care about our life.

On the other hand, a grievance does nothing but take up space in our hearts, exuding ugliness and ever-increasing pain.

One summer, this message — to drop grievances and "let bygones be bygones" — was the theme of an address by Rabbi Ephraim Eliyahu Shapiro for a Chofetz Chaim Heritage Foundation Tishah B'Av presentation. A son who was estranged from his parents heard the lecture in one location. His parents heard it in another. That very day, the parents called their son and reconciled. They chose to clear out the "rotting lumber" and reclaim what was truly valuable, what truly belonged in their hearts.

Looking Within: Do you have unresolved grievances against people who are important to you?

Building Within: Think about how your life would change if these relationships were not marred by negative feelings, and make a plan to create *shalom.*

QUOTE OF THE DAY

"Even if someone bears you ill will, extend a greeting of peace to him."

(Sefer Shmiras HaLoshon, Shaar HaZechirah Ch. 11)

CHAPTER 8

Good Eye — See Hashem's View

Hashem is the Creator, and He is perfect. He created a world that, in His own words, is "good." Everything in creation is invested with Hashem's goodness. Even when we cannot see it, it is sure to be there. Someone with an *ayin tovah* — a good eye — can look past the outer shell and see the spark of goodness in the situations and people he encounters. By gaining this skill, we gain the most precious commodity: the joy of living in a good world filled with good people and guided by a Creator who does only what is good for us.

DAY
69

Living the Mitzvah

What Can I Do About Someone Else's Loshon Hora?

Someone is speaking loshon hora to you. You didn't start it and you're not adding to it, but still, you're hearing it. What should you do?

The Dilemma:

An old classmate finds you at a wedding and starts telling you about the many business failures of someone who graduated with you. His story is clearly geared at describing how inept the person is, rather than soliciting help for him or some other positive purpose. How should you respond?

The Halachah:

We are required to stop someone who is speaking *loshon hora* and let him know that he is doing something improper. This is true even if he will be angry and say something that embarrasses us. If possible, we should rebuke the person in private, and always in a respectful and understanding way. Rebuke is not the proper response, however, if as a result the other person is likely to redouble his *loshon hora*.

Sefer Chofetz Chaim, Hilchos Loshon Hora 6:5

ט כסלו
9 Kislev
Cycle 1

ט ניסן
9 Nissan
Cycle 2

י אב
10 Av
Cycle 3

REMEMBER
Save people from themselves.

9 Kislev – לע"נ בת שבע בת חיים ע"ה נלב"ע י"ד כסלו
Dedicated by the Davidson and Savitzky families

9 Nissan – לע"נ יהושע העשיל בן אליהו ז"ל ואשתו שינא רבקה בת משה אליהו ע"ה
Max Kenigsberg לע"נ מרדכי שמחה בן יעקב ז"ל

10 Av – לע"נ שם טוב בן רחמים הלוי ז"ל נלב"ע כ"ח כסלו
ואשתו בשראת בת דוד ע"ה נלב"ע י' אב

Grow Your Good Eye

Let's Get Real

No one wants to be the naive person who thinks everyone and everything is just what it seems. Anyone with a little experience in the world knows that this is not the case. That is one reason that *loshon hora* sometimes seems to us to be more like "realism" than "evil speech."

If you tend to think that the negative side is a truth that must be spoken, here is a strategy that can help. Think to yourself, "Who says the negative side is 'truer' than the positive side?" Every situation has both. When we focus on the negative, we think and speak the negative. But we are just as "realistic," and infinitely wiser, when we focus, think and speak about the positive.

You can help train your eyes toward the positive by realizing that every trait can act as both a detriment and an attribute. We see this in the Torah when Moshe calls the Jewish nation a "stiff-necked people" just as he is asking Hashem to help them. This is not a mistake; it is meant to point out to Hashem that this is a nation that will cling to Him loyally against all obstacles. "Determined" is the positive side of "stubborn."

If we start with the premise that Hashem made the world and called each of His creations "good," we can find encouragement to look for the good. It's there and it's real; Hashem tells us so.

Looking Within: When you find yourself irritated by, or disapproving of, someone's words or behavior, ask yourself if what you're witnessing is actually evil, or just something that disturbs you personally.

Building Within: Starting with a family member or friend you genuinely love, quash negative thoughts and reactions to that person's foibles by actively recounting something good about him or her.

QUOTE OF THE DAY

"Rebuke that does not come from a sincere caring for the transgressor...will prove ineffective, and the rebuker will be judged for humiliating his fellow Jew unnecessarily and causing him distress." *(Michtav M'Eliyahu, Vol. 3, p. 139)*

DAY 70

Living the Mitzvah

Do I Have to Educate the Whole Crowd?

When one Jew sees another running into the dangerous territory of Torah transgression, he's obligated to warn him. It's cruel and uncaring to stand back while someone walks blindly off a spiritual cliff. But can one person stop a whole crowd from transgressing? Should he even try?

י כסלו
10 Kislev
Cycle 1

י ניסן
10 Nissan
Cycle 2

י"א אב
11 Av
Cycle 3

The Dilemma:

You've been learning *shmiras haloshon* as a *zechus* for your ailing mother. Now you're at a *kiddush* in shul, sitting at a table with a dozen friends, and your heightened awareness kicks in as they begin their half-joking mockery of the members of another Jewish community in town. Should you attempt to stop them?

The Halachah:

You are obligated to let them know that what they're saying may be *loshon hora*. However, if they ignore you, don't persist unless you feel you have a chance of making an impact. Furthermore, if you are in a community in which *shmiras haloshon* is widely ignored and you are unsure whether your words will have an impact, you should not speak up. If they would persist anyway, it's better not to rebuke them and cause them to sin maliciously (*b'meizid*).

Rema, Shulchan Aruch, Orach Chaim 608:2

REMEMBER

You can't give what won't be accepted.

10 Kislev – לע"נ הרב מרדכי בן הרב משה לונדינסקי זצ"ל
הונצח על ידי נכדו שמואל לונדינסקי ורעיתו

10 Nissan – לע"נ מרדכי ניסן בן חיים ארי'ה ז"ל

11 Av – In honor of the Jewish People who want to become closer to the *Ribono Shel Olam*

Grow Your Good Eye

Show Your Children the Sights

Most parents would never think to take their family on a trip to a dark, depressing or dangerous place. They want to show their kids the good things life has to offer: beautiful mountains and beaches, exciting amusements, and points of interest.

But some parents unintentionally show their children a dark and disappointing world every single day. They do it by criticizing people and complaining about events. Little by little, the children get the impression that there's no one worthy of admiration. Their idealism is shattered.

The Manchester Rosh Yeshivah, Rabbi Yehuda Zev Segal *zt"l*, said that such parents are destroying the nutrients their children need to grow up happy and wholesome. The ideals that can help them weather difficulties and challenges have been soured by their own parents.

But children who grow up in a positive atmosphere, hearing their parents assess people and events in a positive light, feel they are living in a good world. They can handle the bumps on the road and still enjoy the journey. It's the best gift a parent can give.

Looking Within: Do you believe that being smart means having a critical eye?

Building Within: Every evening, write down three things that had a positive impact on you that day.

QUOTE OF THE DAY

"It is only proper...that you find moving your heaviest limb easier than your tongue, for the tongue moves swiftly toward sin, and its transgressions are more numerous than all the other [limbs]."
(Chovos HaLevavos, Shaar HaPerishus Ch. 5)

DAY 71

Living the Mitzvah

Isn't It Sometimes Better Not to Rebuke?

Is rebuke always appropriate? Aren't there times when it's better to keep quiet?

The Dilemma:

You've just started a course in computer repair. The class is made up of a disparate group of Jewish men from various towns in the area, and none of you knows one another. During a lunch break a fellow student, a non-observant Jew, strikes up a conversation with you and begins deriding the instructor. Should you rebuke him?

The Halachah:

If you have no relationship with a person, and it is clear that your rebuke will fall on deaf ears, you should not offer rebuke. That applies to any Jew, observant or not. However, if a non-observant Jew is unaware of the prohibition and you feel he would be receptive, you should enlighten him about this beautiful aspect of the Torah's wisdom.

Biur Halachah to Shulchan Aruch, Orach Chaim 608:2 ד"ה חייב

י"א כסלו
11 Kislev
Cycle 1

י"א ניסן
11 Nissan
Cycle 2

י"ב אב
12 Av
Cycle 3

REMEMBER

Care and connect before you correct.

11 Kislev – **In memory of David G. Weiss** לע"נ חיים זאב בן יואל ז"ל
By his children Esther & Baruch Weinstein and family

11 Nissan – **Mr. Harry Cohn** לע"נ החבר חיים בן החבר צבי אהרן הכהן ז"ל
Dedicated by the Cohn family

12 Av – לע"נ שיינדל בת יעקב דוב ע"ה
Dedicated by her children and grandchildren

Grow Your Good Eye

Don't Be a Loser

When someone has a setback, those who care about him share his pain. They feel sympathy for his loss or disappointment. They try to encourage him.

But what if everything is experienced as a setback? People who constantly bring home their gripes and air them in front of their families end up forfeiting their families' respect. The children and spouse perceive a person who seems to never command respect and never seems to inspire kindness from others. They hear only of their loved one's mistreatment at the hands of bosses, friends, professionals, tradesmen — everyone who crosses his or her path. Can everyone else be wrong all the time? The family eventually realizes that this cannot be the case.

Everyone loves a winner. When we paint ourselves as strong, resilient, and understanding of others' shortcomings, we earn the respect of our families. Then, when we really need them to be there for us with empathy and encouragement, they will be.

Looking Within: As you speak, ask yourself, "Would I respect someone who is saying what I'm saying right now?"

Building Within: Call a moratorium on negative conversational topics for three days and see how the tone of your household or office changes.

QUOTE OF THE DAY

[Just as] when there is no wood the fire goes out, [so] when no one complains, strife is silenced.
(Mishlei 26: 20)

DAY 72

Living the Mitzvah

י"ב כסלו
12 Kislev
Cycle 1

י"ב ניסן
12 Nissan
Cycle 2

י"ג אב
13 Av
Cycle 3

Is There Such a Thing as Constructive Listening?

We've learned that when negative information serves a constructive purpose, we are allowed to relate it, subject to certain conditions. But what about listening to negative information? Are there circumstances under which we may listen to negative reports?

The Dilemma:

Your neighbor came to you with a brilliant business idea and you decided to launch a partnership. As you tell your brother about the idea, he says, "Do you know what happened with his last business?" Are you permitted to hear what comes next?

The Halachah:

Just as giving negative information is allowed in order to prevent harm, so is listening to it. Anything that can prevent harm to someone else or to yourself, whether financial, emotional, physical or spiritual, is permitted to be heard. The information should be verified before it is believed and acted upon.

Sefer Chofetz Chaim, Hilchos Loshon Hora 6:2

REMEMBER

Hear what can help.

12 Kislev – לע"נ פילא בת אליעזר ע"ה

12 Nissan – לע"נ קופל בן יצחק ז"ל נלב"ע י"א ניסן
ואשתו גנסי–ה בת משה יהודה וידומלנסקי ע"ה נלב"ע ז' אב

13 Av – **In dedication to our wonderful parents and children,** שיחיו
ברכה והצלחה עמו"ש – **Ahron & Estee Schron**

Grow Your Good Eye

Put in a Good Word

Stopping ourselves from speaking the negative isn't always easy. But there's an alternate route to that all-important destination. Dovid HaMelech advises, "Turn from the bad and do good." If we're speaking *loshon tov,* we are automatically *not* speaking *loshon hora.* We can turn from the bad by doing good.

"You're asking an interesting question," a rebbi tells his student. The student suddenly feels, "I have a good head."

"I'm going to *daven* that you get the job," the man tells his brother. Suddenly the brother doesn't feel alone.

"You're the one who keeps our kids happy and healthy," the husband tells his wife. Suddenly she feels that her hard work is worthwhile.

"I love when we have a little extra time together," the wife tells her husband. Suddenly he knows that his presence is valued.

For the speakers of these words, the cost is zero. For the recipients of these words, the value is infinite. Words that build self-esteem, confidence, appreciation and love are free — not because they're worthless, but because they're priceless.

Looking Within: What is the ratio of positive to negative communication with the people in your life?

Building Within: To pull yourself out of the rut of negative communication, make a conscious effort to speak positive words five times a day. Think ahead if necessary to choose your opportunities and words.

QUOTE OF THE DAY

"The tongue stands as the gate of one's consciousness. And when the gate is guarded, the treasure within is guarded as well."
(Chovos HaLevavos, Shaar HaPerishus Ch. 5)

DAY 73

Living the Mitzvah

Do the Speaker's Intentions Matter?

You might have good reason to listen to someone's negative report. But does he have good reason to say it? Does that matter?

י"ג כסלו
13 Kislev
Cycle 1

י"ג ניסן
13 Nissan
Cycle 2

י"ד אב
14 Av
Cycle 3

The Dilemma:

Your neighbor tells you about his young new assistant at his warehouse. He's not impressed; he complains about the boy's intelligence, work ethic and mode of dress. What he doesn't know is that this information is important to you, because this same boy has been suggested as a *shidduch* for your daughter. May you keep listening?

The Halachah:

If the speaker isn't speaking for a constructive purpose, his words are *loshon hora*, and the listener may not listen. That's because by providing an audience, the listener is "putting a stumbling block" in front of the speaker, encouraging him to go on talking. It's possible, however, to stop the speaker and let him know that you have a constructive purpose for listening. Then, if he meets the other conditions of *to'eles,* he may relate negative information.

Sefer Chofetz Chaim, Hilchos Loshon hora 4:11; Be'er Mayim Chaim 6:3

REMEMBER
If it's intended *as loshon hora, it is loshon hora.*

13 Kislev – לע"נ נתן יהודה בן יצחק יוסף ואשתו פריידה בת יוחנן ע"ה
Dedicated by their children Mr. & Mrs. Alter and Faige Leah Kane

13 Nissan – לע"נ יהושע בן ישראל ז"ל ואשתו הענא פינקל אלטא בת שמחה בונים ע"ה
לע"נ משה נתן בן ראובן פנחס ז"ל ואשתו פערל חי' בת דוד אפרים הכהן ע"ה

14 Av – **In memory of Mr. Etan Savir** לע"נ איתן בן דוד ז"ל
Dedicated by his wife Stephanie Savir and family

Grow Your Good Eye

Peachy Kids

A lemon tree produces sour fruit. A peach tree produces sweet fruit. If parents want their children to be "sweet fruit," they have to make sure that sweetness runs through the fibers of their family tree. This means that they have to keep their observations, conversations and spirit positive.

If you want to know what a child hears at home, simply listen to him talk. Children whose parents see the world in a positive light and express positive ideas within their home are children who exude these traits in their own interactions. On the other hand, parents with a sour view on life often produce "fruit" of the same ilk.

That means that we're not only choosing our own approach to people and relationships when we choose our words; we are choosing the approach our children will have as well. This idea is an effective one to keep on the front burner of our minds as we make our way through the daily interactions of our lives. We all want our children to grow up to be happy people beloved by others. If that's what we want to reap, then that's what we have to cultivate.

Looking Within: What underlying message do you hear when you listen closely to the conversations you have in your home or on your phone with family members and friends?

Building Within: Once in a while, imagine that the words you are saying are coming out of your children's mouths instead of your own.

QUOTE OF THE DAY

"We convey wrong priorities to our children by our reactions to sins... One who realizes he is handling *muktzah* acts like he received an electric shock. Not so for *loshon hora,* which is significantly more stringent."
(Mesillos HaChaim B'Chinuch by R' Chaim Friedlander zt"l)

DAY 74

Living the Mitzvah

May I Go Undercover?

You need information about someone, for legitimate reasons. However, you're afraid that if you reveal your reasons, your source will paint the rosiest possible picture and gloss over the negatives. Are you obligated to reveal your purpose?

י"ד כסלו
14 Kislev
Cycle 1

י"ד ניסן
14 Nissan
Cycle 2

ט"ו אב
15 Av
Cycle 3

The Dilemma:

You've got a great idea for a new business, and you need a partner. You have someone in mind, but you don't know him well enough to know if he's someone with whom you can work. Luckily for you, that person's next-door neighbor is sitting right next to you at a wedding. Are you permitted to get him to talk about his neighbor so you can get a candid impression of the man's personality?

The Halachah:

You have to reveal your purpose for asking, even if it means you might get a more measured response, and even if it means having to disclose your business plan when you'd rather keep it private. That's because if you don't reveal your purpose, you're encouraging the other person to speak *loshon hora*; he has no constructive purpose for speaking if he doesn't know that his information is needed.

Sefer Chofetz Chaim, Hilchos Loshon Hora 4:11 with the first subnote ad loc.

REMEMBER

State your purpose, no matter what.

14 Kislev – **Jack Feldman** לע"נ יעקב בן שושנה ז"ל
Dedicated by his daughter

14 Nissan – לע"נ רות בילא בת ר' אברהם ע"ה
Dedicated by Moshe & Malky Gruner

15 Av – **As a *zechus* for everyone in *Klal Yisrael* who needs a *shidduch***
Dedicated by members of *Klal Yisrael* who love and *daven* for you

Grow Your Good Eye

Deconstruct and Reconstruct

Despite your best efforts at avoiding *loshon hora,* there are bound to be times when you hear it. This in itself violates the laws of speech, but what can you do about it? How can you "un-hear" what you've heard?

The first step is to doubt the accuracy of what you've heard. You might think this is naive, but really it's critical thinking. We have all seen the phenomenon of three eyewitnesses giving three different reports. We've all read newspaper stories about subjects with which we're familiar, and invariably they contain inaccuracies. Why, then, believe what you hear as if it's the unassailable truth?

The next step is to consider the circumstances that might have caused the affront the speaker is reporting. People forget things. They can be preoccupied, short on energy, under pressure or overloaded with anxiety. Any of these conditions can cause a good person to do or say something regrettable. When you filter a negative report through these possibilities, you come out with a different picture: the subject is not someone to disparage, but rather someone who, like all of us, made a mistake.

By following these steps, you can "un-hear" *loshon hora* that you've unavoidably heard. You break through the cloud cast on another person's reputation and let his inherent goodness shine through.

Looking Within: How skeptical are you when someone tells you something negative about another person? Do you assume he speaks the truth, or do you think, "There's probably more to this"?

Building Within: Remember that every story has three sides: the one you inadvertently heard, the subject's version and the objective truth.

QUOTE OF THE DAY

"When *Klal Yisrael* is a single entity with one heart and without dissension, their unity itself is like an immersion in a *mikveh,* as it states in *Zohar,* 'Their congregation is their purity.' "
(Ahavas Shalom, Parashas Ki Sisa, ד"ה ויעמוד משה*)*

DAY 75

Living the Mitzvah

What If Someone Really Needs a Listening Ear?

When people are troubled, they turn to their loved ones and friends to share their burden. Are we permitted to let someone tell us his troubles when doing so involves negative information about another person?

ט"ו כסלו
15 Kislev
Cycle 1

ט"ו ניסן
15 Nissan
Cycle 2

ט"ז אב
16 Av
Cycle 3

The Dilemma:

Your sister is having tremendous difficulties with one of her teenage children. Besides that, her husband isn't handling the situation well. She calls you several times a week to pour out her heart. While you don't have much in the way of practical advice to offer, you do give her an outlet to vent her emotions. Are you permitted to hear about her troubles with her child and husband even though there's no constructive purpose for you?

The Halachah:

Sharing someone's burden is a powerful act of *chessed,* and often just listening to them express their pain, disappointment, fear or frustration is a powerful way to share it. If you can help someone put the situation into a more positive perspective, you should do so. However, the aggrieved person may not be ready to accept anything other than empathetic listening; in that case, just listen and wait for an appropriate time to reframe the issue. Caveat: You are not allowed to believe that what you are hearing is 100 percent true, nor are you allowed to act upon it.

Sefer Chofetz Chaim, Hilchos Loshon Hora 6:4

REMEMBER
Listening is helping.

15 Kislev – לע"נ שולמית בת שמואל ע"ה
Dedicated by Pinchas & Yona Shine and family

15 Nissan – לע"נ אברהם משה בן אליעזר ז"ל נלב"ע י"ט ניסן

16 Av – לע"נ ר' חיים ברוך בן בנימין ז"ל ואברהם בן ברוך ז"ל
Dedicated by their grandchildren, Carolyn & Barry Stein and family

Grow Your Good Eye

Shift Your Focus

When a person feels the urge to speak *loshon hora,* we can be certain of one thing: he is seeing the negative in the other person. There is another thing of which everyone can be certain: no one is without his or her good points. Therefore, if you're doing a slow simmer over someone's irritating behavior, a good way to avoid spouting *loshon hora* is to shift your focus to that person's good points. Can't think of one? Here's a short list of possibilities:

The person has done you a favor; he helps other people; he's sincere; he has good intentions; he's a hard worker; he supports the community; he's learned; he's pleasant; he's talented; he would not have wanted to anger you.

Pinpointing one or two of these positive traits might not undo what the person did or said to upset you. It will, however, shed some light on his value as a human being. That's often all it takes to lead us to a more forgiving, respectful response.

Looking Within: When you are annoyed or angry at someone, are you capable of hearing or saying something complimentary about him, or does your anger cancel out his good attributes?

Building Within: Try to quell your annoyance by looking for the person's good points, no matter how minor they may seem to be.

QUOTE OF THE DAY

"A person who listens will be able to speak forever."
(Mishlei 21:28)

DAY 76

Living the Mitzvah

May I Listen to My Spouse's Woes?

You chose to share your life with this person. May you share in his/her frustrations as well?

The Dilemma:

Your spouse works in the world's most mismanaged office. Her boss is constantly throwing emergencies on her desk and expecting her to stay after hours to take care of them. She comes home every night late, exhausted and frustrated with her inability to change the situation. Are you allowed to listen to her tirade against her boss?

The Halachah:

You are allowed to listen to your spouse's negative feelings for the purpose of letting her/him express it. However, there are two dangers: these kinds of conversations can become so frequent that your home's atmosphere will be overtaken by negativity; or you will be drawn into the negativity and offer your *own loshon hora*. Therefore, if the source of frustration persists, it's best to work on improving the situation or finding help to improve your spouse's perspective.

Caveat: You are not allowed to believe that what you are hearing is 100 percent true, nor are you allowed to act upon it.

Sefer Chofetz Chaim, Hilchos Loshon Hora 10:14 in subnote

ט"ז כסלו
16 Kislev
Cycle 1

ט"ז ניסן
16 Nissan
Cycle 2

י"ז אב
17 Av
Cycle 3

REMEMBER
Help vent the frustration; don't give it a room in your house.

16 Kislev – לע"נ דוד מרדכי בן ר' שמואל הלוי ז"ל

16 Nissan – **In memory of Getzel *ben* Nosson** לע"נ געציל בן נתן ז"ל נלב"ע ט"ו ניסן
Dedicated by his loving daughter Nechama

17 Av – לזכות חיים מרדכי בן חי' שרה נ"י
לזכות אהרן בן הענא נ"י

Grow Your Good Eye

Clean the Windows

When you see everything through a dirty window, the world is not likely to look big and bright. Since you can describe it only the way you see it, your depictions of the people and events in your life are bound to be diminished by your tainted view. This is the plight of the scoffer. He may be surrounded by beautiful ideals, well-meaning people, and great wisdom, but his view is clouded by the shreds of negativity that exists in every aspect of our imperfect world. With that obstructed vision, he turns everything into a jab at someone.

He sits at his neighbor's son's bar mitzvah and listens to Uncle Yankel, the family *talmid chacham,* whose words are wise and warm, but all the scoffer hears is Uncle Yankel's poor command of the English language. "He should have paid a little more attention in English," he says to the person next to him. Then the boy's yeshivah principal makes a speech about spending less time working and more time learning Torah. "I'll bet he doesn't have to pay yeshivah tuitions," the cynic says.

A root cause of *loshon hora,* says the Chofetz Chaim (*Sefer Shmiras HaLoshon, Shaar HaTevunah* 13), is scoffing. Like the person who peers out of a dirty window and sees a dirty world, the scoffer misses the reality. As he shares his vision with others, he often gets a laugh — but at a very high price. It takes no special brilliance to see the flaws in things; they inevitably exist. By appreciating the good, which Hashem embedded in every facet of creation, we save ourselves from living in the dark.

Looking Within: Do you think that there's special insight in seeing the flaw in things? Do you appreciate the input of people who can find the irony or hypocrisy in high ideals?

Building Within: When you think or hear a critique of something good and positive, remember that nothing is perfect, and that the flaw doesn't negate the value.

QUOTE OF THE DAY

"The prayers of one who speaks *loshon hora* do not appear before HaKadosh Baruch Hu, for a spirit of *tumah* clings to them, [until] he returns and does *teshuvah.*"

(Zohar, Parashas Metzora 53a)

DAY 77

Living the Mitzvah

How Do I Squelch Tattling but Encourage Communicating?

We want our children to come to us with their troubles, and yet we have to train them to refrain from speaking loshon hora. How do we find the balance?

י"ז כסלו
17 Kislev
Cycle 1

י"ז ניסן
17 Nissan
Cycle 2

י"ח אב
18 Av
Cycle 3

The Dilemma:

Someone in your son's fifth-grade class picked a fight with him today. He got in trouble and ended up humiliated. He's brimming with indignation and wants to spill out his story for you to hear. Should you listen? Or should you guide him away from the topic, explaining that you would otherwise be listening to *loshon hora*?

The Halachah:

When your child needs emotional support, it's your job — and a constructive purpose — to give it. If he wants to tell you something that he's bothered by but that didn't happen to him, encourage him to relate it without naming names.

Sefer Zera Chaim 9:5

REMEMBER

Train the child's tongue, but hear his heart.

17 Kislev – Leslie Zukor לע"נ יצחק חיים בן יוסף ז"ל
Dedicated by his children and grandchildren

17 Nissan – Harvey Felsen *z"l* לע"נ צבי גרשון בן יואל ז"ל
Dedicated in loving memory by his wife, Esther

18 Av – לע"נ אברהם יהודה בן שלמה זלמן ז"ל
Dedicated by Aroni & Chani Parnes

Grow Your Good Eye

Wield the Weed Whacker

People who take pride in their lawn know that the trick to keeping out the weeds is to make sure the grass is thick. Weeds take root in the bare spots, and then they begin choking off the healthy grass. The thicker the blanket of healthy grass, the less opportunity there is for weeds to take root.

Conversation works the same way. The more positive ideas and thoughts a person expresses, the less room there is for the negative. If we want to ensure that we stay on the right track in our verbal interactions, we can do so by including as much *"loshon tov"* — positive words — as possible. Negative thoughts, words, complaints and criticisms are incongruous in the midst of praise and appreciation. There is simply no place for them to take root.

People often think that a commitment to *shmiras haloshon* means that they must refrain from speaking. However, the best strategy is to fill our conversations with positive words, thereby leaving no room for *loshon hora* to sprout.

Looking Within: What thoughts fill your mind in a neutral moment? Do you fill yourself up with negativity and worries, or positive, appreciative thoughts?

Building Within: Learn how to "change the channel" when you realize that negativity is churning around in your mind. When you're about to complain, think of something to appreciate and voice that instead.

QUOTE OF THE DAY

"Only when people strive for real spirituality is unity and peace possible, for in matters of spirituality there are no limits, and one man's [success] does not interfere with his fellow man at all."
(Michtav M'Eliyahu, Vol. 2, p. 107)

DAY 78

Living the Mitzvah

What Should I Do With What I Hear?

You've heard negative information that has a constructive purpose for you. Now what? Should you believe it? May you act on it?

The Dilemma:
Things have been disappearing from your yeshivah dorm, including your Shabbos cufflinks and your MP3 player. Someone has informed you that he believes the culprit is your roommate and friend. Should you distance yourself from your roommate or ignore the reports? Should you hide your valuables?

The Halachah:
You may not accept the report as true. Nor should you change the way you treat the person in question. However, you should look into the situation further, and meanwhile take precautions to protect yourself based on what you've heard. For instance, don't leave your wallet lying around.

Sefer Chofetz Chaim, Hilchos Loshon Hora 6:2, 6:10

י"ח כסלו
18 Kislev
Cycle 1

י"ח ניסן
18 Nissan
Cycle 2

י"ט אב
19 Av
Cycle 3

REMEMBER

Don't accept, but do protect.

18 Kislev – לע"נ ישכר דוב בן יוסף חיים ז"ל
לע"נ שרה לאה בת יחזקאל שרגא ע"ה

18 Nissan – Nosson Kopolovics לע"נ נתן בן מאיר יוסף הלוי ז"ל
Dedicated by Debbie & Shloimi Kopolovics and family

19 Av – לע"נ דב בער בן הרב צבי הירש ז"ל
לע"נ חי' אסתר בת הרב מרדכי ע"ה

Grow Your Good Eye

Go on a World Tour

If someone arrived from another planet and asked for a tour of Earth, you might show him the Grand Canyon, Yerushalayim, the Alps and many other awe-inspiring sights.

You would probably avoid war zones, toxic waste sites and police states. Those places are also part of Earth, but why go there?

Those who love us, look up to us, and share their lives with us also depend on us to show them the world, and the itinerary we choose paints the picture for them.

"You can't win!"
"People are selfish!"
"What does he know?"
"That teacher can't teach."
"The speaker was boring."
"They're a bunch of phonies."

With words like these, we show others a disappointing, lonely world. Why not bring them on a completely different tour?

"It will work out."
"That was so nice of him."
"It's good to have someone to guide us."
"The teacher is trying to help you."
"I learned something new from that speaker."
"Most people try to do the right thing."

It's a big world. What our loved ones think of it — and their place in it — depends on which tour we give them as we comment on our daily lives.

Looking Within: Does your "truth" tend to be the positive or the critical version of what you observe?

Building Within: When you discuss people, places or issues with others, ask yourself if your goal is to leave them feeling down and disappointed, or happy and hopeful.

QUOTE OF THE DAY

"True peace is when people feel love for one another and are happy for each other's good fortune."
(K'sav Sofer, Esther 10:3)

DAY 79

Living the Mitzvah

Is There a Correct Way to Impart Negative Information?

You know information that you believe would prevent your friend from falling victim to someone. You're allowed — perhaps even obligated — to tell your friend, but if he accepts the information as true, he's violating the halachah. How can you avoid "placing a stumbling block" in front of him?

י"ט כסלו
19 Kislev
Cycle 1

י"ט ניסן
19 Nissan
Cycle 2

כ אב
20 Av
Cycle 3

The Dilemma:

Your coworker informs you that his daughter is engaged. When he mentions the *chassan's* name, you're surprised. You know the young man; you've seen him glued to his Smartphone during *davening*, schmoozing away his night *seder* and inebriated at a wedding. Knowing this is not who your coworker would choose for his daughter, you want to say something. Yet, you're certain that the second you inform your coworker he'll be on the phone breaking off the engagement. Can you tell him the information? How can you prevent him from jumping on your information before he checks it out for himself?

REMEMBER

Advise caution.

The Halachah:

Preface your information with a disclaimer such as "I might not have seen the whole picture, so don't go on my say-so alone..." Don't hide or underplay information that might prove essential for avoiding a disaster, but do discourage your listener from accepting the information without further inquiry.

See Sefer Chofetz Chaim, Hilchos Loshon Hora 2:9; see, however, Zera Chaim 10:2

19 Kislev – לזכות הנכדים אלישבע שתחי' ופנחס נ"י
אליהו ודבורה מילן

19 Nissan – לע"נ ריזל ע"ה בת ר' שמואל שליט"א יבלח"ט
Dedicated by her family

20 Av – Sam Langsner לע"נ שלמה ברוך בן יעקב משה ז"ל
Violet Langsner לע"נ וועלא בת אברהם ע"ה נלב"ע ב' תמוז

Grow Your Good Eye

A Simple Prescription, Available to All

Rebbetzin Reichel Berenbaum, wife of HaRav Shmuel Berenbaum zt"l, penned this verse expressing her view of how to live a happy life. In a time when so many people go to great effort and expense to dispel anxiety and find joy, she shows us that it's not as complicated as we think.

"Guard your tongue"; it's a bonus, not an onus.
May I share with you a phenomenon so profound
Its ramifications really astound?
Since I have committed to guard my tongue
I just can't see anything wrong
With any member of our holy nation
Or with Hashem's magnificent, flawless creation.
My journey in life is filled with love
With Hashem's beautiful blessings showered
from above.
My days are pure joy and ecstasy
Try it; it's guaranteed and it's free.

Looking Within: Do you view *shmiras haloshon* as a way to achieve happiness?

Building Within: Rather than thinking of *shmiras haloshon* as a weighty obligation and struggle, think of the words "bonus, not an onus."

QUOTE OF THE DAY

"One who believes gossipers will ultimately be friendless even if he presently has a cherished and close friend."

(Maalos HaMiddos, Middas Loshon Hora U'Rechilus)

DAY 80

Living the Mitzvah

May I Defend My Son Against His "Mean" Teacher?

School plays a prominent role in a child's emotional health and happiness. When a child complains about his teacher, what should parents do with that information?

כ כסלו
20 Kislev
Cycle 1

כ ניסן
20 Nissan
Cycle 2

כ"א אב
21 Av
Cycle 3

The Dilemma:
Your fourth-grader insists that his rebbi picks on him. All the boys are talking during class, but only he gets into trouble. Six kids forget their homework, but only he is forced to stay in during recess and do it. He's beginning to hate going to school, and you're worried. May you believe and act on your child's complaints?

The Halachah:
Since children are prone to complaining about school, you should not accept their reports as 100 percent true, as with all *loshon hora*, even *l'to'eles*. You should show concern and assure them that you will take care of their issue, and then speak directly to the teacher. Acting upon the complaint as if it is 100 percent true could lead you into especially dangerous territory, where you might needlessly harm a teacher's reputation and endanger his or her position. Instead of moving ahead based solely on the child's complaints, parents must inquire further, preferably in a discreet way that won't embarrass the teacher. Then, if necessary, they can take action.

Sefer Chofetz Chaim, Hilchos Loshon Hora 4:10

REMEMBER
An unhappy student doesn't always mean an unfair teacher.

20 Kislev – In memory of Moshe *ben* Shefia *z"l, yahrtzeit* 18 Kislev
and his wife, Ruth *bas* Esther Rahmey *a"h, yahrtzeit* 22 Kislev

20 Nissan – In memory of Esther *bas* Yaakov *a"h*
Dedicated by the Wasserman family

21 Av – לע"נ שוקת בת משלה שרה ע"ה
לע"נ משיח בן רבקה ז"ל

Grow Your Good Eye

Cast Doubt

What happens when you're the unintentional receiver of a *loshon hora* comment? If you can't get the conversation to stop and you can't walk away, what can you do to mitigate the situation?

One tactic is to quickly step into the victim's shoes and think of a justification for his words or actions. Then voice your perspective. This is especially important if the speaker is speaking to a group of people. As soon as you present some alternative explanation, you've managed to cast at least a little doubt on the truth of the negative story.

Aaron, a young man from Monsey, describes using this strategy: "Our marketing company got a new client — an Israeli electronics importer whose English was terrible. We were having a meeting, trying to figure out what to do for this client, when it became clear that the boss really didn't like him. He found him abrasive, and he quoted a few things the client said that really did sound kind of awful.

"But I know enough Hebrew to know that a lot of things don't translate well, so I said, 'Do you think it could be that he just doesn't have enough English to say things a little more subtly? Because otherwise, he seems pretty warm and friendly.' Another person at the meeting agreed. He even said the client reminded him of his uncle in Netanya. I feel that I succeeded in taking the wind out of my boss's *loshon hora*."

Looking Within: Do you consider it your responsibility to disable the power of *loshon hora* that's spoken in your presence?

Building Within: When you hear someone being criticized in public, think about the assault that's taking place on the person's reputation, and look for a way to save him.

QUOTE OF THE DAY

"When the tongue is good, there is nothing better than it, but when it goes bad, there is nothing worse."

(Midrash cited in Maalos HaMiddos, Middas Loshon Hora U'Rechilus)

CHAPTER 9

Humility — Your True Value

There's only one possession we need in order to be important in this world: a Jewish soul. With this one asset, we have everything — a mission to perform, a connection to the Master of the Universe, and a Torah to guide us to a good and meaningful life. Everything else we have — money, appearance, talents, strength, families, friends and more — is not ours at all. It is a resource Hashem has loaned us for the fulfillment of our purpose. Knowing this keeps us humble, which keeps our words humble as well.

DAY 81

Living the Mitzvah

May I Believe That Someone Has "Done It Again"?

When somebody habitually trespasses certain halachos, or totally disregards the Torah, are we permitted to accept a report that he's engaged in a misdeed?

כ"א כסלו
21 Kislev
Cycle 1

כ"א ניסן
21 Nissan
Cycle 2

כ"ב אב
22 Av
Cycle 3

The Dilemma:

You know someone who drinks too much. You've seen him at many a *kiddush* and many a *simchah*, clearly inebriated and incoherent, embarrassing people and behaving irresponsibly. Now someone tells you that he saw this person leaving a wedding, preparing once again to drive his car while intoxicated, and he took the person's keys away. May you believe this report?

The Halachah:

If you know the person drinks to excess and have seen him overindulge with your own eyes, the prohibition against believing the negative information does not apply. If you know that someone commits a certain sin because of temptation, you may believe he's done so again. However, you may not believe that this time he's done it out of malice, thus taking his transgression up a notch.

Sefer Chofetz Chaim, Be'er Mayim Chaim 7:10 with Hagahah to Hilchos Loshon Hora 6:10

REMEMBER

When there's no doubt, there's no benefit of the doubt.

21 Kislev – לע"נ שלום בן אברהם ז"ל נלב"ע ה' טבת
לע"נ חנה בת אהרן שמואל ע"ה נלב"ע כ"א כסלו

21 Nissan – לע"נ ר' חיים שמעון לייב בן זאב ז"ל
Dedicated by his wife Susan Herskovits and children

22 Av – **Rebbetzin Mindel Potashnik** לע"נ הרבנית מינדל בת הרב שמעון דוב הכהן ע"ה
Dedicated in loving memory by Chavie Feuer and Dina Einhorn

Grow Your Humility

How to Win by Quitting the Game

In a person's drive to distinguish himself in this world, he wants to feel that he excels at something. That means that he needs the rest of the world to be his inferior in that area. This little piece of psychology drives much *loshon hora*. The easiest way to rise above the crowd is to lower everyone else.

Rav Eliyahu Dessler (*Consulting the Wise*, p. 206) explains that this mentality is rooted in the trait of envy. A person feels that he can take pride in his intelligence only if he's at the top of the class. He can take pride in his wealth only if he's the wealthiest person in town. People don't want others to challenge their position, and therefore they resent others' achievements.

To combat that mindset, Rabbi Dessler teaches us to forget about being unique, the best, the top. Give it up in favor of *ahavas Yisrael*. Remind yourself that others' achievements don't lower your value in any way.

Looking Within: Do you bristle when people challenge your expertise in areas in which you consider yourself to excel?

Building Within: If you feel a competitive urge to put down someone else's achievement, make a conscious effort to take the back seat and give the other person center stage.

QUOTE OF THE DAY

"Everyone must have two pockets. In one should be placed the phrase, "The world was created just for me," and in the other, "I am but dust and ash."
(R' Simchah Bunim M'Pshischah, Simchas Yisrael, Maamarei Simchah 12)

DAY 82

Living the Mitzvah

Should I Warn My Friend That Someone Is Speaking Against Him?

When you hear one person speaking negatively about another, especially if the subject is a friend or family member, are you responsible for letting the subject know that someone is tarnishing his reputation?

כ"ב כסלו
22 Kislev
Cycle 1

כ"ב ניסן
22 Nissan
Cycle 2

כ"ג אב
23 Av
Cycle 3

The Dilemma:

You're talking to your neighbor at a *simchah*. Another neighbor, whom you both thought was going to be there, is absent. "I wonder what happened to him?" you ask. "I hope he's okay." To your surprise your neighbor says, "Oh, him? When was he ever okay?" He then begins informing you of the missing neighbor's various emotional challenges. Shouldn't the subject of this report know that someone is out there spreading negative information about him?

The Halachah:

Telling one person that another person spoke ill of him is the definition of *rechilus*. It is forbidden under the Torah prohibition, "Do not go as a gossipmonger among your people" (*Vayikra* 19:16). The outcome of *rechilus* is invariably to stir animosity among Jews.

Sefer Chofetz Chaim, Hilchos Rechilus 1:2

REMEMBER

When you carry a tale, you spread the plague of machlokes.

22 Kislev – לע"נ מרדכי בן צבי ז"ל

22 Nissan – לזכות משה בן צירל נ"י

23 Av – In memory of Rose Nochumson לע"נ רבקה בת יצחק ע"ה
Dedicated by her grandson and great-grandchildren

Grow Your Humility

Live Like a King

Of all the forces that are capable of propelling our negative thoughts from our brains into our mouths and out into the world, anger is the most powerful of all. Someone who can contain his anger can usually contain his words long enough to consider their impact and decide whether or not something needs to be said.

But how does someone with a short fuse access this self-control? He can learn from a short-tempered king, a righteous ruler whose failing caused him endless grief. *Sefer HaMiddos* (p. 239) relates that the king's trusted servant helped him overcome his problem by intervening whenever the king's temper began to rise.

The servant succeeded by showing the king three lines: (1) Always remember that you are merely a creature and not the Creator; (2) always remember that you are flesh and blood and will eventually perish; and (3) always remember that there will be mercy for you in the future only if you have mercy on others.

Keeping in mind that we're not above our fellow man, and that G-d is above us all, can help us see through the illusion that we have the right to debase another person.

Looking Within: Everyone is "king" to someone in his or her life, whether it is employees, children, students or other family members. Do you exercise your "kingship" with humility?

Building Within: Before exercising authority over another person, think first, "I'm not the boss. Hashem is the boss, and He will treat me as I treat my 'subjects.' "

QUOTE OF THE DAY

"A falsely humble person considers himself insignificant, and considers everyone else as insignificant as himself."

(R' Shalom m'Belz cited in M'Gedolei HaChassidus #10)

DAY 83

Living the Mitzvah

May I Tell My Friend Who Voted Against Him?

As a member of a decision-making committee or board that has an impact on someone's life, you are privy to the opinions voiced by the other members. If someone wants to know who stood for him and who stood against him, may you tell him?

כ"ג כסלו
23 Kislev
Cycle 1

כ"ג ניסן
23 Nissan
Cycle 2

כ"ד אב
24 Av
Cycle 3

The Dilemma:

You're one of a three-man team interviewing candidates for a position as a rebbi in the yeshivah where you teach. Your neighbor's son applies for a position, but one of the other interviewers feels he doesn't have the right personality for the job. After a brief discussion, the principal decides not to offer him the job. When the candidate's father hears the news he tells his son, "I don't believe it! I'm going to find out what happened." May you tell him?

The Halachah:

You are not allowed to divulge the identities of people who expressed a negative opinion. This is true even if the decision was in favor of the person in question. The same is true of a *beis din*: judges may not divulge who ruled against a litigant.

Sefer Chofetz Chaim, Hilchos Rechilus 2:11

REMEMBER
Your vote is your business.

23 Kislev – לע"נ אלישבע דינה בת יצחק ע"ה
Dedicated by the Golpariani family and children
23 Nissan – Avraham Chaim Hollander לע"נ אברהם חיים בן מרדכי יצחק ז"ל
24 Av – לע"נ הרב צבי בן ר' פסח זצ"ל
Rabbi Hirsch Diskind of Yerushalayim and Baltimore

Grow Your Humility

Losing to Win

Leah R. is a parent who has always been very involved in her son's yeshivah. She has a Masters in Education, and at one point was despairing at what she saw as a deficiency in the school's reading program.

In the public school at which she taught, she encountered an online reading program. She saw good results with the students, and thought this program would be a great asset to her son's yeshivah.

First she showed the program to the secular studies principal, and he was enthusiastic. Then she started a grassroots movement to get the program into the school. The board of directors finally agreed to consider the proposal. But at the end of a heated debate, the board shelved the idea because a significant number of parents didn't want online learning introduced to the school.

"Everyone told me I should fight the board," Leah says. "And at first I was ready for a fight. After all, reading is so basic in education. Why should we settle for poor skills when there's help to be had?

"But in the end I realized that there was passion on both sides of the argument and it was going to get heated. As bad as a so-so reading program is for a school, *machlokes* is a whole lot worse. I didn't want to be the cause of that, so I dropped the idea. I realized that even if I would have won, the school would lose."

Looking Within: When you go to bat for something you believe is important, is your focus on winning or on the best overall outcome?

Building Within: Even when you feel that truth and justice are on your side, weigh the situation carefully to be sure that you're doing everything possible to avoid *machlokes.*

QUOTE OF THE DAY

"Just as you accept that others do not look like you, accept that they do not think like you."

(the Rebbe Reb Menachem Mendel MiKotzk, cited in Pisgamim Nivcharim)

DAY 84

Living the Mitzvah

May I Tell Others That Your Child Misbehaves?

Sometimes you hear something negative about a child. Are you allowed to tell the child's parent what you heard?

כ"ד כסלו
24 Kislev
Cycle 1

כ"ד ניסן
24 Nissan
Cycle 2

כ"ה אב
25 Av
Cycle 3

The Dilemma:
Your seven-year-old son wants to invite his school friend over to play after school. Rina, another mother in the class who has already hosted this child once, tells you that he's "a hurricane." When the child's mother calls you to make arrangements for her son's visit, you say, "I hear from Rina that he's a whirlwind!" Have you spoken *rechilus*?

The Halachah:
You have. Even though you're speaking of a child, and people usually make allowances for a child's immature behavior, telling a parent that someone has said something negative about his child is bound to stir resentment. This is true even if the parent has said the very same thing.

Sefer Chofetz Chaim, Hilchos Rechilus 3:3

REMEMBER

Everyone wants you to admire their children.

24 Kislev – **In memory of Feivel** ***bas*** **Zev** ***a"h, yahrtzeit*** **24 Kislev**

24 Nissan – לע"נ יוסף בן ציון ז"ל נלב"ע כ"ז ניסן
Dedicated by Gabriel Mairzadeh and family

25 Av – **In memory of my mother** לע"נ שרה לאה בת שלמה מנחם ע"ה
Dedicated by Dovy & Yocheved Brazil and family

Grow Your Humility

Whose Suit Are You Wearing?

If you ever find yourself speaking about others from a high-and-mighty place, you might try remembering this *mashal* given by Rabbi Ephraim Wachsman *shlita*.

A man is invited to a wedding, but he doesn't own a proper suit. He can't afford to buy one, but he has a wealthy friend who's just his size. The friend agrees to lend the man his suit.

The man dons the suit, adjusts his tie, looks in the mirror and is very impressed by what he sees. He stands up a little straighter and heads off to the wedding.

When he enters the hall, a few of his friends come to greet him. "Hmph!" he thinks to himself. "Look how ill-cut their suits are. That one even looks a little frayed around the lapels. Don't these guys know how to dress?"

As Rabbi Wachsman concludes, the man is a fool. His pride is inflated by something that's not even his. But we, too, are only borrowing the money, strength and talent Hashem lends us for our visit to this world. To feel superior because of anything we have is as ridiculous as this man's pride in his borrowed suit.

Looking within: What motivates you to judge another person negatively? What do you gain?

Building within: The next time you begin to look down at someone, ask yourself, "Whose suit am I wearing?"

QUOTE OF THE DAY

"Searching for sins and seeking the good are both admirable traits, provided that the former is for oneself and the latter for one's fellow."
(the Rebbe Reb Levi Yitzchok MiBerditchev, cited in Pisgamim Nivcharim)

DAY 85

Living the Mitzvah

May I Share Your Joke About Your Family?

Some families joke cynically about a family trait. It might be their seemingly bad luck, their lack of talent in some area, such as business or math, their lack of musical ability or some other idiosyncrasy. Even if they freely discuss that trait, may you?

כ"ה כסלו
25 Kislev
Cycle 1

כ"ה ניסן
25 Nissan
Cycle 2

כ"ו אב
26 Av
Cycle 3

The Dilemma:
A teenage girl is visiting her cousins for Shabbos. After a few rounds of beautiful, harmonious *zemiros*, her uncle says to her jokingly, "I'll bet you that the 'Tone-deaf Tannenbaums' don't sound like this." The next week at home, when her family makes a weak attempt at singing, she pipes up: "Even Uncle Sruly knows we're the tone-deaf Tannenbaums!" Is that *rechilus*, or sharing a family joke?

The Halachah:
It's *rechilus*. No matter what people say about their own group, whether it's a family, a school, a community or a company, they don't appreciate hearing that others are joking about them. Such a report is likely to sting a little and thereby stir animosity.

Sefer Chofetz Chaim, Hilchos Rechilus 3:3 [at the end]

REMEMBER
If the joke's about me, it's not funny.

25 Kislev – As a *zechus* for *brachah* for the Dadon family and as a *zechus* for Tzion *ben* Rachel

25 Nissan – Salamon Mandel לע"נ מרדכי שלמה בן בנימן אליעזר ז"ל נלב"ע כ"ו ניסן
In loving memory by his wife, children and grandchildren

26 Av – Anonymous

Grow Your Humility

Remember the Feud of All Feuds

When people are angry with each other, the idea of forgiveness seems far away. The longer they stew and build a case against their adversary, the more *loshon hora* flows out and envelops everyone in their lives. A woman who volunteers her time mediating family disputes says she has one powerful argument that often succeeds in breaking the deadlock.

"It's often a matter of who is going to break down first," she says. "Both sides feel that they are right, and their pride won't allow them to approach the other. So I remind them of the *pasuk* (*Korach* 17:5) 'There will not be another dispute like Korach's.' We usually interpret that to mean that there shouldn't be infighting in Klal Yisrael.

"But there's another meaning, too. This was a dispute in which one person — Moshe Rabbeinu — was 100 percent right and the other person — Korach — was 100 percent wrong. The Torah is telling us that this will never happen again. From then on, in any dispute, each side will bear at least a small portion of the blame.

"This idea often creates a small opening through which humility can enter the person's heart. When they can recognize some way in which they contributed to the fight, they can find grounds on which to reach out to make amends."

Looking Within: Do you sometimes have the feeling that you're completely in the right in a dispute?

Building Within: Ask yourself, what part of the dispute am I willing to take responsibility for?

QUOTE OF THE DAY

"One who guards his tongue is not envied, is universally beloved and trusted...and no one ever speaks ill of him."

(Sefer Shmiras HaLoshon, Vol. 1, Shaar HaZechirah Ch. 11)

DAY 86

Living the Mitzvah

What If Animosity Already Exists?

When people are already at odds with each other, it would seem that the reason for prohibiting rechilus — its potential for stirring animosity — would no longer be relevant. In that case, may negative information be conveyed?

כ"ו כסלו
26 Kislev
Cycle 1

כ"ו ניסן
26 Nissan
Cycle 2

כ"ז אב
27 Av
Cycle 3

The Dilemma:

Your neighbor installed an Olympic-sized swimming pool and promptly let everyone know that no one is invited to enjoy it. "I don't want to run a country club," he explained. Many people on your close-knit block are furious at him. The pool owner seeks your sympathy. "Do you know that your next-door neighbor uninvited me to his son's bar mitzvah? He's causing all this *machlokes* and it's going to come back at him some day." May you tell your neighbor that the pool owner blames him for creating *machlokes*?

The Halachah:

This is *rechilus,* even though your neighbor already has plenty of ill will toward the pool owner.

Sefer Chofetz Chaim, Hilchos Rechilus 1:4

REMEMBER
Don't add new fuel to the old fire.

26 Kislev – **As a *zechus* for my daughter for a *shidduch*** לזכות מרים ארילה בת לאה
Dedicated by her father יהודה מנדל בן אליעזר

26 Nissan – לזכות בני בכורי י–הודה לייב בן צבי–ה נ"י
לבריאות, הצלחה, נחת, פרנסה, שמחה ודורות ישרים מבורכים

27 Av – לע"נ חיים בן אברהם הלוי ז"ל
Dedicated by Alvin Segal and family

Grow Your Humility

Anger and Rebuke Don't Mix

One way the *yetzer hora* finds entry into many people's hearts is when they believe they have a righteous cause. Then they become Pinchas, zealously defending Hashem's honor even if it means, figuratively at least, killing the wrongdoer.

For example, a teenager has trouble waking up in time for *minyan.* His parents rightfully believe that this is a bad habit that needs to be overcome. In their zeal, they scream, yell, threaten and punish him, call him lazy and foretell the troubles awaiting him in life if he doesn't straighten out. They believe they have to come down hard because after all, how can a religious boy justify a lax attitude toward praying to his Creator? Doesn't he believe in Hashem? Doesn't he believe he owes Hashem some punctuality and attention? Would he be late to a basketball game? With such thoughts, *ona'as devarim* and *loshon hora* are almost certain to follow.

To all this, Rav Chaim of Volozhin (*Love Your Neighbor,* p. 285) advises: Work on your temper and anger before you attempt to fulfill the obligation of *tochachah.* "For if you cannot rebuke in a pleasant way, you cannot fulfill this mitzvah." This advice makes perfect sense, because rebuke delivered in anger is simply not heeded (*Erech Apayim,* p. 44, quoted in *Love Your Neighbor*).

Looking Within: Do you address the flaws in people close to you with self-righteous anger that's disguised as concern?

Building Within: Whenever you feel someone needs correction, keep in mind the fact that an angry rebuke doesn't work. Therefore, it's simply a verbal assault with no constructive purpose.

QUOTE OF THE DAY

"It is impossible to help another person grow, whether spiritually or physically, without first having a positive view of that person."
(Shem MiShmuel, Bamidbar, Beha'aloscha 5677)

DAY 87

Living the Mitzvah

Do I Have to Worry About People Repeating My Words?

You know something interesting that you're passing along to a few friends. It's neutral information for them. However, what if they repeat the information to someone else, who finds it insulting?

כ״ז כסלו
27 Kislev
Cycle 1

כ״ז ניסן
27 Nissan
Cycle 2

כ״ח אב
28 Av
Cycle 3

The Dilemma:

Shimon is talking to his coworker Levi about changes in his community. "My neighbor Reuven told me that a boy in his son's class was kicked out of school for smoking in the playground. An 11-year-old — smoking!"

A few days later, Levi is at a wedding. The table conversation turns to troubled youth. Levi jumps in: "Listen to this! Shimon's neighbor Reuven told him that a kid in his son's fifth-grade class got kicked out of yeshivah for smoking!"

Levi didn't know that the fifth-grader's father was at the table. He is now furious at Reuven for discussing his son's mistake. Was Shimon speaking *rechilus* when he told Levi the story, even though he didn't know it would eventually cause bad feelings between Reuven and the boy's father?

REMEMBER
The results, not the intention, make words rechilus.

The Halachah:

You are responsible for where your words go once they leave your mouth. You are not allowed to say something that could cause strife if it is repeated. When Shimon spoke to Levi his words were not *rechilus*; ultimately they became *rechilus*. Hence, sharing the information with Levi was prohibited.

Sefer Chofetz Chaim, Hilchos Rechilus 3:3

27 Kislev – לע״נ זלמן נפתלי בן ר׳ שמואל מיכל ואשתו לאה בת ר׳ שבתי שפטל ז״ל
לע״נ משה בן ר׳ מנחם זאב ואשתו זלאטא בת ר׳ אברהם חיים ז״ל

27 Nissan – **May today's learning be a *zechus* for our family.**
Rabbi & Mrs. Yossi Spanier

28 Av – לע״נ אברהם בן חיים ז״ל
Dedicated by Mr. & Mrs. Chaim Mordechai Abramson

Grow Your Humility

Saved by the Bell

A successful international businessman gave this account of how a quick, well-timed reminder of the power of speech saved the day.

There is a company in Japan with which I do a lot of business. Recently the company made a huge, costly mistake. I was so furious that I decided to go to Japan and blast them in person.

The morning of the meeting, I was walking into the building rehearsing in my head everything I was going to say. Then, just as I entered the conference room, my phone gave a "ping." It was my daily *shmiras haloshon* email from the Chofetz Chaim Heritage Foundation.

Right then and there, I decided that I would not speak until I heard their side. As it turned out, I had completely misinterpreted what happened and they really were not to blame. Can you imagine the damage to this relationship and to my company if I had marched in and humiliated them?

In one second, this man's mind switched tracks from anger and blame to holding his tongue. All it took was a little "ping" from heaven, and a place in his heart for shmiras haloshon.

Looking Within: Do you tend to get into a state of righteous indignation when things don't go your way? Does this sometimes lead you to say things you later regret?

Building Within: When anger and outrage take over your better nature, realize that you are walking across a minefield. Take time to consider the possibility of another side of the story, and then proceed with caution.

QUOTE OF THE DAY

"Whoever loses his temper — if he is a scholar, he will lose his wisdom; if a prophet, he will lose his holy spirit."
(Talmud Pesachim 66b)

DAY 88

Living the Mitzvah

May I Provide Someone Access to Something Negative That Was Written About Him?

Someone you care about is being spoken about in a negative, harmful way. You know better than to tell your friend what the person has been saying, but may you let him find out by reading about it?

כ"ח כסלו
28 Kislev
Cycle 1

כ"ח ניסן
28 Nissan
Cycle 2

כ"ט אב
29 Av
Cycle 3

The Dilemma:

Your local newspaper carries a parenting advice column written by your next-door neighbor, who is a therapist. She brings a very unflattering example of a mother who overprotects her children, and despite the fact that she uses a pseudonym, it's clear to everyone who knows your family that she is talking about your wife. Your friend gives you a copy of the paper and says, "Read Mrs. Levine's parenting column," believing that you and your wife should know not to trust the therapist as a friend. Is the neighbor's report *rechilus*?

The Halachah:

Despite the fact that your neighbor hasn't spoken *rechilus*, his effort to give you access to written material that can cause ill feelings is still considered *rechilus*. This is true even though the subject's name isn't mentioned, because she is identifiable nonetheless. Recorded material used in this way can also be *rechilus*.

Sefer Chofetz Chaim, Hilchos Rechilus 1:9,11

REMEMBER

Don't show and don't tell; neither story ends well.

28 Kislev – Dedicated as a *zechus*

28 Nissan – As a *zechus* for Ari Yosef, Ariela, Yehuda and Odelyah Cohentov
Dedicated by their parents, Mr. Hirbod E. & Mrs. Arvin Cohentov

29 Av – לע"נ דוד יוסף בן הרב יהודה לייב זצ"ל
By his wife, Gloria Pearl, and children, Sara, Asher Zelig and Chananya Yisrael

Grow Your Humility

Can You Give Me a Lift?

Did you ever consider the old adage, "Pick yourself up by your bootstraps"? How can you lift your own weight?

In all our endeavors in life, we put in the effort and Hashem decides either to crown those efforts with success, or allow failure to teach us a needed lesson. The only area in which our own efforts determine our success is in spirituality. If we want to grow, we can. We must, in effect, pull ourselves up by our own bootstraps. We may want to grow in *shmiras haloshon,* but our habits and surroundings comprise a weight we can't lift by ourselves. We will never succeed if we believe we can do it all on our own. Therefore, we have to pray for Hashem's help.

When we humbly turn to Hashem for help, He has plenty of help to offer. He can limit the temptations in our lives; the gossipy neighbor can move out. Or, He can arrange our lives so that we have less stress and more sleep, making us less likely to snap. He can give us a friend who inspires us to grow. He can make our task easier, even though spiritual growth is our task to do.

Each morning, when we reach the end of *Shmoneh Esrei* and ask Hashem *"netzor leshoni mei'ra"* (guard my tongue from evil), we have a chance to humbly ask Hashem to help us through the day.

Looking Within: Is success in *shmiras haloshon* among your requests when you *daven*?

Building Within: Stop and place extra focus on the words, *"Elokai netzor leshoni mei'ra."*

QUOTE OF THE DAY

"Sometimes people learn the *halachos* [of *shmiras haloshon*] and they still have a hard time keeping them. It's because they forget that they need to ask Hashem for help."

(Rabbi Moshe Mordechai Lowy)

DAY 89

Living the Mitzvah

What If My Father Asks Me?

You're privy to something that your father feels he should know. Are you allowed — or perhaps even obligated — to supply the information if it might arouse negative feelings?

The Dilemma:

This year, for the first time ever, your brother did not bring his family to your parents' house for Pesach. He told your father that the reason was the poor sleeping habits of his new baby, which were made much worse when he didn't sleep in his own room in his own crib. However, you know the real reason: your brother wanted to make his own Seder for his family. Your father suspects as much and he demands that you tell him the "real reason." Should you?

The Halachah:

Even though we are obligated to honor our parents' requests, in this case, doing so would violate the Torah prohibition against *rechilus* if you suspect that your answer would create hard feelings between your father and your brother. Likewise, we are not permitted to speak *rechilus* when a mother, teacher, or *rav* request information from us.

Sefer Chofetz Chaim, Hilchos Rechilus 1:5

◆כ"ט כסלו◆
◆*29 Kislev*
Cycle 1

כ"ט ניסן
29 Nissan
Cycle 2

ל אב
30 Av
Cycle 3

REMEMBER
You may not "honor" parents by serving them rechilus.

◆ *When this month has only 29 days, the lesson for 30 Kislev should also be studied today.*

29 Kislev – לזכות בני א–ליהו זוסע בן צבי–ה נ"י
לבריאות, הצלחה, נחת, פרנסה, שמחה ודורות ישרים מבורכים

29 Nissan – לע"נ שלמה זלקא בן משה ואשתו פעסיל בת נחום ז"ל

30 Av – **Mike Greenfield** לע"נ מאיר בן ברוך ז"ל
Dedicated by his children Sari & Ari Bacon

Grow Your Humility

All Cleaned Up

This account comes from Miriam Pessie, a girl who started a group called Word Watch *when she was only in fifth grade. Four years later, as she was entering high school, the group already had 400 members nationwide, and was changing girls' lives.*

When Miriam was in fifth grade, a relative gave birth to a preemie. The baby was in need of a *refuah* and the women of the family organized a nightly conference call to learn *shmiras haloshon* and recite *Tehillim* as a merit. Miriam wanted to join the effort, but she wanted to do it with girls her own age.

That's how her group got started. She got two cousins to join. Then she invited classmates. Then the classmates invited their neighbors and friends and before she knew it, Word Watch had grown from a project into a movement. It's a nightly commitment that Miriam has kept, "no matter what."

Miriam Pessie describes the impact of the nightly conference call. "My friends are so good. We have gotten to a point where we have clean conversations. There's no *loshon hora*. That's what we wanted to accomplish."

She describes the feeling as "like being a new person." In her class, where everyone is a Word Watcher, she has seen girls become more sensitive to and caring for each other. "Everyone knows us as the class that has *achdus*."

Miriam Pessie is proof positive that when shmiras haloshon is close to a person's heart, it can become a life-changing positive force. With a budget of zero and a little help from her parents and friends, she illustrates what can be done.

Looking Within: Have you given up the dream of being the positive person you want to be because it seems impossible?

Building Within: Whenever you feel yourself slipping in your commitment to *shmiras haloshon,* push yourself forward just a few short inches and reclaim your momentum. Stop every so often to recall where you started and acknowledge how far you've come.

QUOTE OF THE DAY

"Perfecting one's character demands even greater sacrifice than *mesirus nefesh* [sacrificing one's life to Hashem]."

(R' Naftoli Amsterdam, Chayei HaMussar [Bnei Brak ed.], p. 53)

Teves

לע"נ בונא בת חיים חנונה ע"ה נלב"ע ה' טבת

Beatrice Gordon

Dedicated by
Dr. & Mrs. Joseph & Susan Furman

As a zechus for brachah and hatzlachah
Dedicated by
Munnell and Goodman families

לע"נ רחמים בן אדל ז"ל

Raymond Kairey

לע"נ משה בן מרג'י ז"ל

Morris I. Gindi

Iyar

לע"נ יוסף בן ר' דוד הכהן ז"ל
ואשתו חי' ריזל בת ר' ישראל אשר זעליג ע"ה

Dedicated as a zechus for our family

By Yoey & Andi Schochet

לע"נ שלוה ראכל בת ישראל מנחם ע"ה
נלב"ע א' אייר

לע"נ ישראל מנחם בן שלום ז"ל
נלב"ע כ"ו טבת

Elul

להצלחה בכל הענינים חנה בת יוכבד תחי'

לזכות חנינה חנה בת לאה לולו שתחי'

L'zechut Chanina Chana bat Leah Lulu

Dedicated as a zechus for the Adler family

CHAPTER 10

Idealism — Spread Your Light

When a spark of inspiration strikes, there are only two choices — fan it into a flame or let it die out. Some of the greatest leaps in Shmiras Haloshon in homes, shuls and communities across the globe have been ignited by one person's spark — a spark that he fanned, fueled and empowered by getting others on board. Ordinary people can inspire extraordinary changes, and when they do, the benefits live on forever.

DAY 90

Living the Mitzvah

What If I Have to Lie to Keep the Peace?

You've been asked a loaded question. If you refuse to answer, that alone will reveal that the answer is hurtful. Should you then state something that isn't true in order to avoid this "silent rechilus"?

ל כסלו*
30 Kislev
Cycle 1

ל ניסן
30 Nissan
Cycle 2

א אלול
1 Elul
Cycle 3

The Dilemma:
Your friend's daughter has just been turned down for a teaching job at an elementary school where you've worked for many years as the principal's administrative assistant. In fact, you were in on the interview. You know that your friend's daughter wasn't hired because the principal felt she didn't project enough energy to engage a class. Your neighbor asks you, "What did she say about my daughter? Do you have any idea why she didn't hire her?" She knows you're in the principal's inner circle; you can't pretend not to know. What should you say?

The Halachah:
Whether you refuse to answer or tell the truth, the mother is bound to feel animosity for the principal. Therefore, you should say something as neutral as possible, even if it isn't exactly true: "She decided she wants someone who has more experience with third grade." The Torah teaches that "One may alter the facts for the sake of peace" (Rashi on *Bereishis* 50:16).

Sefer Chofetz Chaim, Hilchos Rechilus 1:5,8

REMEMBER
Weigh the truth against the consequence.

* *When this month has only 29 days, the lesson for 30 Kislev should be learned together with 29 Kislev.*

30 Kislev – **In memory of my parents Lillian and Sol Blackman** ***a"h***
Dedicated by their daughter Phyllis Blackman

30 Nissan – לע"נ זאב ואלף בן רפאל שראגא פייויל ואשתו רבקה ליבא בת משה הכהן ע"ה
לע"נ תחיה אסתר ע"ה בת רפאל שרגא יוסף יבלח"ט

1 Elul – **Dedicated by Yehuda and Yosefa Bunker**

Grow Your Idealism

Special Delivery From the Chofetz Chaim

Machlokes (divisiveness) often spreads quickly and, like an ugly weed, overtakes everything in its path. But sometimes, as the account below demonstrates, a sudden burst of awareness can nip this noxious weed in the bud:

A shul was bitterly divided over the question of renewing its rabbi's contract. Prior to the members' vote on the issue, the shul president sent out a letter advising against renewal. On the day the letter went out, a woman who learns Shmiras Haloshon Yomi from *The Chofetz Chaim***:** *A Daily Companion* received her daily email containing a lesson called "Playing with Fire," which discussed *loshon hora* about rabbis. In the lesson, the Chofetz Chaim explains the grave danger of this type of *loshon hora,* as it defames someone who represents Hashem, and furthermore, rips apart communities.

The woman immediately copied the email and distributed it to the shul members. The timing was not lost on them: on the exact same day as the president sent out his derogatory letter, the *sefer* carried the Chofetz Chaim's words of warning about that form of *loshon hora.* "It was as if the Chofetz Chaim were crying out from his grave to our community," said the woman. "And the rabbi did win."

Looking Within: When a flash of inspiration hits you, what do you do with it? Do you try to act on it, or shake it off and move on?

Building Within: Pay attention to the messages Hashem sends you and try to act on them with enthusiasm and energy.

QUOTE OF THE DAY

"Guard your tongue from speaking evil: This is a greater *segulah* for success than all other *segulos* that people seek out."

(Sefer Shmiras HaLoshon, Chovas HaShemirah Ch. 6)

DAY 91

Living the Mitzvah

Are There Any Shmiras Haloshon Pitfalls in Expressing My Gratitude?

You're touched. You're grateful. You want to let others know what a nice thing someone has done for you. Can that be rechilus?

א טבת
1 Teves
Cycle 1

א אייר
1 Iyar
Cycle 2

ב אלול
2 Elul
Cycle 3

The Dilemma:

You are making a wedding and the expenses are overwhelming. Your neighbor, a wealthy man, comes to you and hands you an envelope with $5,000 in cash. "Just a little something to help out," is all he says. When you see your neighbor's wife, you want to tell her how grateful your family is for her husband's generosity. Does she know what a *tzaddik* her husband is? Well, she should! Is there any violation of halachah in telling her this?

The Halachah:

You can run into a problem if the wife resents her husband's gesture, perhaps because she feels that he shouldn't give away so much money, or because she has someone in mind to whom she would rather give it. However, because creating ill will wasn't your intention, your words are called *"avak rechilus,"* meaning the "dust" of *rechilus,* which is a Rabbinic prohibition.

Sefer Chofetz Chaim, Hilchos Rechilus 8:2

REMEMBER
Even praise can kick up the dust.

1 Teves – לע"נ הרב שרגא פייוול בן הרב שאול ז"ל נלב"ע י' תשרי
Dedicated by his grandchildren

1 Iyar – Jack Friedman לע"נ יעקב יוסף בן נתן נטע ז"ל
Dedicated by his children, grandchildren and great–grandchildren

2 Elul – As a *zechus* for a *refuah shleimah* for all *cholei Yisrael*
Dedicated by Eliezer & Shaindel Bliss, Edmonton, Canada

Grow Your Idealism

Crowd Out Complaints

One of the most powerful — and pleasant — ways to stop *speaking loshon hora* is to start speaking *loshon tov.* It's hard to be negative when you're busy noticing and speaking about the positive. And as one man discovered, positive vibes spread fast:

Duvi was standing in a long line of customers at a popular bagel shop. Everyone was annoyed at the slowness of the service. They started grumbling to each other. One man accidentally jarred the elbow of the man in front of him and got an irate "Watch what you're doing!" in response.

Duvi turned to the man behind him. "Got a minute for a *dvar Torah*?" Duvi asked the man. The man shrugged and smiled. "Sure, why not?" Duvi offered a quick *vort* on the *parashah.* He then asked his new friend to hold his place and he made his way down the line, wishing people a nice day, complimenting them on their patience, offering some other brief Torah insights.

Soon the line was filled with smiling people, all talking amieably to each other. Some might have thought Duvi a little odd, but no one could deny that he had sucked the poison right out of the atmosphere and replaced it with the sweet taste of *ahavas Yisrael.*

Looking Within: Do you believe that you have the power to turn around a negative situation?

Building Within: When you realize that the atmosphere is being poisoned with negativity, think of a way to reverse the tide with positive words.

QUOTE OF THE DAY

"When *Klal Yisrael* is unified, their blemishes are not recognized...for when one purchases an entire flock of sheep one does not inspect each one individually for flaws."

(Yaaros Devash, Part II, Derush 2, p. 36)

DAY 92

Living the Mitzvah

Can Rechilus Ever Be Constructive?

Just as loshon hora may be allowed l'to'eles, so too might a person be obligated to speak rechilus to protect others from harm. But how do we know if our purpose is truly considered constructive?

ב טבת
2 Teves
Cycle 1

ב אייר
2 Iyar
Cycle 2

ג אלול
3 Elul
Cycle 3

The Dilemma:

You're at a wedding when Levi, sitting next to you, asks Shimon, on the other side of him, what he knows about the Stern family, as he was given as a reference for a *shidduch*. Your ears perk up, because Rachel Stern, the wife of that family, is your sister. Shimon says he tells everyone who asks that he knows your brother-in-law from yeshivah, 25 years ago, and he was "totally unfocused, a real character." He adds "If his kids turned out normal, it's a miracle." May you inform your brother-in-law that Shimon is giving out this demeaning, outdated information?

The Halachah:

There are three questions to gauge whether *rechilus* qualifies as *l'to'eles*: (1) Does it provide warning that someone intends to harm another person so that he can prevent it? (2) Does it inform someone that another person is presently harming him, so he can put an end to it? For this reason you may tell your brother-in-law to remove Shimon's name as a reference. (3) Does it inform someone that another person has harmed him, so that the victim can seek restitution?

Even with these guidelines, it's wise to consult a *rav* to make sure you're judging the situation objectively.

Sefer Chofetz Chaim, Hilchos Rechilus 9:3-10

REMEMBER
Negative words can have positive impact — when used with guidance.

2 Teves – **In memory of Faygel Yentel *bas* David Meier *a"h***
Dedicated by her grandchildren

2 Iyar – **Dedicated as a *zechus* for the Goldwasser family**

3 Elul – **Ruth Stromer *a"h*** לע"נ שפרה רייזל בת צבי ושרה ע"ה
Dedicated by Sue and Arthur Talansky

Grow Your Idealism

Shmiras Haloshon x 1,000 = A Revolution

When someone decides he wants to improve in *shmiras haloshon,* he sometimes faces a major obstacle: everyone else! He has to build the strength to keep quiet when others are involved in an interesting topic, and perhaps even change locations to avoid hearing what he shouldn't hear. The best way to ensure your own growth is to bring others along on the journey, as one man discovered:

For Zev Beinenstock, it wasn't enough to learn *shmiras haloshon,* observe its tenets, and enjoy the vast benefits it brings to life. He had to share what he found out, and that is what he did through his campaign to get members of his Flatbush community and his shul, Khal Zichron Mordechai, involved in Shmiras Haloshon Yomi.

Through his hard work and persistence, as well as his enthusiastic endorsement of his "product," Zev got more than 1,000 people to sign up for learning from *Chofetz Chaim: The Daily Companion.* The result is a community where the tone and content of conversations has taken a giant leap upward, all because one man decided to make it so.

Looking Within: Do you live and work in an environment that's conducive to *shmiras haloshon?*

Building Within: Take a step to improve your own *shmiras haloshon* and invite others in your home, community or office to join you.

QUOTE OF THE DAY

"[At Sinai] every angel revealed its secret and its power to [Moshe Rabbeinu]. The Angel of Death did too. It divulged that its secret is rooted in *loshon hora.*"

(Pri Tzaddik, Parashas Korach)

DAY 93

Living the Mitzvah

What If My Negative Report Can't Help the Victim?

You know that someone has harmed another person, but there's no fixing the situation. Furthermore, there's no chance that the harm will continue or be repeated. Does the victim have the right to know who harmed him?

ג טבת
3 Teves
Cycle 1

ג אייר
3 Iyar
Cycle 2

ד אלול
4 Elul
Cycle 3

The Dilemma:
Your new son-in-law, in an effort to be helpful, offers to fix your wife's computer. Ultimately, his tinkering actually makes the problem worse. Now your wife wants to use the computer and it's completely frozen. "What happened?" she says in a state of annoyance. Should you tell her that your son-in-law tried to fix it?

The Halachah:
You should not share this information, as it would give your wife a negative feeling toward your son-in-law. She is not likely to ask him to fix what he did, nor will she ask him to pay for the repair. Furthermore, he is not going to have the opportunity to do further damage to the computer; there's no purpose to her knowing.

Sefer Chofetz Chaim, Hilchos Rechilus 9:3-10

REMEMBER
If there's nothing you can do about it, there's nothing you can say about it.

3 Teves – **Moshe Azulai** לע"נ ר' משה בן ר' מרדכי ושמחה אזולאי ז"ל
Dedicated by Elchonon & Shuli Nakdimen — Monsey, NY

3 Iyar – **In memory of Marcia Alta *bas* Chaim Hillel *a"h***
In memory of Yeshaya *ben* Avraham Nuta *z"l*

4 Elul – לע"נ פרומא שרה בת ר' חיים יצחק ע"ה
Dedicated by Mr. Hersh & Mrs. Debbi Granek

Grow Your Idealism

"Kamocha"

One sign of how precious *shmiras haloshon* is to Hashem is the amazing *siyata d'Shmaya* that accompanies efforts to spread the mitzvah. It sometimes seems that all a person has to do is get the ball rolling, and Hashem carries it all the way to the goal post.

That's what happened in Chicago, when a well-known businessman named Barak Baver decided to do something to improve the *bein adam la'chaveiro* climate of the city's Jewish schools. With his support and activism and the Chofetz Chaim Heritage Foundation's expertise, a pilot project called Kamocha, involving 1,200 fourth- through eighth-graders, took place in the four weeks before Shavuos.

The project focused the children's attention on one *pasuk*, Hillel's famous summation of the Torah: "That which is hateful to you, do not do to your fellow." The children learned to apply this maxim by asking themselves, "How would I feel?" before interacting with others. Each class thought about this question and pinpointed ways they could prevent causing each other to feel isolated, slighted or humiliated.

When the month was up, children wrote down their impressions. The accolades were universal. In one short month, school had become a friendlier, happier place for Chicago's children.

Looking Within: Do you have a vision of what the world could be like with a greater awareness of *shmiras haloshon?* Do you believe things can change?

Building Within: Consider joining a *shmiras haloshon* learning program or perhaps even start your own learning group, knowing that when you take the initiative, *siyata d'Shmaya* will follow.

QUOTE OF THE DAY

"What is hateful to you, do not do to your fellow."

(Shabbos 31a)

DAY 94

Living the Mitzvah

What If My Information Is Constructive, but Secondhand?

You've found out information that your friend ought to know in order to prevent him from harm. However, you didn't witness the negative situation firsthand. May you repeat it anyway?

ד טבת
4 Teves
Cycle 1

ד אייר
4 Iyar
Cycle 2

ה אלול
5 Elul
Cycle 3

The Dilemma:

Your friend is on the scholarship committee of your yeshivah. He tells you that another member of the committee told everyone that the information on your brother's scholarship application for his sons does not look correct. May you tell your brother what this person said?

The Halachah:

Since your brother stands to be injured by the words — he might not get needed financial help for his children's education — there is a constructive purpose to your telling him. However, because you didn't hear the words firsthand, you must tell him clearly that you're only repeating what you heard, and he should not accept it as fact.

Sefer Chofetz Chaim, Be'er Mayim Chaim, Hilchos Rechilus 9:9

REMEMBER

Secondhand goods come with a disclaimer: "Buyer beware."

4 Teves – R' Levi Yoselovsky לע"נ ר' לוי בן ר' בן ציון יוסלובסקי ז"ל
Dedicated by the Yoselovsky family, Lakewood, NJ

4 Iyar – לזכות שלום עלינו ועל כל עם ישראל

5 Elul – Louis Schulman לע"נ נפתלי ליפה בן שמואל הלוי ז"ל
Dedicated in loving memory by his daughter Sara Stobezki

Grow Your Idealism

The Shabbos Game-Changer

We're accustomed to putting aside our choicest food and most decadent dessert for the Shabbos table. Now, for a growing number of families, *shmiras haloshon* is being added to the menu. The Shabbos Table Machsom l'Fi, with its Shabbos Menu newsletter and beautiful *shmiras haloshon kabbalah* table card, turns the Shabbos meals into a "*loshon hora*-free zone." It ensures that this special time of family togetherness is a time of positive energy and bonding.

"We weren't big on Shabbos table projects," says Daniel G. from Flatbush, Brooklyn. "Anything we tried usually got a lot of eye-rolls and bored expressions. But this really changed things. First of all, you do it as a *zechus*. When we started my father was in the hospital, and everyone wanted to do something for him. The other important thing is that it's so easy. It doesn't take over your table.

"Someone just says a short *tefillah* and *kabbalah* to remind everyone what we're doing. Then, if everyone's into it, there's The Shabbos Menu, which gives you an interesting question on *shmiras haloshon,* a good, real-life situation, and a great story. Everyone has their ideas about what the right answer is, and the discussion sometimes gets really intense. Then we read the answer, and half the time that sparks another debate.

"Then we go on with our meal, but no one's talking about their neighbors or school friends or sisters or brothers. My wife and I also steer completely clear of criticizing the kids at the table. This was a game-changer for our family. And by the way, my father is now home recuperating."

Looking Within: Could the conversation at your Shabbos table use an upgrade?

Building Within: Envision what your optimal Shabbos table could be and take a small step toward that vision. To join The Shabbos Table Machsom l'Fi, text Shabbos to 313131 or visit powerofspeech.org/shabbos

QUOTE OF THE DAY

"You stumbled this morning and spoke the forbidden? Then strengthen yourself and do battle once more! Surely, Hashem will help you succeed."

(Sefer Shmiras HaLoshon, Preface)

DAY 95

Living the Mitzvah

If I'm Not Sure Who's in the Wrong, May I Warn Someone of Another Person's Plan to Harm Him?

ה טבת
5 Teves
Cycle 1

ה אייר
5 Iyar
Cycle 2

ו אלול
6 Elul
Cycle 3

You heard someone say that he intends to wrong another person. You know these two parties are at odds with each other, but you don't know the whole story. Are you obligated to report what you heard to the potential victim?

The Dilemma:
You have neighbors who are in the middle of a contentious divorce. You hear the wife tell her sister, "I'm taking the kids and moving as far away from him as I can get." May you tell the husband what you heard?

The Halachah:
If you aren't familiar with the whole story, you should not repeat what you heard even though it was firsthand. That's because there may be abuse or some other reason that the wife is considering the move. Even though what you heard seems to indict the wife, she may in fact be the real victim. By telling the husband, you might be leaving her vulnerable.

Sefer Chofetz Chaim, Hilchos Rechilus 9:2-4

REMEMBER
A story can't stand on half the necessary information.

5 Teves – **In memory of Jack Gordon** לע"נ יעקב אליהו בן אליעזר ז"ל
Dedicated by his daughter Tracy Gordon

5 Iyar – **Orion Jacob Silverman** לע"נ אהרן יעקב בן ישעי' ז"ל
Dedicated by the Silverman family

6 Elul – **In honor of my children and grandchildren with love, Bubby (Rachel Devorah)**

Grow Your Idealism

From Grassroots to Nationwide

There are people who see a need and think, "Someone should do something about this." Then there are people who see a need and think, "I have to do something about this." And there are people who see a need and *do* do something about it.

Two seminary graduates in Lakewood certainly qualify for that last group. Mimi N. and Nechama M. were inspired to do something to increase the power of *shmiras haloshon* in the world — and they got to work.

Their idea was as simple and low-tech as could be: Every Friday in neighborhoods around Lakewood, high-school girls would gather the younger girls in someone's home and learn *shmiras haloshon* with them. The two girls contacted 11 high schools in Lakewood, explaining their idea and asking for an opportunity to recruit neighborhood leaders. The schools gladly welcomed them, and in the end, almost 200 girls from all the various high schools volunteered to take part in the program, named Achoseinu. A pair of high school girls each led a group of 10 or so younger girls.

When the season was over (the summer candle-lighting time became too late), they made a town-wide Melaveh Malkah celebrating the *shalom* and *achdus* they had built together by enhancing *shmiras haloshon* through Achoseinu. Then, CCHF got on board; not content to confine the program to the Lakewood border, it is helping the girls to take it nationwide, and perhaps worldwide as well. The two young Achoseinu founders couldn't have anticipated how much light would be spread by the single candle they lit.

Looking Within: Do you have an idea that could increase *shalom* and *achdus* in your home, school, office or neighborhood?

Building Within: Share your idea with a like-minded person and work together to turn it into reality.

QUOTE OF THE DAY

"Imagine one who is hopelessly mute, but a doctor comes along and restores his speech... He certainly would not dare to use his speech itself against the trusted doctor's wishes!"
(Sefer Shmiras HaLoshon, Shaar HaTevunah Ch. 1)

CHAPTER 11

Self-Control — Build Real Strength

Who wants to be wishy-washy and weak? Who wants to be a push-over? We all want to be thought of as strong, and sometimes that leads us to be aggressive, arrogant or insulting. We "say it like it is" and think we've shown courage and strength. But as *Pirkei Avos* (4:1) informs us, the strong person is the one who controls his negative urges. He's the one who thinks, "This is something I shouldn't say," and stops before the hurtful words come out of his mouth. Those are the muscles we expend effort to build when we really want to live like heroes.

DAY 96

Living the Mitzvah

Should I Assume That Someone's Outrageous Plot Against Another Person Is True?

You overhear someone plotting against another person, but you have real doubts that the speaker would ever do what he's threatening. Should you warn the potential victim?

ו טבת
6 Teves
Cycle 1

ו אייר
6 Iyar
Cycle 2

ז אלול
7 Elul
Cycle 3

The Dilemma:

A secretary in your office feels very oppressed by her boss. You hear her telling a coworker that she's going to delete hundreds of important emails, quit her job, and "let him figure it out." Should you tell the boss?

The Halachah:

If someone is speaking about an outrageous plot that is out of character for him, you can usually assume that he is fantasizing his revenge for a situation in which he feels stuck. In that case, repeating the information would be a toxic combination of *loshon hora*, *rechilus* and *motzi shem ra* (slander).

Sefer Chofetz Chaim, Hilchos Rechilus 9:3 with Be'er Mayim Chaim 11,12

REMEMBER

If it's unbelievable, it's unrepeatable.

6 Teves – לע"נ מיכיל בן לייב פרידלנד ז"ל
Dedicated by Avraham Gershkovich

6 Iyar – *L'zechut* Gilah *bat* Sarah v'Avraham — Gretchen Glaser
In honor of our dear friend, by Marci & Dennis Brumberg

7 Elul – לע"נ בילא בת מאיר ע"ה

Grow Your Self-Control

The Better of Two Evils

Sometimes a person is burning to speak *loshon hora,* not because he wants to ruin another person, but because he knows the truth. For instance, a couple is in the process of getting a divorce and everyone is siding with the husband, who is a beloved figure in the community. People voice their shock at the wife's insistence on breaking up the family, but you are not shocked at all. You know that she has been suffering in a cold, manipulative relationship for many years and you want to blurt out the truth. It drives you crazy to hear what people are saying. You control yourself and say, "There are always two sides," but no one believes you.

Falsehood is indeed an evil. However, *loshon hora* is its own evil. If you remain quiet, nothing will change. However, if you speak *loshon hora* you will set loose a whole host of negative repercussions on yourself and the Jewish people. There is little to be gained in most disclosures, and much to lose in the act of disclosing.

Looking Within: Do you sometimes have information that feels as if it's burning a trail from your mind to your tongue, just waiting for the moment to emerge?

Building Within: Make a very high fence for this information. Tell yourself that you will not divulge it and stick to your word.

QUOTE OF THE DAY

"It is only right for a person to be more concerned about his speech than his property."
(Rambam, Iggeres HaShmad Ch. 1)

DAY 97

Living the Mitzvah

May I Dramatize a Little to Make Sure the Intended Victim Takes the Threat Seriously?

You heard something that could save your friend from harm. However, you're worried that he'll just shrug it off. May you dramatize what you heard to make your point?

ז טבת
7 Teves
Cycle 1

ז אייר
7 Iyar
Cycle 2

ח אלול
8 Elul
Cycle 3

The Dilemma:

Your son is entering seventh grade in yeshivah. Your friend told you that her son had a hard time with that particular rebbi because he often raised his voice and made the child nervous. You want your husband to get your son transferred into the other seventh grade, but his philosophy is that children should learn to deal with teachers they don't particularly like. To make sure your husband sees the potential damage, you want to say, "I heard he's always screaming and embarrassing the kids. They're petrified of him!" Are you allowed to?

The Halachah:

You're not allowed to exaggerate. The information must be accurate, and it should be the minimum facts necessary to accomplish the constructive purpose.

Sefer Chofetz Chaim, Hilchos Rechilus 9:2

REMEMBER
Drop the drama.

7 Teves – לע"נ אריה זכריה בן אביגדור ורעיה נוימן ז"ל
לע"נ מרדכי בן אשר הלוי ז"ל ואשתו רבקה בת יוסף חיים ע"ה

7 Iyar – Gavriel Iskhakbayev לע"נ גבריאל בן ברוריא ז"ל נלב"ע כ"א אב
Dedicated by Rabbi & Mrs. Nissan Gavrielov

8 Elul – Leo Presser לע"נ אריה לייב בן ירחמאל שלמה הכהן ז"ל
Dedicated by Marilyn and Jaime Sohacheski

Grow Your Self-Control

Edit the News

Talking to others is one of our main ways of creating bonds. We share our happy news, empathize with each other's woes, offer useful advice, exchange opinions, and of course, share ideas and thoughts that inspire us.

The key to preventing these conversations from turning into *loshon hora*, says the Chofetz Chaim, is to limit our conversations that revolve around other people. There are things we should know because they are relevant to us. There might be something we can do to help someone who is facing a challenge. We certainly would want to hear good news — an engagement, a new baby and so forth.

However, when it comes to the soap opera-type tales of other people's personal woes and foibles, we're treading on dangerous ground. If there's no constructive purpose to knowing the information that's forthcoming, our safest strategy is to cut the conversation short or change the subject. The fewer names that come up in our conversations, the freer they are bound to be from *loshon hora*.

Looking Within: Do you have a fascination with other people's personal lives and dramas?

Building Within: Use the sound of other people's names as an alarm bell to warn yourself that *loshon hora* is likely to be forthcoming.

QUOTE OF THE DAY

"About that which enters your mouth you scrutinize and investigate, but about that which leaves it, you have no questions!"
(from Sefer Niflaos HaYehudi)

DAY 98

Living the Mitzvah

Is My Rechilus Constructive If I Dislike the Subject of My Report?

One of the conditions of to'eles, for both loshon hora and rechilus, is that the speaker should not take satisfaction from revealing the subject's destructive plans. But what if you really don't like that person?

ח טבת
8 Teves
Cycle 1

ח אייר
8 Iyar
Cycle 2

ט אלול
9 Elul
Cycle 3

The Dilemma:

The man who opened a competing pizza shop a block away from yours and cut your business in half is standing at a shul *kiddush*, talking to his friend about your friend's ice-cream shop. "I can't stand that guy! I'm gonna tell people his cones are stale and his chocolate ice cream is a cheap imitation. He doesn't stand a chance!" the man brags. "Ah-ha!" you think. "He does these things on purpose! He's a snake!"

Your friend needs to know this information, but may you be the one to tell him when in your heart you are delighted to paint this evil man a few shades darker?

REMEMBER
Clean up your heart before you start.

The Halachah:

Your friend should be told. If someone else at the *kiddush*, who doesn't have bad feelings for the speaker, heard his comments, that person should be the one to tell your friend about the threat. However, if there is no one else, you should work on yourself to dispel your spiteful feelings before relating the information.

Sefer Chofetz Chaim, Hilchos Rechilus 9:2, #3 with Be'er Mayim Chaim 3

8 Teves – לע"נ חיים ראובן שלמה בן שבח אלעזר ז"ל נלב"ע ט' טבת
Dedicated by Dr. & Mrs. Jeremy Simon

8 Iyar – לע"נ הרב אליעזר בן שלמה ז"ל נלב"ע ט' אייר
לע"נ פסיא פנינה בת אפרים מנשה ע"ה נלב"ע י"ב אב

9 Elul – *L'ilui nishmas* **Sarah** *bas* **Dovid** *Halevi z"l*
Dedicated by R' Chaim & Leah Tatel

Grow Your Self-Control

Here's an Offer You Can't Refuse

There's a saying, "Everyone has his price." It suggests that people will uphold their principles only until the reward for betraying them becomes tempting enough. But what if a wonderful reward were given not to abandon your principles, but to adhere to them?

Boruch M. from Boro Park relates: "I knew some unflattering information about an important person in my community. Whenever people praised this person, I felt like exploding. I thought, 'If only people knew!'

"This same guy was being honored by my sons' yeshivah. I had to go, and I honestly didn't know how I was going to stand hearing him being praised and making a speech. I said to my wife, 'Someone there is going to be getting lots of attention. I won't tell you who it is or what he's done, but I can tell you that the last thing he deserves is an honor. I don't know how I'm going to hold myself back from telling people what he is.'

"She gave me good advice. She said to do it as a merit for our daughter Shani, who was having trouble finding her *bashert*. She said, 'Just picture Shani under the *chuppah* when you feel like opening your mouth.' "

Boruch's wife's idea worked. Boruch had his price. And Chazal tell us that if we knew the reward our *shmiras haloshon* earns us in the Next World, we too would be sold on this mitzvah: "For every moment a person refrains from speaking the forbidden, he earns a reward beyond the comprehension of angels" (Vilna Gaon, citing *Midrash*).

Looking Within: When you're bursting to impart negative information, do you maintain your restraint or give up, feeling that the *loshon hora* is going to come out eventually?

Building Within: Think of something in your life that requires great *zechus* to accomplish, and dedicate your restraint to that goal.

QUOTE OF THE DAY

"For every moment that a person refrains from speaking the forbidden, he merits the Hidden Light, which neither angel nor creature can fathom."
(Iggeres HaGra)

DAY 99

Living the Mitzvah

May I Speak Rechilus to Help Someone If I Don't Think the Listener Will Act on My Advice?

Sometimes we see the cause of another person's problem far more clearly than the person himself sees it. We may know who is causing him grief, but we also know he won't do anything to help himself. May we offer our advice?

ט טבת
9 Teves
Cycle 1

ט אייר
9 Iyar
Cycle 2

י אלול
10 Elul
Cycle 3

The Dilemma:

Your coworker, Shmuel, has been passed over for a promotion and a raise many times during the ten years he's worked in your organization. He's depressed and miserable, but afraid to say anything for fear of antagonizing the boss. You've heard Shmuel's immediate supervisor paint him as a bumbling incompetent, and you know that this is why the boss lacks confidence in him. May you tell Shmuel what his supervisor has been saying?

REMEMBER
If it won't help, it's not constructive.

The Halachah:

If you've seen from Shmuel's behavior over the years that he lacks the confidence to confront his superiors, you can be fairly sure that he won't change now. Your information will only deepen his agitation. Since nothing positive is likely to be accomplished, your report, despite its good intentions, is *rechilus*.

Sefer Chofetz Chaim, Hilchos Rechilus 9:12

9 Teves – לע״נ ר׳ אהרן בן ישראל ז״ל נלב״ע י׳ טבת
As a merit for שלום for the family

9 Iyar – **In memory of Batya Brenda *bat* Mazal *a"h***
Dedicated by the Levy and Azoolay families

10 Elul – לע״נ חיה דרייזל מערקא בת יעקב אריה לייב הכהן ע״ה
Dedicated by the Kroll family and Faigy & Meir Altman

Grow Your Self-Control

You Can Do It

People often see *shmiras haloshon* as an impossibility because of the pervasive, fluid nature of conversation. We are constantly making split-second decisions about what to say and what to withhold. How can we possibly expect ourselves to always make the right decision?

The truth is, success is possible only when we get into the habit of thinking before we speak. Can such a level of self-monitoring really happen?

A man is learning late one Friday night. The dining room light has gone out and he is learning at the kitchen table. He feels sleep overcoming him and decides to go upstairs to bed. As he leaves the kitchen, he instinctively reaches for the light switch, but just before he touches it, he pulls his hand back. It's Shabbos!

He comes to a sudden realization. Only because Shabbos is so ingrained in him does his awareness override his instinctive motion. *Shmiras haloshon,* too, could become so deeply ingrained. Then, if he were to instinctively "reach" for a negative word to say, his awareness would hold back his tongue. It can be done!

Looking within: To what extent is *shmiras haloshon* ingrained in your mindset?

Building within: Find ways to increase the *shmiras haloshon* awareness in your life so that improper speech will ring an inner alarm bell and you will have the opportunity to pull back.

QUOTE OF THE DAY

"One who has accepted upon himself not to hurt another even through words will certainly be careful not to physically hurt another...so that eventually he will be free of all sins between man and his fellow."
(Sefer Shmiras HaLoshon, Shaar HaZechirah Ch. 1)

DAY 100

Living the Mitzvah

Do I Have to Be Concerned About the Retaliation My Rechilus Might Cause?

What if you have every good reason to tell someone that another person is harming him, but you know that this will result in harmful retaliation? May you still give the warning? Are you obligated to do so?

י טבת
10 Teves
Cycle 1

י אייר
10 Iyar
Cycle 2

י"א אלול
11 Elul
Cycle 3

The Dilemma:

You heard your neighbor Yosef tell another neighbor, Shaul, that he shouldn't let his children play in the home of still another neighbor, Reuven. "Reuven's wife is a space-cadet," Yosef said. "She doesn't keep an eye on the kids. My four-year-old once played there and he wrote all over himself with permanent marker." You feel that Reuven should know that his home and family are being besmirched, but he has a bad temper, and will very likely retaliate harshly against Yosef. What should you do?

The Halachah:

If your report might cause undue harm to the subject, either through physical or financial revenge or even *loshon hora*, then the *rechilus* is not justified by your constructive intent.

Sefer Chofetz Chaim, Hilchos Rechilus 9:2, #5, with Be'er Mayim Chaim 9

REMEMBER
Don't do more harm than good.

10 Teves – לע"נ צבי ארי' בן אלתר חיים ישעי' ז"ל
Dedicated by the Steger, Jacobovitch and Wesson families

10 Iyar – לע"נ חנה שושנה בת ברוך צ'רנר ע"ה
Dedicated by Dr. Mechel & Cheftzi Wiederkehr

11 Elul – לע"נ פעסא בשא בת אליהו ע"ה
Dedicated by the Steger, Jacobovitch and Wesson families

Grow Your Self-Control

Give It a Rest

Somebody does something wrong and you have a legitimate need to set him or her straight. For instance, your son uses your tools without your permission. Not only that, but he doesn't put them away properly; and now you want to finally fix the shaky table leg but you can't find your toolbox.

You're angry, and rightfully so. Your son shouldn't use other people's things without their permission and then, to make matters worse, be careless with them.

Right now, in the heat of your anger, you want to tell your wife how careless your son is. But instead of this being a constructive conversation about how to teach your son to be more responsible, it is likely to be nothing more than a complaint against him. Anger and *loshon hora* go hand in hand.

The solution, says Rabbi Simcha Zissel Ziv (*Chochmah U'Mussar,* Vol. 1, p. 161) [cited in *Love Your Neighbor*, p. 370] is to wait until the anger abates before speaking. We're not only allowed to correct someone who does wrong; we're obligated. By waiting until we're calm, even if it takes days or weeks, we can prevent our mitzvah from turning into *loshon hora* or *ona'as devarim.*

Looking Within: Do you tend to look for the nearest person to vent your frustrations on when you become angry with someone?

Building Within: Tell yourself, as you're about to complain about someone, "I can still discuss this later. It doesn't have to be now." In this way, you give yourself a chance to gain perspective.

QUOTE OF THE DAY

"As water extinguishes fire, so does silence nullify the strength of anger."
(Pele Yoetz, Ka'as)

DAY 101

Living the Mitzvah

Do I Have to Give the Perpetrator the Benefit of the Doubt?

You find out that someone is planning to do something to harm your friend, but according to the mitzvah of judging others favorably, you feel that you should assume there's some other explanation and not stir up trouble. Are you right?

י"א טבת
11 Teves
Cycle 1

י"א אייר
11 Iyar
Cycle 2

י"ב אלול
12 Elul
Cycle 3

The Dilemma:

Your friend tells you that he's had it with his business partner and he's going to "line things up" so that he can break up the business in a way that gives him more than his fair share of the assets. In fact, he has already begun the process. Although you're not personal friends with the partner, you know he is a good, honest person and hate to see him victimized. On the other hand, maybe your friend is just talking big and will calm down. Is this just an instance of bravado, or something about which you should warn the other party?

The Halachah:

Judging favorably is a mitzvah; however, it shouldn't come at someone else's expense. The partner should be warned. Be careful to report only the words you heard without exaggeration.

Nesiv Chaim, Introduction to Klal 10, Hilchos Loshon Hora

REMEMBER
Prevent harm even when no harm is meant.

11 Teves – לע"נ צבי בן חיים יעקב ז"ל
Dedicated by the Panish family

11 Iyar – לע"נ שרגא בן זאב ז"ל נלב"ע י"א אייר תשע"ח

12 Elul – In memory of Noson *ben* Avraham Moshe Alter *z"l*
By his loving daughter and son-in-law, Devorah & Ken Rich

Grow Your Self-Control

Try Saying Nothing at All

People love to talk. If you're sitting with a group of people, they are likely to look askance at you if you seem to have nothing to say. Keeping up your end of the conversation is part of the social contract.

However, Chazal see things differently: "All my life I have been raised among the wise, and I have found nothing better for the body than silence" (*Pirkei Avos* 1:17). What is the value of saying nothing? One benefit is that it builds the power of restraint. If you can sit quietly when you feel like jumping in to give your two-cents-worth, you can keep yourself still when negative words come to mind.

One rebbi says that he practices this skill at yeshivah staff meetings. "People love to discuss everything from discipline to how some kids still can't read Chumash to scheduling. They even debate what's on the lunch menu every day. The truth is, a lot of people like to have their say, but nothing really changes as a result. So I just let everyone else have the floor. I certainly have my thoughts, but I'm content to just think them. It's very empowering."

Looking Within: Do you tend to talk just to fill up "dead air" time, or to keep the conversation going?

Building Within: Choose an appropriate venue, in which your input is not really needed, to practice the art of silence.

QUOTE OF THE DAY

"Even a house full of *sefarim* requires a *mezuzah* at its door. Similarly, man cannot become internally holy without first sanctifying the doorways of his mouth."
(Chasam Sofer, Parashas Korach)

DAY 102

Living the Mitzvah

If My Student Discloses to Me in Confidence Information That Could Harm Someone, Do I Have to Keep the Confidence?

י"ב טבת
12 Teves
Cycle 1

י"ב אייר
12 Iyar
Cycle 2

י"ג אלול
13 Elul
Cycle 3

Teachers are on the receiving end of a lot of personal information, especially from young children who don't yet understand the boundaries of privacy. If the information is alarming, what should the teacher do?

The Dilemma:

Your third-grade student comes over to you during recess and tells you a secret: His Mommy got so mad that she yelled lots and lots of not-nice words at his Tatty. "Me and my sister got so scared. We hid in the closet so Mommy wouldn't find us and yell not-nice words at us too." What do you do with that information?

The Halachah:

Generally, a teacher shouldn't disclose family secrets leaked by an unsuspecting child. However, if there is abuse or danger involved, the proper authorities should be told. A halachic authority should be consulted without giving the family's name.

See Choshen Mishpat 388:9

REMEMBER
Keep a confidence, but prevent a calamity.

12 Teves – **Gloria Gordon** לע"נ חי' גלדא בת ברוך ע"ה נלב"ע י"א טבת
Dedicated by her daughter Tracy Gordon

12 Iyar – לע"נ ר' ישראל ארי' בן ר' ברוך יוסף הלוי ז"ל ואשתו שרה אלטא בת ר' גרשון ע"ה
לע"נ הרב שמוען צבי בן ר' שלמה דוד ז"ל

13 Elul – לע"נ יוטא בת צבי פרנקל ע"ה
מאת משפחת פרנקל

Grow Your Self-Control

The Side of Caution

The nature of conversations is that they flow. A good conversation with lots of give-and-take is sometimes called "fluid," and like fluid, the flow of words is often difficult to stop in midstream. Therefore, one of the greatest *loshon hora* prevention skills a person can acquire is the ability to close the dam. Stop speaking. Think: Should I say what I'm about to say?

The Chazon Ish observed that people very rarely regret having kept quiet when in doubt. If you later decide that you should share information, you can usually still do so, having first thought through your actions and perhaps asked a *shailah*. If, on the other hand, you spill your words without a thought, you are far more likely to end up with regrets.

Just as "counting to ten" helps people avoid blowing up in anger, "closing the dam" helps curtail *loshon hora*. In both cases, the brief delay gives our better judgment a chance to take hold. Is this piece of information really so important? Is it worth the negativity it will set in motion? Erring on the side of caution rarely turns out to be an error.

Looking Within: Are you uncomfortable with silence?

Building Within: The next time a conversation starts becoming negative, think to yourself that you have "the right to remain silent" rather than going with the flow.

QUOTE OF THE DAY

"When I speak, I [sometimes] regret it; when I do not speak, I never do. Before I speak, I control my words; once I speak, they control me."
(Sefer Chassidim 86)

DAY
103

Living the Mitzvah

Is There Any Rule Against Hearing What People Are Saying About Me?

A well-meaning friend wants to let you know that someone has been speaking negatively about you or your family. May you listen?

י"ג טבת
13 Teves
Cycle 1

י"ג אייר
13 Iyar
Cycle 2

י"ד אלול
14 Elul
Cycle 3

The Dilemma:
You're at a *simchah* when Mrs. Segal makes a beeline to your table and says, "I'm so glad you're here. I've been meaning to call you. I think you should know what people are saying about you!" May you listen to this report, or is that a violation of the Torah's law, "Do not accept a false report"?

The Halachah:
You should ask Mrs. Segal if there is any *to'eles* in your hearing the information. If there's no potential harm in the negative information that is being related, listening to it is not allowed. It will only cause you to dislike the subject of the report.

Sefer Chofetz Chaim, Hilchos Rechilus 5:2

REMEMBER
Letting negative words into your ears lets negative feelings into your heart.

13 Teves – לזכות Rena Bracha Siff & Nesanel Zvi Nagelblatt upon their marriage
י"ג טבת תשע"ו — Dedicated by Yisroel Moshe & Shoshana M. Siff

13 Iyar – As a *zechus* for our family for health, happiness, *shidduchim*, and *parnasah*
Dedicated by Dovid Yona *ben* Meir

14 Elul – לזכות אריכות ימים ושנים טובות בשמחה לאמינו מורתנו
צבי–ה בת חנה דבורה שתחי'

Grow Your Self-Control

Just Say "Later"

Forever is a long, long time. That's why, when the *yetzer hora* wants to take down our self-improvement plans, it encourages us to make grand, total and final resolutions. "I will never speak another word of *loshon hora* again!" we might say in a moment of inspiration. Sounds good to our ears, but eventually, when that inspiration starts to wane, a few words of *loshon hora* manage to sneak out of our mouths and we think, "I might as well face it. I can't change."

Therefore, a powerful strategy for maintaining our resolve is to "never say never." Instead, say "later." A thought pops into your mind in the midst of a conversation. You know somewhere inside you, where the little kernel of truth resides, that the words you are thinking are *loshon hora*. Instead of falling into the *yetzer hora's* "never" trap, tell yourself that you'll hold back for now. You're not promising yourself to never reveal the information — you're just holding back for the present.

Not surprisingly, once "later" arrives, the urge to speak has usually dissipated. Eventually we find that by winning these little battles, we win the war.

Looking Within: Have you made "never again" commitments to *shmiras haloshon* or other self-improvement resolutions? Have you succeeded?

Building Within: Recognize that you can honestly commit only to refraining from the *loshon hora* that is right in front of you at this moment. Focus on the doable rather than making shaky commitments for the future.

QUOTE OF THE DAY

"*Loshon hora* is the root and essence of most sins between man and his fellow."

(Sefer Shmiras HaLoshon, Shaar HaZechirah Ch. 1)

DAY 104

Living the Mitzvah

Should I Rebuke Someone Who Is Speaking Rechilus in Front of a Group of People?

When you're among a group of people and someone begins speaking rechilus, what's more important: *that you try to end the rechilus or that you avoid embarrassing the speaker?*

י"ד טבת
14 Teves
Cycle 1

י"ד אייר
14 Iyar
Cycle 2

ט"ו אלול
15 Elul
Cycle 3

The Dilemma:

You're at a family Chanukah party, sitting at a table with cousins. Your sister half-jokingly tells a cousin, "My mother always says that growing up, your mother had a crazy temper. She says she fought so much that she was more like a little brother. Right?" she asks, looking to you for confirmation. Meanwhile, you notice that everyone at the table is listening to your sister's tale, and your cousin isn't amused. Should you inform your sister that she's speaking *rechilus*?

The Halachah:

Even though a person is obligated to rebuke a wrongdoer, he must do so without causing embarrassment. Instead you should comment in a non-confrontational manner, "That sounds like it might be *rechilus*." The best strategy would be to try to contain the damage by changing the topic, and later on, in private, point out to the speaker that she was speaking *rechilus*.

Rambam, Hilchos Dei'os 6:8

REMEMBER
Nothing is ever repaired through shame.

14 Teves – **In loving memory of Mayer *ben* Dov Halevi *z"l***
Dedicated by the Rubinstein family, Sharon, MA

14 Iyar – **Edmund Breiner** לע"נ מנחם מענדל בן פנחס ז"ל
Deedicated by the Lipson family

15 Elul – לע"נ יוסף מאיר בן חיים ישעי' ז"ל ואשתו בילא בת מרדכי קיפפעל ע"ה

Grow Your Self-Control

Think Cool

When a certain challenging situation comes up repeatedly in your life, there are two ways to go: Each repetition of the situation can get you more and more irritated, like a pebble that rubs your foot over and over again with each new step. Or, you can decide, "If this is going to be part of my life, I'm going to figure out a way to face it without letting it get under my skin."

By choosing the second path, you eliminate a great potential source for *loshon hora* in your life. And you're following the timeless advice of the Ramban, who says in the opening of his famous *Iggeres HaRamban,* "Accustom yourself to speak gently to all people at all times."

"Accustom yourself" means prepare yourself. Think in advance of a way to deal with a stressful situation so that you can keep your cool and avoid feeling or saying anything rash. Every time you repeat your stay-cool strategy in the face of challenge, you're strengthening your self-control and building a solid barrier against the *loshon hora* that might otherwise flood into your life.

Looking Within: Think about one recurring situation that tends to upset your emotional balance, and ask yourself what's going on in your mind when that happens.

Building Within: Reframe that situation, either by trying to see it from the other person's perspective or by some other means that gets rid of the feeling of personal affront.

QUOTE OF THE DAY

"A person whose main focus in life is self-improvement will feel the greatest joy on those days that his challenges are most difficult."

(Rabbi Yosef Yozel Hurvits, the Alter of Novardok)

DAY 105

Living the Mitzvah

If Someone in a Position of Authority Wants to Tell Me Rechilus, Do I Have to Rebuke Him?

Your boss loves to confide in you. How far do you have to go in an effort to stop him and protect yourself?

ט"ו טבת
15 Teves
Cycle 1

ט"ו אייר
15 Iyar
Cycle 2

ט"ז אלול
16 Elul
Cycle 3

The Dilemma:
You are a young attorney who works for your father-in-law, a partner in a large, successful firm. In an effort to give you a "heads-up," he occasionally comes into your office, asks how you're doing, and then tells you what each of the other partners and senior attorneys think about your performance. You learn that there's a lot of jealousy toward you as the boss's son-in-law, expressed in cruel comments. May you listen to your father-in-law's reports? Must you rebuke him for speaking *rechilus*?

The Halachah:
You should not be listening to *rechilus* and you may not believe it. If you feel that rebuking your father-in-law/boss will come at the price of your job, you're not required to do it because we're not required to sacrifice money for the mitzvah of *tochachah* (rebuke). You should try not to listen and make every effort to change the subject or end the conversation. Where possible you should try to convey that you prefer not to hear. You should make some attempt to show that you don't want to hear this information, so that you won't be guilty of flattery.

Sefer Chofetz Chaim, Hilchos Loshon Hora 6:5 with Be'er Mayim Chaim 9

REMEMBER
If you can't beat 'em, at least don't join 'em.

15 Teves – **In memory of Noach *ben* Yehuda *z"l***
Dedicated by Mr. & Mrs. Eli Friedman

15 Iyar – לע"נ הרב אהרן בן אליהו ז"ל נלב"ע כ"ט תמוז
ואשתו הרבנית לאה בת אריה מרדכי חיים ע"ה נלב"ע ט"ו אייר

16 Elul – לזכות הלל בן אלעזר הכהן נ"י
Dedicated by his parents

Grow Your Self-Control

Quiet Down

Were you ever in a noisy place, a wedding for instance, at which the music was blaring full blast, when all of a sudden the noise stopped? You could almost feel your body relax and your senses calm down, even if you hadn't realized that you were tense. Quiet has a way of instilling tranquility in our hearts.

That's why the Ramban, in his famous letter of advice called *Iggeres HaRamban,* advises that we "speak gently (*b'nachas*) to all people at all times." Speaking *b'nachas*, even when we're not happy with what's going on at the moment, has the power to center us, keep our emotions from taking over, and thereby allow us to react wisely.

We've all seen the magic of a teacher who quiets a noisy class by lowering his own voice. Instead of yelling above the din, the teacher gets the students to quiet down so that they can hear what he is saying. We can use this trick on ourselves. By quieting our voice, we get our raging emotions to quiet down too. Then, we can truly hear what our wise inner teacher is saying.

Looking Within: Does your tone get loud and strident when you're trying to make a point?

Building Within: *Nachas* is a word that denotes inner peace and pleasure. Lower your voice by thinking about doing so as a pleasant experience, as an embrace of tranquility, rather than a mighty battle to restrain your emotions.

QUOTE OF THE DAY

"The gentle words of the wise are heard."
(Koheles 9:17)

DAY 106

Living the Mitzvah

What Can I Do If There's Someone in My Life Who Is Always Gossiping?

Whether it's out of a desire for attention, a cynical view of life or some other reason, there are those who always have tales to tell. If such a person is in your life, how can you mitigate the damage?

ט"ז טבת
16 Teves
Cycle 1

ט"ז אייר
16 Iyar
Cycle 2

י"ז אלול
17 Elul
Cycle 3

The Dilemma:
Once a month, you and your family go to your sister's home for Shabbos. Everyone enjoys the time together, but there's one glitch. Your sister is an inveterate gossip. Her conversation is filled with stories — most of them negative — about neighbors and friends. Your husband feels you should limit your visits to avoid hearing her tales. You, however, feel it's more important to maintain the closeness with your sister. Do you have to curtail your visits to avoid hearing *rechilus*?

REMEMBER

Steer clear of flying rechilus.

The Halachah:
If you can influence your sister to improve, that is the ideal response. If you know that wouldn't work, then avoiding her and the situation would be the next option if this won't cause any hard feelings. If, however, the situation is unavoidable, then it should be minimized as much as possible.

Sefer Chofetz Chaim, Hilchos Loshon Hora 9:4

16 Teves – As a *zechus* for finding a *zivug* for Dalia Rivka *bas* Tamara

16 Iyar – Mina *bas* Moshe לע"נ מינה בת משה ע"ה
As a *zechus* for my family by Syvia Felendler (Linker)

17 Elul – Naomi Benyowitz לע"נ נעמי ליבא בת ר' אברהם ע"ה
Dedicated by her children

Grow Your Self-Control

Be Your Own Mentor

Anger is a human trait that only the rarest individuals conquer completely. That means that the rest of us, if we want to avoid hurting others, are in a constant battle to rein ourselves in. Many people think that even if they win some battles, they'll ultimately lose the war against anger. And when that's a person's outlook, he may not try so very hard to maintain his equanimity when it's challenged.

But there's another way to look at the situation. Rather than focusing on the inevitability of failing once in a while, one man tried instead to build upon the skills he employed on the occasions that he succeeded.

"I thought back to times when I reacted to a setback in a way I was proud of. I tried to think, 'What kept me calm?'" He explains, "I realized that whatever worked in those instances were tools I had inside me. After all, I don't blow up every time something goes wrong. So that means that I *can* control myself. It's *not* a futile effort, because I do have the ability."

He stresses that this isn't a one-time exercise. The more time a person puts into thinking about how he manages to succeed against anger, the stronger those tools become.

Looking Within: Do you think of yourself as someone who is in control of your anger?

Building Within: Think of a situation that tends to set off your anger and mentally rehearse how to deal with it. Then, when the situation comes up, you will be prepared with a calm, productive response.

QUOTE OF THE DAY

"Who is mighty? One who conquers his evil impulse!"

(Ben Zoma, Pirkei Avos 4:1)

DAY 107

Living the Mitzvah

What If I Have Good Reason for Listening to Rechilus, but the Speaker Doesn't Know It?

Your friend starts telling you a story that would be rechilus if not for the fact that the information is useful to you. However, the speaker doesn't know that. Is the speaker speaking rechilus?

י"ז טבת
17 Teves
Cycle 1

י"ז אייר
17 Iyar
Cycle 2

י"ח אלול
18 Elul
Cycle 3

The Dilemma:
Walking home from shul one Friday night, your friend confides in you that Mr. Blumberg, a financial adviser, is being investigated for fraud, and your friend himself lost money with him. Your friend doesn't know that you've just begun to invest with Mr. Blumberg and he's trying to persuade you to invest more, with promises of great returns. Is your friend speaking *rechilus*? What should you do about it?

The Halachah:
Unless the speaker knows that there's a constructive purpose to your listening, he is speaking *rechilus*, and you, by listening to it, are encouraging him. Therefore, as soon as you become aware that he's telling you something important, let him know as well.

Sefer Chofetz Chaim, Hilchos Loshon Hora 4:11

REMEMBER
If you're listening for a good reason, say so.

17 Teves – James Victor לע"נ החבר חיים בן החבר יהודה הלוי ז"ל
Dedicated by Aryeh & Yehudis Victor

17 Iyar – *Brachah* and *hatzlachah* for the whole family
Mr. and Mrs. Moshe Gewirtz

18 Elul – לע"נ חיים שמואל בן אברהם דוב שערמאן ז"ל

Grow Your Self-Control

Don't Get Stuck With the Bill

If *loshon hora* caused the same immediate reaction as anger or violence, we would find it much easier to control. Most people try very hard not to strike anyone or yell at them because, besides the inherent wrong in doing so, they don't want to cause tears or rage.

With *loshon hora,* however, the people around us more often dissolve into laughter or lean toward us with interest. They're eating it up. It doesn't *feel* like we're doing something wrong, at least in the moment.

The Chofetz Chaim offers this analogy: Your friend invites you to dinner. He says, "It's on me. The sky's the limit!" He urges you to order the prime rib. "How about a nice bottle of wine?" he adds. As your pareve ice cream *flambé* with shaved chocolate arrives at the end of the feast, your friend excuses himself. The minutes tick by. The bill comes. Your magnanimous friend has disappeared. Now the meal's on you.

Loshon hora can be delicious, fascinating and hysterically funny. But when we get to *Olam Haba,* the bill arrives, and all the people who were sharing the table with you, listening and laughing, are nowhere to be found. If we remember this, says the Chofetz Chaim, then no matter how great the *loshon hora* seems to taste, we'll pass up the momentary pleasure so as not to get stuck with the eternal debt.

Looking Within: How do you react when a *loshon hora* conversation gets going? Are you enjoying it, eager for the next detail, or feeling uncomfortable?

Building Within: Use the Chofetz Chaim's image of being stuck with the bill — one you cannot begin to afford — to help you change the subject to a positive or a neutral one.

QUOTE OF THE DAY

"A man's entire essence and station [in his spiritual life] is determined by how much he values his potential."
(Mishnas R' Aaron, Vol.1, p. 151)

DAY 108

Living the Mitzvah

May I Ask for Pertinent Information That Would Otherwise Be Rechilus?

Someone knows something that you need to know for a constructive purpose. Are you allowed to ask him for the information?

י"ח טבת
18 Teves
Cycle 1

י"ח אייר
18 Iyar
Cycle 2

י"ט אלול
19 Elul
Cycle 3

The Dilemma:

Three times already you've gotten through the interview process for a new job, only to be turned down once the references were checked. You are fairly certain that one of your references at your last job is speaking against you. May you ask someone at the company to find out if there are people speaking against you?

The Halachah:

You're allowed to ask for information that is constructive for you to know, but you have to let the speaker know clearly that this is permitted. Also, you can only listen to the information that's pertinent. If your informant goes further, you have to stop him.

Sefer Chofetz Chaim, Hilchos Loshon Hora 4:11 [with the first note ad loc.]

REMEMBER

If you need to know, you can ask with caution.

18 Teves – לע"נ יעקב בן שמאול חיים ואסתר מלכה ז"ל נלב"ע י"ז טבת
Dedicated by the Badani family

18 Iyar – לע"נ שלום דובער בן הרב יעקב ישראל זובער ז"ל
Dedicated by Izzy Zuber and family

19 Elul – **Dedicated to my daughter Yael in honor of our daily learning**

Grow Your Self-Control

Me vs. Me

People who struggle with *loshon hora* often say, "I know it's wrong, but I can't stop myself." Indeed, how does a person stop himself? When your "self" is on both sides of the fight, straining to hold back and at the same time, urging you to speak, how can you give the "home-team advantage" to your better self?

Rav Eliyahu Dessler (*Consulting the Wise*, p. 225) advises: "See the negative urge as an outside intruder, the *yetzer hora* buzzing in your ear. The real you, the *neshamah* that wants a strong connection with Hashem, can then fight back.

"Speak to the *yetzer hora* as if you were speaking to a different person. As Rabbeinu Asher says, 'Shout at the evil inclination who tries to entice you to do improper things'... Also we find in the Talmud (*Nedarim* 9b) that someone said to the *yetzer hora*, 'Why are you conceited about a world that is not really yours?' "

If the *yetzer hora* were a small child nagging you to do something dangerous, you'd have no trouble saying "That's enough! I don't want to hear another word about it." Although you know he's bound to continue nagging, you and he both know that he's not in control.

Looking Within: Do you head into a battle against *loshon hora* feeling like the conquering hero or the victim of an ambush?

Building Within: Follow Rabbeinu Asher's advice. Think of a powerful phrase you can say out loud or to yourself that will put your better self in control of your conversation.

QUOTE OF THE DAY

"If only [those who fast and afflict themselves] would realize that they would be better off eating and drinking and instead accepting upon themselves a "fast of speech."

(Toldos Chofetz Chaim in Sefer Me'oros HaGedolim)

DAY 109

Living the Mitzvah

Why Shouldn't I Believe Credible Rechilus?

Someone tells you what another person said about you. You're not supposed to believe it, but it certainly sounds believable. What can you tell yourself?

The Dilemma:
Your brother tells you that your father has said that you don't put enough effort into controlling your children's behavior. Sounds right to you — he's said the same thing to your face many times. Nevertheless, it's insulting to think he's saying it to your brother as well. You know you shouldn't believe the *rechilus,* but what else can you think?

The Halachah:
Rechilus, by its nature, is secondhand information that cannot be trusted. The reason is that there is no way to have the whole picture of what was said, how it was said and under what circumstances. You should be *dan l'chaf zechus* that your father was trying to get your brother to speak to you about this issue.

Sefer Chofetz Chaim, Hilchos Rechilus 5:1

י"ט טבת
19 Teves
Cycle 1

י"ט אייר
19 Iyar
Cycle 2

כ אלול
20 Elul
Cycle 3

REMEMBER
Don't believe what you don't hear with your own ears.

19 Teves – As a *zechus* for our family
Dedicated by Nathan & Dvora Liebster

19 Iyar – In honor of our children
Zoey & Eitan Rosenfeld and Elijah Abraham & Nili Rose Glaubach

20 Elul – לע"נ יהושע בן חיים יצחק ז"ל נלב"ע ב' כסלו
לע"נ צירל בת משולם דוב ע"ה נלב"ע כ' אלול

Grow Your Self-Control

As Popular as a Snake

People who speak *loshon hora* often do so because they think it's entertaining for their listeners. Being in the know and having a good story to tell seem to be the path to popularity. However, the Torah teaches us a different view.

In Gan Eden, the world's first sin came about because of the *loshon hora* of the snake, who told Chava that Hashem had forbidden the fruit of the *Eitz Hadaas* because He wanted to prevent mankind from acquiring His knowledge. It was just a power play, the snake implied, and Chava believed his story. The result was mankind's downfall and all the troubles of mortal man. But the snake's punishment was, in effect, unpopularity. "And I shall place hatred between you and the woman, and between your seed and her seed. They shall bruise your head, and you shall bruise their heel" (*Bereishis* 3:15).

"When you feel like passing along a negative story, think of the snake hissing spiteful words into people's ears," one high school teacher told her students. "You might imagine that people are going to enjoy what you have to tell them, but in the end, if you act like the snake, you end up like the snake. People run from you."

Looking Within: Do you sometimes find yourself enjoying the position of being the one "in the know" about someone else's flaws or troubles?

Building Within: Think about how you feel toward people who always have something critical to say, and try not to let that type of attitude become part of your personality.

QUOTE OF THE DAY

"When someone speaks *loshon hora,* he becomes contemptible even in the eyes of his listeners."
(Shaar HaZechirah Ch. 11)

DAY 110

Living the Mitzvah

If I Receive Necessary Information Through Rechilus, May I Believe It?

When you've met the standard of rechilus for a constructive purpose, are you allowed to believe what you've heard and act on it?

כ טבת
20 Teves
Cycle 1

כ אייר
20 Iyar
Cycle 2

כ"א אלול
21 Elul
Cycle 3

The Dilemma:

Your son is suddenly reluctant to go to yeshivah every morning, and comes home every afternoon in a low mood. When you ask his rebbi about this change, he informs you that a certain boy has been picking on your son. "I spoke to the boy's father about it a couple of times but unfortunately, he didn't seem very concerned. He says your son is too sensitive and he should learn how to take care of himself," the rebbi said. You want to call the boy's father and discuss the situation. May you take as a fact the rebbi's impression that the father doesn't care about his son's aggressive behavior?

The Halachah:

While you certainly have a constructive purpose for finding out what's going on in your son's school life, the information you've gleaned may not be believed as truth. When you launch your discussion with the aggressive boy's father, you are allowed to be prepared for the possibility that he *might* not feel that his son is at fault, but you may not assume that this is so. Certainly, you may not form a negative opinion of him for allowing his son's tactics to go unchallenged when you don't know firsthand that this is the case.

Sefer Chofetz Chaim, Hilchos Rechilus 5:4

REMEMBER

Believe only your own eyes and ears.

20 Teves – לע"נ אשר בן שלום ז"ל
Dedicated by Rivka Prescott

20 Iyar – As a *zechus* for our family in honor of the בר מצוה of Aaron Kerper's נ"י
Dedicated by his grandparents Sam & Esther Gross

21 Elul – As a *zechus* for *hatzlachah*, good health and *nachas* for
Shmuel *ben* Miriam and Elisheva *bas* Elianora

Grow Your Self-Control

Because You Can't Un-send

Tzippy, a young woman who learns shmiras haloshon each day, gave this account of how her increased awareness saved her from an irreversible mistake.

I got an email from a cousin asking for information for my aunt (my cousin's mother) about a girl she knew. I thought she wanted the information for *shidduch* purposes, so I started writing some personal information that would have been important for that. But then I started thinking. If I send my cousin the information, and she passes it on to her mother, then two people are going to know personal information that they don't need to know. So I decided to delete that information and I sent her back an email saying that her mother should get directly in touch with the person who knew this information.

A couple of days later, I saw my cousin and she told me that I had completely misunderstood her email. She just needed the girl's contact information because her mother had something to send her. I was so glad that I thought before I sent that email with all that personal information in it, because it wouldn't have been *l'to'eles* at all.

Looking Within: When you communicate via social media or email, do you get caught up in the back-and-forth without thinking too much about what message you're transmitting?

Building Within: Make it a habit to ask yourself before sending any instant communication: "Do I have to say this? Do I have to say it now?"

QUOTE OF THE DAY

"Do not demean any man, nor discount any thing. For there is no person without his time, nor a thing without its place." *(Pirkei Avos 4:3)*

DAY 111

Living the Mitzvah

May I Accept One Person's Negative Interpretation of Words or an Act That, According to Another Person, Was an Innocent Occurrence?

כ"א טבת
21 Teves
Cycle 1

כ"א אייר
21 Iyar
Cycle 2

כ"ב אלול
22 Elul
Cycle 3

Two people hear the same words said about you. One relays the incident to you innocently, believing there was nothing offensive involved. The other, however, interprets the situation as an insult to you. May you believe the second person?

The Dilemma:

You missed out on a family *simchah*. A few weeks later, you bump into two cousins who were there. "How was the wedding?" you ask. One tells you, "It was great! Everyone at our table was asking where you were, though. They said they were glad you didn't make the long drive!" The other cousin adds, "Certainly, they said they were glad you didn't make the long drive! They meant that they were enjoying the evening and you would have ruined it." May you believe that the comment was meant as an insult?

REMEMBER

Don't look at the dark side.

The Halachah:

First of all, the negative report is *rechilus* and shouldn't be believed. Second, when there is an insight that transforms an innocent word or act into something malicious, we are not permitted to believe that interpretation.

Sefer Chofetz Chaim, Hilchos Rechilus 4:1

21 Teves – As a merit for protecting the *Yidden* in *Eretz Yisrael*, America and throughout the world all united together.

21 Iyar – In honor of our children, Miri, Shlomo, Esti, Avigayil and Gila Dedicated by their loving parents

22 Elul – As a *zechus* for our children Tova and Dovid Tzvi Dedicated by Bob & Liora Refua

Grow Your Self-Control

Keep the Water Cool

What happens when you put a pot of cold water on a low flame? It heats up. You might not even notice; perhaps there are a few little bubbles around the edges. But then, if you suddenly turn the flame up to its highest setting, your pot of "cool" water boils over.

This is what happens to us, as well, when we keep our thoughts and mood on a constant low flame. The *Iggeres HaRamban* advises, "Accustom yourself to speak softly to everyone at all times," in order to avoid becoming angry. Rabbi Ephraim Wachsman says that while the words "at all times" are usually interpreted to mean "even in the worst of times," we should also apply that advice to the quiet, calm times in life.

When nothing in particular is happening, when we're sitting on the subway heading home, when we're washing dishes or eating dinner or working out at the gym…where are our thoughts? If they are on irritating, anxiety-producing subjects, we are keeping our emotional pot on a low flame. Then if something arises to challenge us, we'll instantly boil over. Therefore, a powerful way to maintain our equilibrium when things get tough is to nurture our sense of serenity when things are normal. Pleasant subjects are just as easy to contemplate as unpleasant ones. By noticing what we're thinking and switching tracks when necessary, we get the full measure of benefit from the Ramban's advice. "All times" means the good times, too.

Looking Within: What do you think about when your mind is wandering?

Building Within: Write a list of 15 or 20 constant positives in your life that you can switch to when you find yourself caught up with negative thoughts.

QUOTE OF THE DAY

"A powerful way to maintain our equilibrium when things get tough is to nurture our sense of serenity when things are normal."

(Rabbi Ephraim Wachsman)

DAY 112

Living the Mitzvah

If I Can't Believe Constructive Rechilus, of What Purpose Is It to Me?

There seems to be a contradiction in the idea of constructive rechilus. If we're not allowed to believe it, how is it constructive?

כ"ב טבת
22 Teves
Cycle 1

כ"ב אייר
22 Iyar
Cycle 2

כ"ג אלול
23 Elul
Cycle 3

The Dilemma:

You worked for several years as a successful salesman for a clothing store. Now you're opening a store of your own in another locale. A former coworker tells you that your ex-employer is angry that you'll be competing with him and has been telling people that you "walked off with all my proprietary information" and should be considered "a thief." These negative rumors could ruin your business, but what can you do with this information if you're not allowed to believe it?

The Halachah:

You're not allowed to accept your coworker's report as fact or let it change your feelings about your former employer. However, you are allowed to investigate the situation and, if you find it to be true, to take whatever allowable action you can to prevent further harm to yourself.

Sefer Chofetz Chaim, Hilchos Rechilus 5:4

REMEMBER
Don't believe, but don't be naive.

22 Teves – **Dedicated to my dear children and all children of *Klal Yisrael* May they be *shomrei Torah u'mitzvos* with great joy all their life.**

22 Iyar – **Dedicated as a *zechus* by the Grunfeld family**

23 Elul – **Rose Honikman *a"h*** לע"נ זקנתי רשקה בת אליעזר ע"ה
Dedicated by Peretz Chaim & Zahava Levin and family

Grow Your Self-Control

The No-Call List

You have the right to remove your name from telemarketers' lists if you don't want to be bothered with their calls. Once you're on that no-call list, you won't be annoyed with salesman after salesman, all calling you to decide if you want to donate to this cause or that, purchase this product or that, attend this event or that. You're free to seek out the information that's relevant to you and be spared the rest.

People who refuse to listen to *loshon hora* discover that they end up in that very same enviable position. Knowing that they're not interested in the tales of their fellow Jews, people stop "selling" it to them. There's simply no point. Like people on the no-call list, they've announced to the world, "Don't bother me with this nonsense. I'll find out what I need to know and I don't want to hear about the rest."

This means that avoiding *loshon hora* gets easier the longer a person consistently rejects it. The challenges dwindle as people stop thinking of you as a potential buyer of their wares. You get to live in peace.

Looking Within: Do people think of you as someone who would be offended by *loshon hora,* or as someone who might be interested?

Building Within: Remember that every time you turn away a *loshon hora* "salesman," you are making the mitzvah easier for yourself in the future.

QUOTE OF THE DAY

"All worlds depend upon [man's words]; their entire bearing corresponds to man's actions, words and conduct."

(Derashos R' Chaim M'Volozhin)

CHAPTER 12

Tolerance — Let Hashem Be the Judge

What our eyes take in, our minds will inevitably assess. Do we like what we see? Do we think it's good, bad or somewhere in between? While we work on developing a positive perspective on our world and its inhabitants, we might still generate some negative thoughts about others. That's when tolerance becomes our greatest tool. Learning to keep in mind that Hashem has created us all and that each of us is a "work in progress" can prevent a negative thought from becoming negative feelings and words.

DAY 113

Living the Mitzvah

If Someone Who I Know Really Cares About Me Tells Me Constructive Rechilus, May I Believe It?

כ"ג טבת
23 Teves
Cycle 1

כ"ג אייר
23 Iyar
Cycle 2

כ"ד אלול
24 Elul
Cycle 3

There are people in your life who you know would never mislead you. Therefore, when they tell you rechilus for a constructive purpose, you are inclined to believe it. Does the reliability of your source make a difference?

The Dilemma:

One day, you call a paper-goods supplier that your bagel shop has been using for years and put in an extra-large order to accommodate the Chanukah rush. Much to your surprise, the supplier asks for payment on delivery. When you question him, you find out that rumors of your impending bankruptcy have ruined your credit. However, your business is not in trouble at all; it's thriving! Where are the rumors coming from? You have a real need to know. Your brother, well-connected in the business world, discovers that a new local caterer is the source of the false rumor. May you believe him?

REMEMBER
The best intentions don't guarantee the best information.

The Halachah:

Even though your brother clearly has only your benefit in mind, you are not allowed to accept his report as fact. However, if you can't convince yourself that his report might not be true, you must at least admit that he might have misinterpreted something he heard. At the same time, you have to do what you must to protect yourself from harm in the event that his information is accurate.

Sefer Chofetz Chaim, Hilchos Rechilus 6:5

23 Teves – לע"נ יהושע בן יהודה ז"ל ואשתו מרים חנה בת יהושע גוטווירן ע"ה
לע"נ יעקב יצחק בן יהושע ז"ל

23 Iyar – לע"נ קלמן בן יעקב ז"ל נלב"ע כ"ה אייר ואשתו אסתר בת חיים ע"ה
Dedicated by their loving children Devora Berger and Reuven Sarett

24 Elul – לע"נ חי' מלכה בת יעקב שלמה הכהן שכטר ע"ה
מאת משפחת פרנקל

Grow Your Tolerance

No Offense

Three hours past his bedtime, a toddler has a meltdown. He's lying on the floor kicking his legs, and when his mother comes to pick him up she gets a good hard kick in the shin. As soon as the initial pain passes, she resumes her effort to get her cranky son ready for bed. She doesn't think, "How dare he kick me!" She knows he's not acting out of dislike or disrespect. There's no evil intention, just a lack of self-control.

Our anger is much less aroused when we don't ascribe negative intentions to people who do or say things we don't like. Therefore, a great strategy to avoid anger and the *loshon hora* it spawns is to stop looking for insults. Realize that most people "kick" because they aren't paying attention to what they're doing. They're tired, overwrought, emotional, forgetful, or even angry at something else. Once we squelch the voice that says, "He *intentionally* insulted me," our own anger subsides.

Looking Within: When someone does something that irritates or upset you, do you assume that the person doesn't care about you?

Building Within: The next time you take offense at someone's actions or words, tell yourself that he didn't realize how you would be affected — even if he should have realized.

QUOTE OF THE DAY

"Through developing the quality of *savlanus*, tolerance, the quality of *shmiras haloshon* is easily attainable."

(Sefer Shmiras HaLoshon, Shaar HaTevunah Ch. 8)

DAY 114

Living the Mitzvah

If Someone Relates Rechilus in Public, Where It Is Likely to Be Challenged If It's Untrue, Does That Make It More Believable?

כ"ד טבת
24 Teves
Cycle 1

כ"ד אייר
24 Iyar
Cycle 2

כ"ה אלול
25 Elul
Cycle 3

The speaker is speaking in front of a whole group of people. He's not being secretive at all, and sounds quite authoritative. Is his rechilus still not to be believed?

The Dilemma:

You are the division head of a large summer camp. You're having a planning meeting with the counselors and staff. The head counselor says, "I was speaking to Rabbi Funshein (the camp's owner) and he told me that you don't seem like the right person for the job. The ideas you came up with so far are not exciting and the kids are bored with your program!" Should you believe his report, which he is repeating in front of 16 counselors, two lifeguards, and the arts and crafts director?

The Halachah:

A person's willingness to repeat *rechilus* in front of others is no proof that it's true or accurate. However, if you feel that the information is important for you to know — perhaps Rabbi Funshein is unhappy with your work and your job is in jeopardy — then you may seek further information.

Sefer Chofetz Chaim, Hilchos Rechilus 6:1

REMEMBER
An air of authority doesn't prove authenticity.

24 Teves – **Dr. Albert Hornblass** לע"נ אברהם בן משה ז"ל נלב"ע כ"ז טבת
Dedicated by the Hornblass and Dushey families

24 Iyar – **In memory of Aryeh Leib *ben* Zev Wolf *z"l***
Dedicated by Mildred Goldczer

25 Elul – **As a *zechus* for *hatzlachah* for our children**
Dedicated by Mr. and Mrs. Isaac Ash

Grow Your Tolerance

It's Not You, It's Them

People have a natural tendency to strike back when they're insulted. If they can't strike back directly, they will do so indirectly by telling others about the insult they endured. This is often the dynamic that spawns *loshon hora*.

The Ralbag suggests a different way to react. "There is no need to take to heart the emotional outbursts of people who insult you," he says, "because this is only a reflection of their own suffering and bitterness. When people are in pain they are likely to say thoughtless things, and this is not necessarily an accurate reflection of the reality of the situation" (*Consulting the Wise*, p. 62). Knowing that, Moshe and Aaron didn't reply when the Jewish people complained against them. They realized that the angry words arose from the people's fears.

Using that idea, Tova B. says she found a way to make peace with a difficult boss and to encourage workers to be more forgiving of her as well. "I told my coworkers, 'Imagine what it's like to wake up every day and have her level of anxiety. We only have to deal with her a few hours a day. She has to deal with herself all day, every day.' Somehow this calmed everyone down. And with less friction, my boss also calmed down."

Looking Within: Do people who annoy or insult you realize they are doing it or is it part and parcel of their personality? Does this make a difference in how you process their words and actions?

Building Within: If there are people in your life with poor self-control, poor social skills or perhaps some psychological issues, deal with their offensive behavior by being grateful that you do not have their challenges.

QUOTE OF THE DAY

"One must skimp on his basic needs to buy [a *Sefer Chofetz Chaim* and *Shmiras Haloshon*], because without them, a Jew may never open his mouth to speak, nor his ear to hear."
(HaGaon Rav Shmuel Haminer, introduction to Sefer Ikkarei Dinim)

DAY 115

Living the Mitzvah

May I Believe a Report Conveyed by Someone Whose Integrity Is Above Reproach?

A highly respected individual tells you something another person said about you because he feels you must protect yourself. Can you believe the information based on this person's unassailable integrity?

כ"ה טבת
25 Teves
Cycle 1

כ"ה אייר
25 Iyar
Cycle 2

כ"ו אלול
26 Elul
Cycle 3

The Dilemma:

You encounter your former Rosh Yeshivah at a *simchah*. He calls you aside and tells you that he's glad he met you, because there was something you need to know: He had met Moshe K., your roommate from yeshivah days, who is on your resume. "He told me that you used to have a serious drinking problem when you were in yeshivah, and that when people call him for information about you he tells them to watch out. I told him of course that it wasn't true at all, but you need to know what's going on." May you believe the Rosh Yeshivah?

REMEMBER
Nowadays, no one's that perfect.

The Halachah:

Although there is a halachah that permits believing individuals of great integrity, the Chofetz Chaim ruled that in his day, no one could claim to meet that standard. Therefore, in our own day, that halachah should not be relied upon. Hence, you are not allowed to believe outright that Moshe K. is saying this about you. However, as in other instances of constructive *rechilus*, you should take steps to investigate and protect yourself from harm.

Sefer Chofetz Chaim, Hilchos Rechilus 6:7

25 Teves – לע"נ שרה אסתר ע"ה בת ר' ישראל חיים יבלח"ט נלב"ע כ"ה טבת תשע"ב
Sorala (Follman) Krigsman

25 Iyar – לע"נ הרב שלמה בן נפתלי מרגלית זצ"ל–נלב"ע י"ד שבט
והרבנית חוה רבקה מרגלית בת אברהם ע"ה–נלב"ע כ"ה אייר

26 Elul – לע"נ הרב שמואל אליהו ז"ל בן הרב רפאל אומן יבלח"ט
Dedicated by Rabbi & Mrs. Refoel Auman and family

Grow Your Tolerance

Nature's Bounty

Some people have a critical eye. Even those they love and respect are subject to their scrutiny. In their view, seeing the flaws is important. It means having high standards and pushing others to be the best they can be. However, if our eyes always zoom in on what's wrong, we set ourselves a monumental *shmiras haloshon* challenge. How do we keep ourselves from saying what we are constantly thinking?

One answer might be to reframe our definition of "flaw." If we change the word to "nature," we will realize that there are many types of people with many varying perspectives and ways of doing things. The aggressive person may see the easygoing person as lazy, but this is simply not true. The easygoing person is exactly what Hashem created him to be, in order to accomplish what Hashem put him on earth to accomplish. Likewise, the creative person may not be very well organized. The well-organized person might be unimaginative. The accepting person might lack boundaries. The disciplined person might lack empathy.

Every person is on this earth to work on himself. When we accept people for who they are and stop expecting them to be who we want them to be, our critical eye stops feeding our minds disparaging thoughts about others. Once we appreciate and accept others, we can be effective in helping them to improve.

Looking Within: Are you generally critical of others, either because of a negative attitude or out of a positive desire to correct and help them?

Building Within: Try the above strategy of recognizing someone's innate nature and note the impact on your relationship.

QUOTE OF THE DAY

A piece of dry bread with tranquility is better than a house full of offerings with strife.
(Mishlei 17:1)

DAY
116

Living the Mitzvah

May I Believe Rechilus That Is Said by Someone Who Has No Idea That the Information Is Hurtful?

You overhear something that someone said about you. However, the person who made the remark had no idea that he was stirring up animosity. May you believe what he said?

כ"ו טבת
26 Teves
Cycle 1

כ"ו אייר
26 Iyar
Cycle 2

כ"ז אלול
27 Elul
Cycle 3

The Dilemma:

You invited a family in your neighborhood to join you for a Shabbos lunch. The wife politely declined, saying that she had been sick in bed all week and wanted to rest as much as possible on Shabbos. Later that week, you meet another neighbor who tells you that the same family that declined your invitation is going to join her for Shabbos lunch. "Michal said she was so happy to have a lunch out. She, in fact, was just invited to another house, but made an excuse because but made an excuse because she couldn't take one of those meals that go on forever."

The Halachah:

As in the case of *loshon hora*, such a report should not be believed. You should make every effort to reject or explain away the actions.

Sefer Chofetz Chaim, Hilchos Loshon Hora 7:6-7, Hilchos Rechilus 6:8

REMEMBER
Innocent remarks can still be inaccurate.

26 Teves – **In memory of Max Traeger** לע"נ מרדכי בן דוב ז"ל
Dedicated by the Mendelsons and the Mendelson great-grandchildren

26 Iyar – **Dedicated as a *zechus* by the Grunfeld family**

27 Elul – לע"נ שמואל בן משה ז"ל
Dedicated by the Metzger family

Grow Your Tolerance

The Test

Do you ever wish there was a gauge for spirituality — some gizmo that could scan your eyeballs and tell you where you stand in terms of meeting your spiritual potential? That way you couldn't fool yourself into thinking you were more righteous than you actually are, or on the other hand, you might find out that you're not giving yourself enough credit.

As it turns out, there is such a test, and Rav Yeruchem Levovitz describes it simply: "The test of a person's spirituality is how he treats other people."

What's the connection? Every person is a creation of Hashem. The more we show respect to Hashem's creations, the more we express our awareness of Hashem. Rav Yeruchem further explains, "If someone is devoted to speaking positively about others, this is strong proof that he is a *tzaddik*. This trait shows that he relates to his soul" (*Consulting the Wise*, p. 139).

This teaches us that the more we make an effort to look past someone's misjudgments, character flaws, or irritating traits, and to see instead the pure soul inside him, the more we will be able to overcome the urge to speak ill of him. Eventually, we'll find that we're measuring up to our spiritual potential.

Looking Within: When you think about prodding yourself onto higher spiritual levels, do you envision yourself becoming more — or less — tolerant of others?

Building Within: Use Rav Yeruchem's advice as a tool for jump-starting your spiritual growth. If you feel stuck and uninspired, try focusing on the Divine spark within other people in your life.

QUOTE OF THE DAY

"The test of a person's spirituality is how he treats other people."

(Rav Yeruchem Levovitz)

DAY 117

Living the Mitzvah

May I Believe a Report That's Supported by Evidence I've Seen Myself?

You hear a negative report about someone and it provides the perfect explanation for a situation you have observed with your own eyes. May you believe the report?

כ״ז טבת
27 Teves
Cycle 1

כ״ז אייר
27 Iyar
Cycle 2

כ״ח אלול
28 Elul
Cycle 3

The Dilemma:
Lately, you've been noticing that your formerly outgoing neighbor barely speaks to you as you stand together waiting for your children's school bus to arrive. One day a different neighbor tells you, "Miri decided that the people in this neighborhood are snobbish and she is looking to move out." Since Miri's standoffish behavior seems to prove the truth of the report, may you believe it?

The Halachah:
In the case of both *loshon hora* and *rechilus,* you're allowed to accept as truth a report that's backed up by conclusive circumstantial evidence. In the case at hand, though, you are not allowed to accept it as truth. There may be countless other reasons why your neighbor is not her normal ebullient self.

Sefer Chofetz Chaim, Hilchos Loshon Hora 7:10

REMEMBER
Even when you think you see what you hear, think again.

27 Teves – **Florence Presser** לע״נ פייגא נעשא בת בנימין הכהן ע״ה
Dedicated by Marilyn and Jaime Sohacheski

27 Iyar – לע״נ אסתר בת יעקב ע״ה
Dedicated by Allan and Sheila Bleich

28 Elul – לע״נ ברוך משה אברהם בן חנה דבורה ז״ל
לע״נ בת שבע בת חוה אילת ע״ה

Grow Your Tolerance

Change Seats

Two people are sitting across from each other in a restaurant. One has a view of the parking lot and the other has a view of the harbor. The one with the parking lot view complains that the restaurant doesn't have much atmosphere. "It's a beautiful atmosphere!" the one looking out at the harbor protests. "What are you talking about? You really don't appreciate anything!"

Often, our irritation with others comes from a lack of understanding of their perspective. Without living through their lives, feeling their feelings and enduring their challenges, we have no way to relate to life as they see it. A great strategy for curtailing judgmental thinking, and thereby opening the way for positive thoughts and speech, is to take the time to sit in their seat.

That doesn't mean we need to put someone through psychoanalysis before we can have a conversation with them. It simply means that if we take even one moment to contemplate the possibility that they see things from a different perspective, we can go far in our effort to judge and speak favorably of others.

Looking Within: When someone differs with you, how likely are you to try to see the situation from his side?

Building Within: Recall some times when the other person's view turned out to be right, and use that experience to motivate yourself to be open to a different perspective.

"All of creation is finite except for two things: Torah and peace."

(Menoras HaMaor, Gadol HaShalom)

QUOTE OF THE DAY

DAY 118

Living the Mitzvah

What Can I Do to Repair the Situation If I've Spoken Rechilus?

You slipped up and repeated information that caused animosity between two friends. Is there any way to make amends?

The Dilemma:
You told your husband something his older sister said about him that wasn't flattering. She felt that as his sister she had the right to make a judgment. You thought he would find it funny, but he didn't. Is there any way to undo the mess and repair the pain your report has caused?

The Halachah:
If you have spoken *rechilus*, your first step should be to tell the person you spoke to that your report was not accurate. "It sounded a lot worse when I repeated it. Your sister didn't mean an insult at all!" If the report caused friction between your husband and his sister, you should try to make *shalom* between them, and ask your sister-in-law for forgiveness.

Sefer Chofetz Chaim, Hilchos Rechilus 4:3

כ"ח טבת
28 Teves
Cycle 1

כ"ח אייר
28 Iyar
Cycle 2

כ"ט אלול*
**29 Elul*
Cycle 3

REMEMBER

Clean up your mess.

** On 29 Elul, the lesson for Day 119 should be learned together with today's lesson.*

28 Teves – לע"נ ישראל חיים בן נחום הלוי ז"ל ואשתו שרה בת יהודה לייב ע"ה
Dedicated by their sons Robert & Eddie Lowinger

28 Iyar – לזכות לחינוך הבנים

29 Elul – Mechel *ben* Yoel Wolf *Halevi* לע"נ מעכל בן יואל וואלף הלוי ז"ל
As a *zechus* for my family by Sylvia Felendler (Linker)

Grow Your Tolerance

The Best Response

Shimon is a young man who grew up in a traditional Jewish household. His family attended a Conservative synagogue and he went to Hebrew school for a few years prior to his bar mitzvah. He had no more formal contact with Judaism until 10 years later, when a Birthright trip to Israel got him interested in learning. By the age of 30, he had returned to his home town, was married, religious and the father of a little boy. That's when the problems began.

"If my parents believe in G-d as they say they do, how can they not keep the Torah?" he often wondered. "They can't pretend to be ignorant anymore, because I've explained everything to them a thousand times!" He spoke about his frustrations to his friends, resulting in oceans of *loshon hora* that he saw as completely justified.

However, the Ralbag (*Consulting the Wise,* p. 50) tells us that this is a counter-productive way to view others' mistakes. "Whenever you see that someone has made a mistake, view the situation as a learning experience to prevent yourself from making similar mistakes," he says. In Shimon's case, he could ask himself, "Aren't there areas in which my actions don't live up to my knowledge of what I should be doing?" The answer, if Shimon is human, will be "yes." With that realization, he can calm his frustrations and change a spur to *loshon hora* into a spur for growth.

Looking Within: Do you lose patience with people who don't mend their ways once you've pointed out their mistake?

Building Within: Rather than condemning such people, try to learn from their error and work to improve yourself.

QUOTE OF THE DAY

"*Loshon hora* kills three people: the speaker, the listener, and the one who is spoken about."

(Yerushalmi Peah 1:1)

DAY 119

Living the Mitzvah

How Can I Make Amends for Hearing Rechilus About Someone?

The damage is done. You've heard that someone has said something unflattering about you and you feel angry at that person. Should you ask his forgiveness?

כ"ט טבת
29 Teves
Cycle 1

כ"ט אייר
29 Iyar
Cycle 2

כ"ט אלול
29 Elul
Cycle 3

The Dilemma:

Your son told you that his friend isn't allowed to play at your house because his mother says your food isn't kosher. You're not the least bit surprised. The woman has always come across to you as elitist and critical. You are, however, furious. She doesn't know the first thing about you, your house or your *kashrus*. Later, you meet the woman at the market and she approaches you to ask if her son can come over to play on Shabbos. "He really loves your son. I think they'll be good friends!" You realize that your son must have gotten the message wrong. Should you apologize to the mother?

The Halachah:

You should not apologize. Your *teshuvah* for accepting *rechilus* is between you and Hashem. However, even if you had not met the mother, you would have been required to convince yourself that the report may not have been accurate.

Sefer Chofetz Chaim, Hilchos Rechilus 5:6,7

REMEMBER
Not everything people say is true.

29 Teves – **Harold Palokoff** לע"נ הירשל בן מאטל הכהן ז"ל נלב"ע כ"ח טבת
Molly Palokoff לע"נ מאשא בת אברהם יצחק ע"ה נלב"ע כ' אדר

29 Iyar – ***L'zechus* our children** תמימה ברכה, טלי'ה, מאירה, שיינא גיטל
Grow happily לתורה מצוות ומעשים טובים בדרך ה' — **the Mendelsons**

Grow Your Tolerance

Don't Shoot the Messenger

Imagine if no one could hurt you. You'd have nothing negative to say about anyone.

Rabbi David Ashear, the author of *Living Emunah,* explains that indeed, no one can hurt us. When people slight us or disappoint us, they cannot do us any real harm. Rather, Hashem finds another "messenger" to deliver His bounty in exactly the time and manner that is best.

One woman, a seamstress, related how this idea helped her hold her tongue. "I had a big job to do for a wedding. The whole family came to me for alterations on their gowns. I was hoping this job would cover a high summer electric bill. However, my customers didn't pay on time. I tried to tell myself that this was part of Hashem's plan. I borrowed money to pay my bill and stayed calm. A month later, my car needed an expensive repair. No sooner had I hung up from the mechanic than my customer rang the bell. She had my money — exactly what I needed to fix the car."

If we dig down beneath any positive *middah,* we come to the same root — *emunah. Shmiras haloshon* is all about knowing in our hearts that everything comes from Hashem, and that Hashem deals with us purely out of love. There is no one to scorn, reject or attack. There is only Hashem, placing challenges before us — sometimes in the form of challenging people — to strengthen us, elevate us and prime our souls to revel in the incomparable joy of His Presence.

Looking Within: Do you stop to remember that whatever is happening to you, even if it's not what you expected or believed was due to you, is what Hashem has orchestrated?

Building Within: Remember not to "shoot" or disparage the messenger. Instead, look within and assure yourself that you will always get your due, all in due time.

QUOTE OF THE DAY

"Let Heaven and Earth bear witness that after I finished studying *Sefer Chofetz Chaim* and *Shmiras Haloshon,* I sensed within myself a positive change."

(letter of the Imrei Emes)

Master Your Words, Master Your Life — Tools for Mastery

Master Your Mind

*When we think negative, we end up speaking negative. Learning how to formulate positive impressions of others is a skill that takes patience, wisdom and practice. That skill — judging others favorably — is where shmiras haloshon begins.**

Six Questions to Getting the Story Straight:

When we hear something negative about someone, our instincts tell us, "Where there's smoke, there's fire." But the Torah tells us, "Judge according to the merit." We might feel a bit foolish looking for excuses and justifications to explain someone's questionable behavior. But very often, the fool is the one who believes it without looking any deeper. Here are six questions that help you play it smart:

1. Are you sure it happened at all? *Sometimes we see it or hear it wrong.*
2. Are you sure the details are correct? *One inaccurate detail can make a big difference.*
3. Do you know if the other person intended harm? *Often the consequences are unforeseen.*
4. Do you know what the other person was thinking? *It might explain why he did what he did.*
5. Could it be an innocent, human error? *Everyone makes mistakes.*
6. Do you know what was going on at the time? *Pain, frustration, stress, illness or loss, might be a factor.*

* *Although the Torah requires us to judge others with favor and compassion, physical, verbal or emotional abuse must be addressed and corrected.*

Master the Rules

Sometimes life presents complicated scenarios in which the decision to remain silent about someone's wrongdoing can cause harm to another person. The Torah gives us the rules of *to'eles — loshon hora* for a constructive purpose — to guide us in saying what needs to be said without causing unnecessary harm.

Seven Rules of To'eles:

At times, negative information may [or must] be repeated for a constructive purpose. For instance, if you are speaking in order to:

a. help the person you are speaking about.
b. help someone victimized by the person or prevent others from being victimized.
c. resolve major disputes.
d. help others refrain from improper behavior.

Provided that:

1. **The information is accurate, based on firsthand information and careful investigation.** You must have seen the person's behavior yourself. The only time that you may repeat secondhand information is to protect someone from potential harm. Even then, it is necessary to state that you are relating secondhand information.

2. **The situation is well understood.** Any possibilities to judge the person favorably have been explored.

3. **All other options were tried.** If there is any other way to achieve the desired result, without relating the negative information, then one may not relay the negative information.

4. **You tried to speak to the person yourself, before speaking about him.** Note: This condition does not apply if speaking to the person yourself will make it impossible to achieve the desired result.

5. **Your intent is pure.** You do not bear a grudge against this person or have any reason to take pleasure in relaying this negative information.

6. **You will relate the information accurately**, without exaggeration or altering of the facts. You may also not leave out information that would minimize the severity of the person's behavior. In addition, you may say only the minimum necessary for the intended purpose.

7. **No undue harm will be caused.** If the person will receive a more severe punishment or incur more damage than *beis din* would assess, you may not relate the incident.

In addition, there must be a reasonable chance of bringing about the desired result; otherwise your words will not be *l'to'eles*.

Reminder: You must preface your words by saying that you are speaking *l'to'eles*.

Master Your Words — Put Your Words to the Test

When Something Negative Must Be Said*

Knowing the rules of *to'eles* is a vital first step, but how do we act on those rules as our day-to-day life experiences unfold? How do we avoid fooling ourselves and making mistakes? Here are six questions to ask yourself to make sure that your *to'eles* is truly constructive.

1. Is it definitely true?

Did I see it myself or hear it from a trustworthy source?

2. Is it clearly wrong?

Could I have misinterpreted it?

3. Did I try speaking directly to the person involved?

Is there any necessity to involve others?

4. Am I exaggerating?

Am I adding a little extra drama to make my point?

5. Are my words truly meant to help?

Do I dislike the person? Are my words likely to be accepted? Can the person I'm speaking to do anything about the situation?

6. Have I tried all other possible solutions?

Is there a *loshon hora*-free way to accomplish the goal?

7. How much harm will my words cause?

Will it be more than what halachah allows [the person to suffer] in this instance?

---

* These rules apply to normal "*to'eles*" situations, such as information regarding *shidduchim* or employment. However, if you know that someone is causing mental or physical harm to another, it is prohibited to keep quiet, and a *rav* should be consulted immediately.

Questions Before Asking

Whether we're making conversation, satisfying our curiosity or trying to express interest in another person's life, we often find ourselves in the position of asking a question. Sometimes, an innocuous question opens up a sore topic or causes pain we never intended. To avoid that outcome, question yourself first:

1. Do I really need (to know) the answer to this question?
2. What kind of talk will this question generate?
3. Can I rephrase this question so that it will lead to only "kosher" talk?

Master Your Hour — The Power of Machsom L'fi

The Power of Shmiras Haloshon — Multiplied!

When you form a Machsom L'fi group, you are taking the amazing merit of *shmiras haloshon* and multiplying it many times over as you and your group work together to bring the blessings of *shmiras haloshon* into the world.

What Is a Machsom L'fi?

It's really very simple. A group gets together and divides the day into one- or two-hour periods. Each person takes one time-slot in which he or she commits, *bli neder*, to be extra-careful to avoid hearing or speaking loshon hora or other forms of forbidden speech.

Isn't *Shmiras Haloshon* an Obligation All the Time?

When you break down your commitment into short periods, you'll find that you can succeed. You'll quickly realize that you really do have the power to control what you say.

Of course we are always obligated to guard our speech. But you are sure to find that these hours of special focus make you much more aware of the words you say all day, every day.

How Do I Get a Machsom L'fi Started?

The best motivation to get a Machsom L'fi started and keep it going strong is to do it as a *zechus* for someone in need of a *yeshuah, refuah* or *shidduch*.

Get enough people to cover the waking hours of the day in one- or two-hour periods.

Have each person choose a time-slot until the entire day is covered. Each person commits, *bli neder*, to be especially careful not to speak, hear or write *loshon hora* or hurtful words during his or her hour(s). A good way to start your time-slot is to say the Declaration and Prayer for Proper Speech. If you slip up (we're all human!) try again during the next hour(s) if you can, or give some *tzedakah* according to your ability.

By joining a Machsom L'fi you are taking a concrete step toward making *shmiras haloshon* a centerpiece of your life. Harness the power of your commitment by learning two *halachos* of *shmiras haloshon* each day. Not only will you gain the knowledge you need to keep the mitzvah correctly, but you will also merit the *siyata d'Shmaya* everyone needs to conquer *loshon hora* and bring Hashem's most beautiful *brachos* into our lives.

A Speech Problem and a Speech Solution: The Story of Machsom L'fi

About 30 years ago, Hindy H. had a young child who was being treated for a severe stutter, and she was very concerned. She contacted her sister, a well-known educator who lived in Eretz Yisrael, and asked her to please go to a *gadol* and ask for advice in finding a *refuah*. The sister approached Rav Meir Bransdorfer of the Eidah Hachareidis in Yerushalayim, who suggested that the family focus on *shmiras haloshon*.

Hindy's sister asked Rav Bransdorfer if he could be more specific, and Rav Bransdorfer proceeded to outline the rules for the Machsom L'fi:

A group of people should divide up the waking hours of the day, with each one committing to three hours of *shmiras haloshon* — being extra careful to refrain from loshon hora and all other forbidden speech (such as anger, hurtful words, and so on). The commitment should be taken on for a one-month period, *bli neder,* and each participant could do it as a *zechus* for a *shidduch, children, refuah,* etc.

Hindy, a reserved person, couldn't see herself pulling a group of women together, so she called up a former teacher.

"Morah," she said, "I'm not the type to organize something like this. Can you help me?" And that was the beginning of the Machsom L'fi groups. Baruch Hashem, Hindy's son's stutter went away.

Over the years, this teacher organized many more groups. Seeing how difficult it was for women to keep three hours, she sent someone to ask Rav Bransdorfer if the commitment could be for two hours. After some consideration, he agreed.

Today the Machsom L'fi is used all around the world as a way to strengthen one's grasp of *shmiras haloshon,* unite groups of Jews in a powerful spiritual enterprise, and bring merit for the many *yeshuos* needed by *Klal Yisrael.*

Machsom L'fi Sign Up Sheet

Date ______________________

Our Machsom L'fi is being done as a zechus for: ____

HOURS	NAME	ADDRESS / ZIP	PHONE#
6-8 AM	____________________ ____________________	____________________ ____________________	______________ ______________
8-10 AM	____________________ ____________________	____________________ ____________________	______________ ______________
10 AM-12 PM	____________________ ____________________	____________________ ____________________	______________ ______________
12-2 PM	____________________ ____________________	____________________ ____________________	______________ ______________
2-4 PM	____________________ ____________________	____________________ ____________________	______________ ______________
4-6 PM	____________________ ____________________	____________________ ____________________	______________ ______________
6-8 PM	____________________ ____________________	____________________ ____________________	______________ ______________
8-10 PM	____________________ ____________________	____________________ ____________________	______________ ______________
10 PM-12 AM	____________________ ____________________	____________________ ____________________	______________ ______________

This form may be copied as needed for your Machsom L'fi group.

Kabbalah/ Verbal Acceptance (without a vow)

Please recite the following prior to your Machsom L'fi hours: *I accept upon myself (without a vow) to observe the laws of shmiras haloshon, in regard to both what I say and what I listen to, during the hours of _____ to _____ as a merit for ______________________________.*

א לומר נוסח זה קודם המחסום לפי:
ני מקבל על עצמי, בלי נדר, שמירת הלשון
דיבור ושמיעה משך שעות ______ עד ______
זכות ______________________________.

The Shmiras Haloshon Shaila Hotline

Call for answers to your halachic questions regarding proper speech. 718-951-3696 • 9-10:30pm, Sun. 10:30am-12 noon ES

Master Your Meal —
The Shabbos Table Machsom L'fi

A powerful place to begin building a home imbued with *shmiras haloshon* is the Shabbos table, where the family is together and the holiness of the day sets the stage for our best selves to emerge.

Create a Shabbos of Sweetness and Harmony in Your Home:

Machsom L'fi is a program in which people commit themselves to focusing for a set period of time on the proper use of their words. Often, a Machsom L'fi is undertaken as a *zechus* for someone who is in need of a *refuah*, a *shidduch* or a personal *yeshuah*. During the set time, people concentrate on avoiding speaking and hearing *loshon hora*, gossip, slander, or *ona'as devarim* (hurtful words).

The Shabbos Table Machsom L'fi is a free CCHF program that takes the concept of a Machsom L'fi and uses it to enhance and uplift every Shabbos meal. When you exercise this particular "spiritual muscle" at your meals, you build control over your speech, and you enhance your ability to keep the mitzvah throughout the week.

Thousands of families around the world are experiencing the beauty of a warm, upbeat Shabbos table, and you can too. We provide the tools you need and you use them as best suits your family:

- **The Shabbos Menu**, a family-friendly weekly newsletter featuring a thought-provoking *shmiras haloshon* dilemma to discuss, as well as a short, inspiring story.
- An elegant reminder card for your table that includes a *kabbalah* some families use to launch the meal in the right direction.
- A weekly reminder text or call.

To join, visit: *powerofspeech.org/Shabbos* or in the USA, text: *shabbos* to 313131.

Master Your Conversations — Lessons in Listening

Mastering our relationships relies not only on how we speak to others, but on how we listen to them as well.

ARE YOU LISTENING?

Listening seems to be a simple, one-way street. Words leave the speaker's mouth and enter our ears; they have been spoken, and we have heard them.

But Shlomo Hamelech teaches us that ears are not quite enough. When he ascended to the throne, Hashem allowed him to choose the gift he most needed to succeed in his position. He asked for a "*lev shomeia,*" a "listening heart." He knew that to deal effectively with his people, he would not only have to open his ears, but open his heart to their words so that they would feel understood.

Here are some ways to evaluate your listening style and find out if the people in your life walk away from a conversation with you feeling that they've been heard.

Are You a Competitive Listener?

1. You ready your response while the speaker is speaking.
2. You love to debate and disprove others' points.
3. You don't tend to see the matter from the other person's point of view.

The speaker doesn't usually feel heard or understood.

Are You a Passive Listener?

1. You really want to hear what the other person has to say.
2. You don't feel the need to respond or probe further.
3. You're satisfied even if you don't fully understand what the speaker meant.

The speaker might not feel that you're really interested.

Are You an Active, Reflective Listener?

1. You listen attentively without formulating your response or judging.
2. You engage with the speaker, asking questions and reflecting back his comments to make sure you really understand.
3. You listen with full attention, making sure to have quiet surroundings and a clear mind.

Both the speaker and the listener end the conversation feeling they have a greater understanding of one another.

Master Your Inner World — Words From the Wise

The words that come out of our mouths are drawn from the hidden depths of our hearts and minds. When we sweeten and purify our thoughts and feelings, our words and the relationships they build automatically become sweeter as well.

1

Daven to Hashem to see the good.
Rabbi Dr. Abraham J. Twerski

When we seek to grow spiritually, our first line of action must be to ask Hashem to help us. The Rebbe Reb Elimelech of Lizhensk composed a beautiful *tefillah* (which some say before davening) in which he asks Hashem, "Help me that I should see the good in other people, and not their faults and defects."

Fulfilling *v'ahavta l'rei'acha kamocha* by seeing the good in other people is a wonderful way to prepare for *tefillah*, and a great merit and virtue through which our prayers will be answered.

2

Understand people's motivations
Rabbi Simcha Feuerman

A good way to cut down on frustration in relationships and to transform our negative view of others into a positive one, is to seek to understand others. By seeking to understand why something is important to them or why they act or think a certain way, we open a new world of harmony, respect, and happiness within our relationships.

3

Be an easy grader — give partial credit.
Dr. Meir Wikler

It's not all or nothing! Learn to see the good in those around you by giving partial credit. When someone does a favor, runs an errand, etc. — even if he didn't do exactly what you wanted — it's important to give partial credit and express appreciation for the effort and for what he *did* do.

4

Accept differences.
Rabbi Doniel Frank

We need the humility to understand that just because we do things a certain way doesn't mean that's how others need to do it. Acceptance of these differences is key to keeping negativity out of our relationships.

5

We find fault... where *our* faults lie.
Rabbi Dr. Abraham J. Twerski

The Baal Shem Tov said that the world is a mirror in which the faults we see in others are really those within ourselves.

If you find a fault in another person, stop and consider, "Where is that fault in myself?"

6

Don't keep score.
Rabbi Simcha Feuerman

The idea that things have to be fair is an illusion that blocks our happiness. When people keep score and think or say, "I did this for you yesterday, why can't you do this for me today?" that's where negativity takes over and hijacks the relationship.

7

Everyone has faults...that's Hashem's design.
Rabbi Doniel Frank

The first principle of relationships is that people are born with deficits. Everyone has faults; that's part of being human. The quality of our relationships hinges upon our learning to embrace people as a whole, with all their good points and their faults.

Master the Meanings — Index of Hebrew Words

a"h – may he (she) rest in peace
ahavas Yisrael – love of one's fellow Jew
apikorsus – heresy
avak loshon hora – a hint ("dust") of loshon hara
b'nachas – calmly
bachur – yeshivah student
bashert – pre-destined
bein adam lachaveiro – between man and his fellow man
beis din – rabbinic tribunal
chassan – bridegroom
chavrusa – study partner
chessed – lovingkindness
chillul Hashem – desecration of G-d's Name
Chol HaMoed – the intermediate days of the festivals of Passover and Sukkos
chuppah – marriage canopy
dan l'chaf zechus – judging favorably
daven – pray
davening – praying
dvar Torah – explication of a Torah topic
Eitz Hadaas – the Tree of Knowledge in the Garden of Eden
emunah – faith in G-d
halachah (pl. *halachos*) – Torah laws
hechsher – kosher certification
Kabbalah – the esoteric Torah
kashrus – the laws of kosher food
kavanah – concentration, intent (esp. in prayer)
Kiddush – sanctification of Shabbos and holidays, usually over wine; collation at which *kiddush* is recited
loshon hora – forbidden derogatory speech
Maariv – the evening prayer
machlokes – dispute
Machsom L'fi – a program for extra zealousness in refraining from *loshon hora* for a specific time period
Mashiach – the Redeemer
mesirus nefesh — self-sacrifice
mezuzah – doorpost; also the parchment that we nail into the doorpost, with special prayers written on it
middah – (pl., *middos*) traits or qualities
middah k'neged middah – measure for measure: the Divine system of reward and punishment
Minchah – the afternoon prayer
minyan – a quorum of ten men
mitzvah (pl. *mitzvos*) – positive Torah commandment(s)
mashal – a parable
motzi shem ra – speaking slander
neshamah – soul
Olam Haba – the World to Come
ona'as devarim – hurtful speech
Parashah – the weekly portion of the Torah read on Shabbos in the synagogue
pareve – neutral; a food that is neither a meat nor a dairy product
Pesach – Passover
pasuk – a "sentence" in the Scriptures (Tanach)
rabbanim (sing. *rav*) – rabbis
rebbi – Torah teacher
rechilus – gossip
refuah – recovery from illness
savlanus – patience
Seder – the ritual Passover-night meal
sefer – book
segulah (pl. *segulos*) – favorable omen
Shabbos – the Sabbath
shailah – a question of halachah (Torah law)
shalom – peace
shamayim – heaven
shidduch (pl. *shidduchim*) – marriage matches
shiur – Torah lecture

shlep – drag
shlit"a – "May he live a long and healthy life"
shmiras haloshon – guarding one's tongue (from derogatory speech); a positive commandment
simchah – happiness, happy occasion
sinas chinam – baseless hatred
siyata d'Shmaya – the help of Heaven
talmid chacham – Torah sage
tefillin – phylacteries
tefillos (sing. *tefillah*) – prayers
Tehillim – the Book of Psalms
teshuvah – repentance
to'eles – constructive purpose (*l'to'eles* – for a constructive purpose)
tochachah – rebuke
tzaddik (pl. *tzaddikim*) – saintly person
v'ahavta l'rei'acha kamocha – love your friend as yourself
vort – engagement celebration [lit., a word]
yeshivah – Talmudical academy
yeshuah – salvation
yetzer hora – the evil inclination
yetzer hatov – the good inclination
Yom Tov – holiday
zechus – merit
zemiros – songs for the Shabbos table
zt"l – abbreviation for "the memory of the righteous is a blessing"

MASTER THE MITZVAH—
Tools for Shmiras Haloshon

C TALK

Talk is the CCHF free Teen Inspiration
d Chizuk hotline for high-school girls.
ovative, intriguing and timely segments
uploaded daily. Features include
sonal Stories of Wow!, Lessons for Life,
e Playlist, Q&A, Spotlight on Schools, and
erialized story. TIC Talk currently receives
re than 50,000 calls weekly from teens
rldwide. **Call 201.855.8255**

Shabbos Table Machsom L'fi

Thousands of families are making their Shabbos tables warmer, sweeter and more elevated with this simple, FREE family-friendly program. It consists of observing a Machsom L'fi at the Shabbos table, enhanced by our weekly discussion-provoking Shabbos Menu newsletter, a weekly reminder, and our *tefillah* and *kabbalah* table card. Join at **powerofspeech.org**. or, in the USA, **text Shabbos to 313131** to receive your start-up materials.

*The Shimras Haloshon **Shaila** Hotline*

This telephone hotline puts callers in contact (anonymously) with expert *rabbanim* who can answer their halachic questions concerning correct speech. This free service is available at **718.951.3696** from 9 to 10:30 p.m., including Motzoei Shabbos and Sunday mornings from 10:30 AM to 12:00 PM. EST.

Email

Thousands participate in Shmiras Haloshon Yomi through one of our daily learning emails, which include three choices of text to study from, and our MP3 daily 5-minute SHY audio. Additionally, more and more people are receiving our daily email reminders for the Morning Machsom L'fi, as well as daily learning from Lessons in Truth, Loving Kindness and our popular bi-weekly newsletter, Chosen Words. Thousands more receive Shabbos Menu, the weekly newsletter of the Shabbos Table Machsom L'fi program, in their inbox each week. **Email: editorial@chofetzchaimusa.org**

ooks

ith over 450,000 volumes in print, our best-selling books for daily
arning for both adults and children have created a worldwide
volution in speech and deed. Building on that success, MASTER
OUR WORDS, MASTER YOUR LIFE shows us how to harness the
credible power of words to nurture and uplift the people in our lives.
order, **call 845.352.3505** x 116 or visit **powerofspeech.org**

Prayer for Proper Speech

תפילה על הדיבור

מאת מרן החפץ חיים זצ"ל

רִבּוֹנוֹ-שֶׁל-עוֹלָם, יְהִי רָצוֹן מִלְּפָנֶיךָ
אֵ-ל רַחוּם וְחַנּוּן שֶׁתְּזַכֵּנִי הַיּוֹם
וּבְכָל יוֹם לִשְׁמֹר פִּי וּלְשׁוֹנִי
מִלָּשׁוֹן הָרַע וּרְכִילוּת: וְאֶזָּהֵר
מִלְּדַבֵּר אֲפִילוּ עַל אִישׁ יָחִיד, וְכָל
שֶׁכֵּן עַל כְּלַל יִשְׂרָאֵל, אוֹ עַל חֵלֶק
מֵהֶם וְכָל שֶׁכֵּן מִלְּהִתְרָעֵם עַל
מִידּוֹתָיו שֶׁל הַקָּדוֹשׁ בָּרוּךְ הוּא.
וְאֶזָּהֵר מִלְּדַבֵּר דִּבְרֵי שֶׁקֶר, חֲנוּפָה,
מַחֲלוֹקֶת, כַּעַס, גַּאֲוָה, אוֹנָאַת
דְּבָרִים, הַלְבָּנַת פָּנִים, לֵיצָנוּת, וְכָל
דִּיבּוּר אָסוּר. וְזַכֵּנִי שֶׁלֹּא לְדַבֵּר כִּי
אִם דָּבָר הַצָּרִיךְ לְעִנְיָנֵי גּוּפִי וְנַפְשִׁי,
וְיִהְיוּ כָּל מַעֲשַׂי וְדִיבּוּרַי לְשֵׁם שָׁמַיִם.

Master of the World, may it be Your will, compassionate and gracious G-d, that You grant me the merit today and every day to guard my mouth and tongue from speaking loshon hora and rechilus. May I be zealous not to speak ill of an individual, and certainly not of the entire Jewish people or a portion of it; and even more so, may I be zealous not to complain about the ways of the Holy One, Blessed is He. May I be zealous not to speak words of falsehood, flattery, strife, anger, arrogance, hurt, embarrassment, mockery, and all other forbidden forms of speech. Grant me the merit to speak only that which is necessary for my physical and spiritual well-being, and may all my deeds and words be for the sake of Heaven.

This volume is part of
THE ARTSCROLL® SERIES
an ongoing project of
translations, commentaries and expositions on
Scripture, Mishnah, Talmud, Midrash, Halachah,
liturgy, history, the classic Rabbinic writings,
biographies and thought.

For a brochure of current publications
visit your local Hebrew bookseller
or contact the publisher:

Mesorah Publications, ltd

4401 Second Avenue
Brooklyn, New York 11232
(718) 921-9000
www.artscroll.com